Israel Lottery Council
for the Arts

Drawn & Quarterly; Post Office Box 48056, Montreal, Quebec, Canada H2V 4S8. www.drawnandquarterly.com; Second hardcover edition: September 2007. Printed in Singapore.10 9 8 7 6 5 4 3 2; Library and Archives Canada Cataloguing in Publication; Modan, Rutu; Exit wounds / Rutu Modan. ISBN 978-1-897299-06-7; I. Title. NC1729.M63A64 2007 741.5'95694 C2006-905526-2; Distributed in the USA and abroad by Farrar, Straus and Giroux; 19 Union Square West, New York, NY 10003; Orders: 888.330.8477. Distributed in Canada by Raincoast Books; 9050 Shaughnessy Street, Vancouver, BC V6P 6E5; Orders: 800.663.5714; Distributed in the United Kingdom by Publishers Group U.K.; 8 The Arena, Mollison Avenue, Enfield, Middlesex EN3 7NL; Orders: 0208 8040400. Story advisor: Yirmi Pinkus. Translation: Noah Stollman. Lettering: Rich Tomasso. Acknowledgements: I would like to thank Yirmi Pinkus, for his eye-opening comments, ingenious solutions and advice; and Batia Kolton, who, in her nonchalant way, helped me more than I can say. There would be no book without either of you. Thanks to Chris Oliveros for convincing me that I was capable of creating this book. Thanks to my younger sister, Dana Modan, for guiding me through the writing process and to Noah Stollman for translating, editing, and giving me a title. Thanks To Rachel Marani of the Israel Cultural Excellence Foundation for her attentive support and to Thomas Gabison for his good words and intentions. For support and friendship: thanks to Itzik Renert, Mira Friedmann, Moran Palmoni and Lilian Bareto, Alona Palmoni, Orit Bergman, Orit Mazor and Yotam Burnstein, Meirav and Amnon Salomon-Dekel, Ephrat Beloosesky, Tamar and Zeev Bergman, and Zvia Cagan. Thanks to Tom Devlin for the design and for being so nice; to Shachar Kober—such a faithful assistant; to the real Koby Franco for his name; and to David Ofek—whose documentary No 17. inspired this story. Most of all, thank you to my patient husband Ofer Bergman.

exit wounds rutu modan

exit wounds rutu modan

drawn & quarterly
montréal

To Yirmi and Ofer.

chapter one
father figure

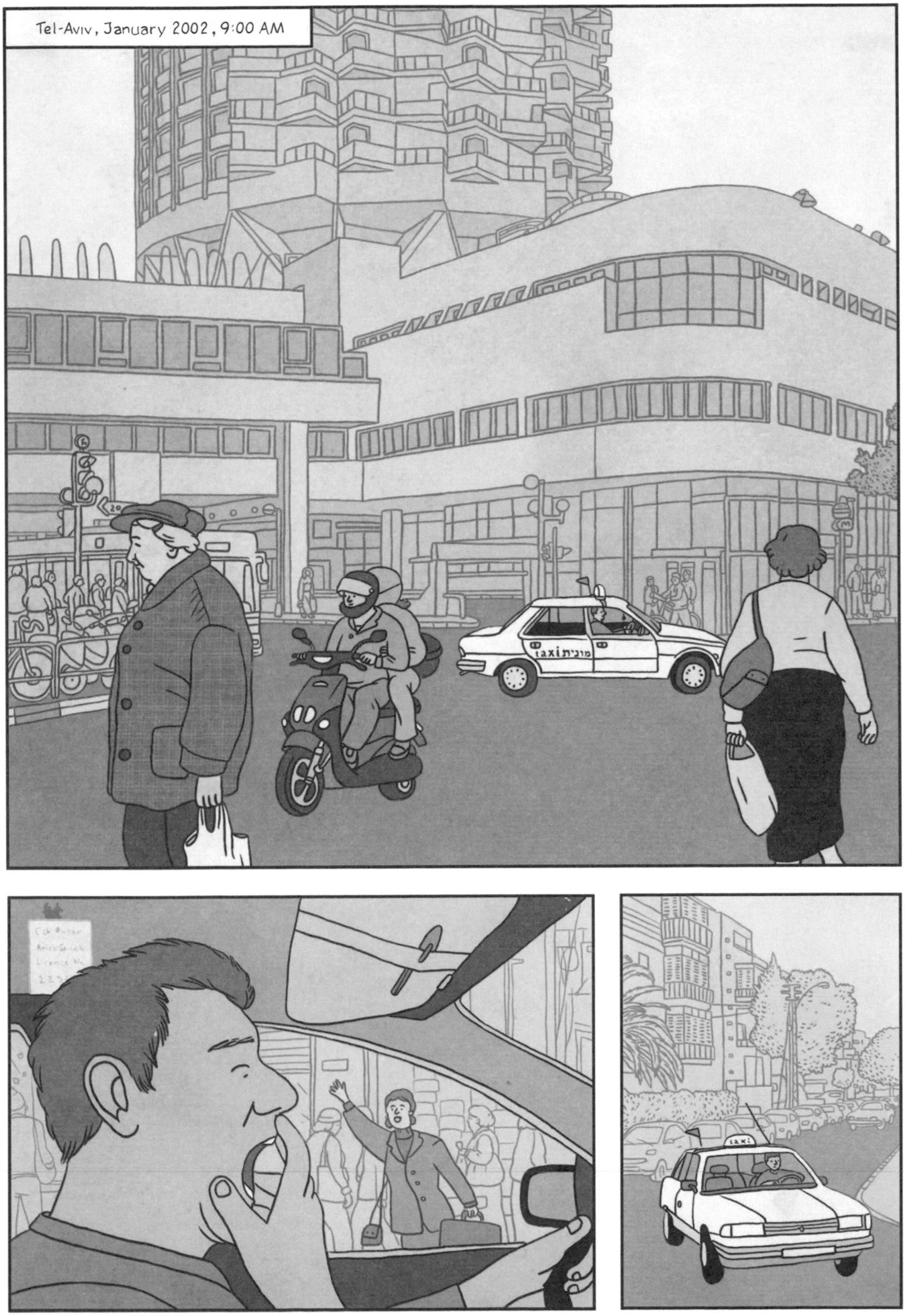
Tel-Aviv, January 2002, 9:00 AM

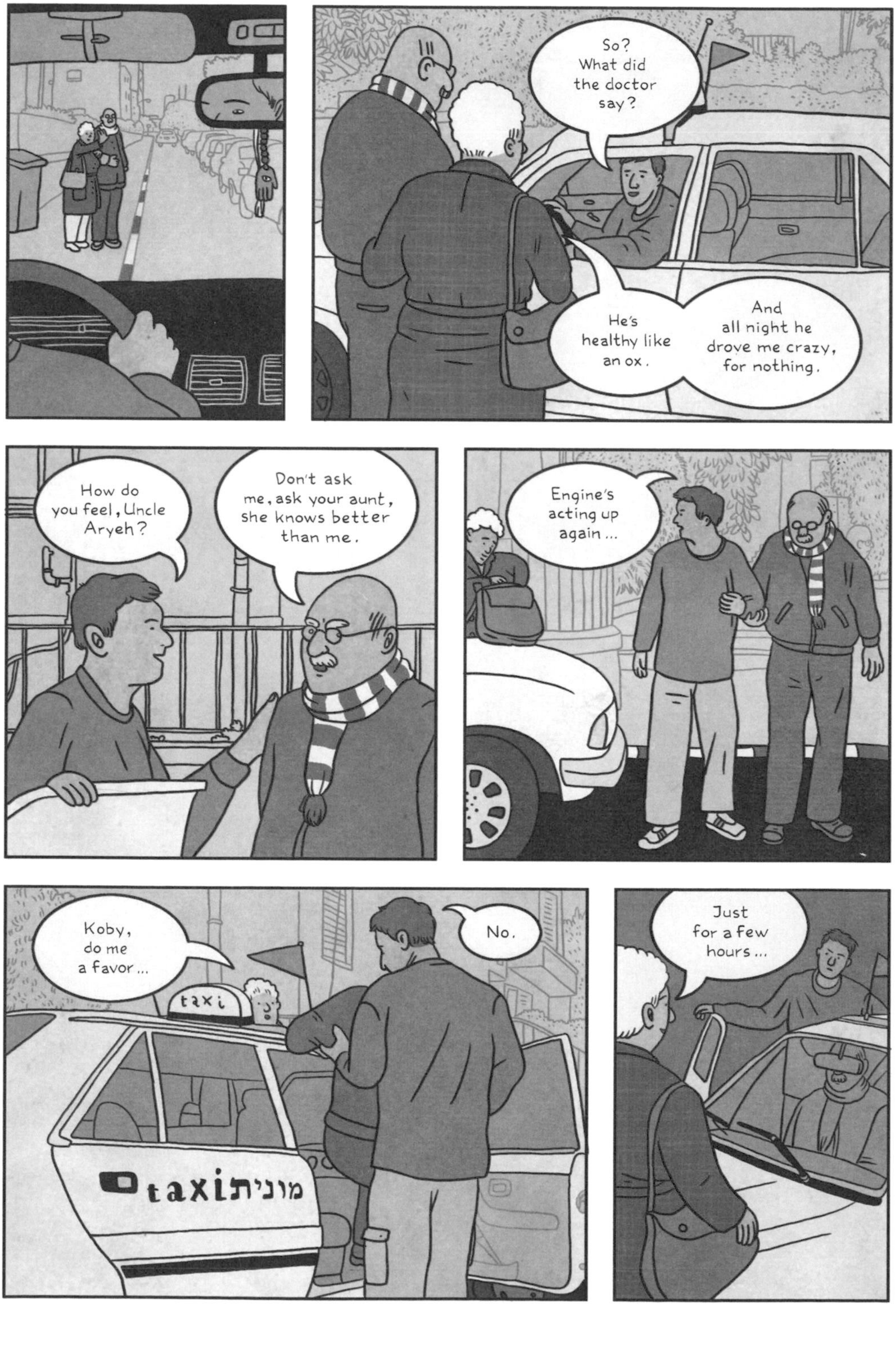
So? What did the doctor say?
He's healthy like an ox.
And all night he drove me crazy, for nothing.
How do you feel, Uncle Aryeh?
Don't ask me, ask your aunt, she knows better than me.
Engine's acting up again...
Koby, do me a favor...
No.
taxi
taxi מונית
Just for a few hours...

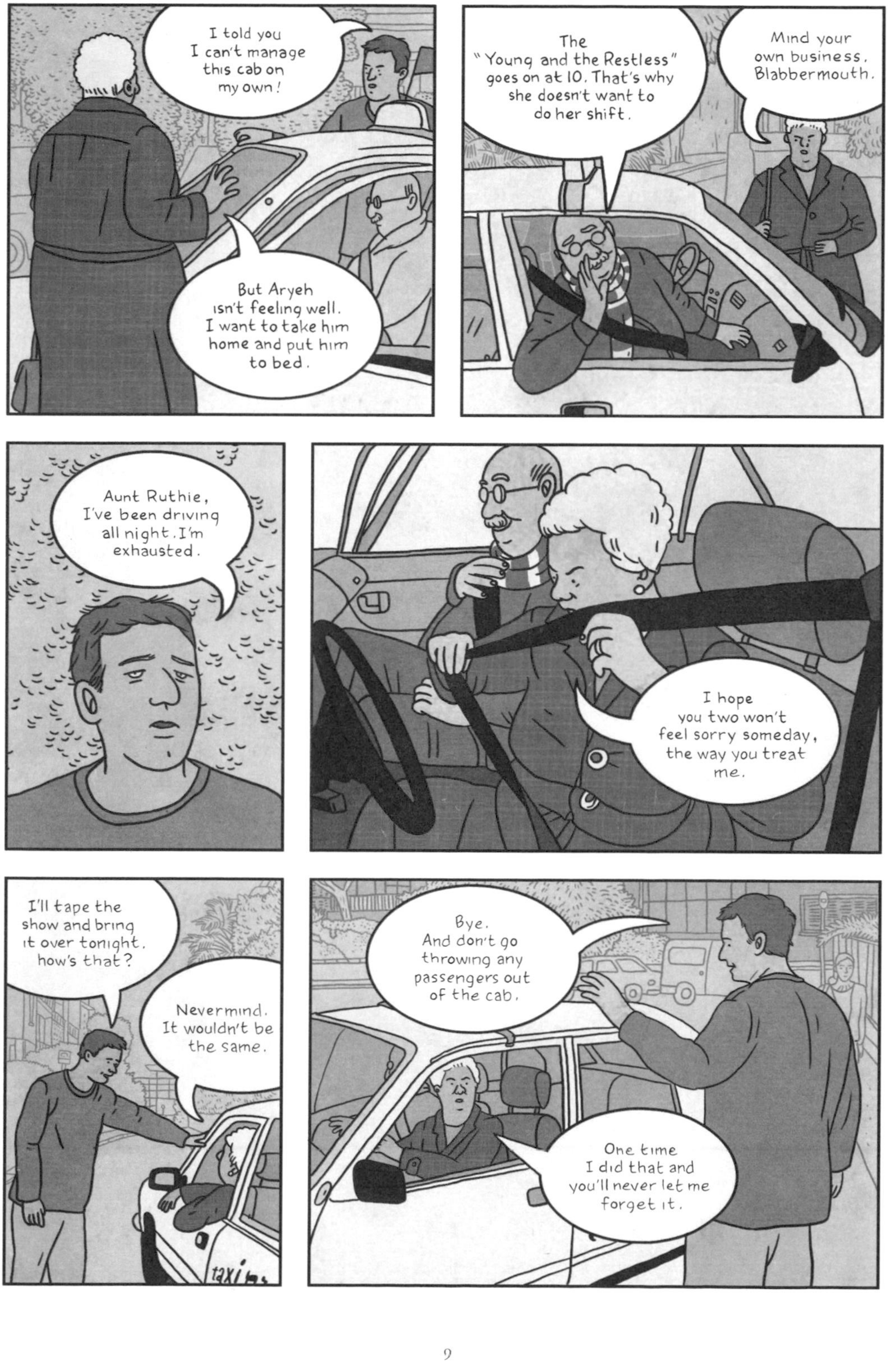
I told you I can't manage this cab on my own!
But Aryeh isn't feeling well. I want to take him home and put him to bed.
The "Young and the Restless" goes on at 10. That's why she doesn't want to do her shift.
Mind your own business, Blabbermouth.
Aunt Ruthie, I've been driving all night. I'm exhausted.
I hope you two won't feel sorry someday, the way you treat me.
I'll tape the show and bring it over tonight, how's that?
Nevermind. It wouldn't be the same.
Bye. And don't go throwing any passengers out of the cab.
One time I did that and you'll never let me forget it.
taxi

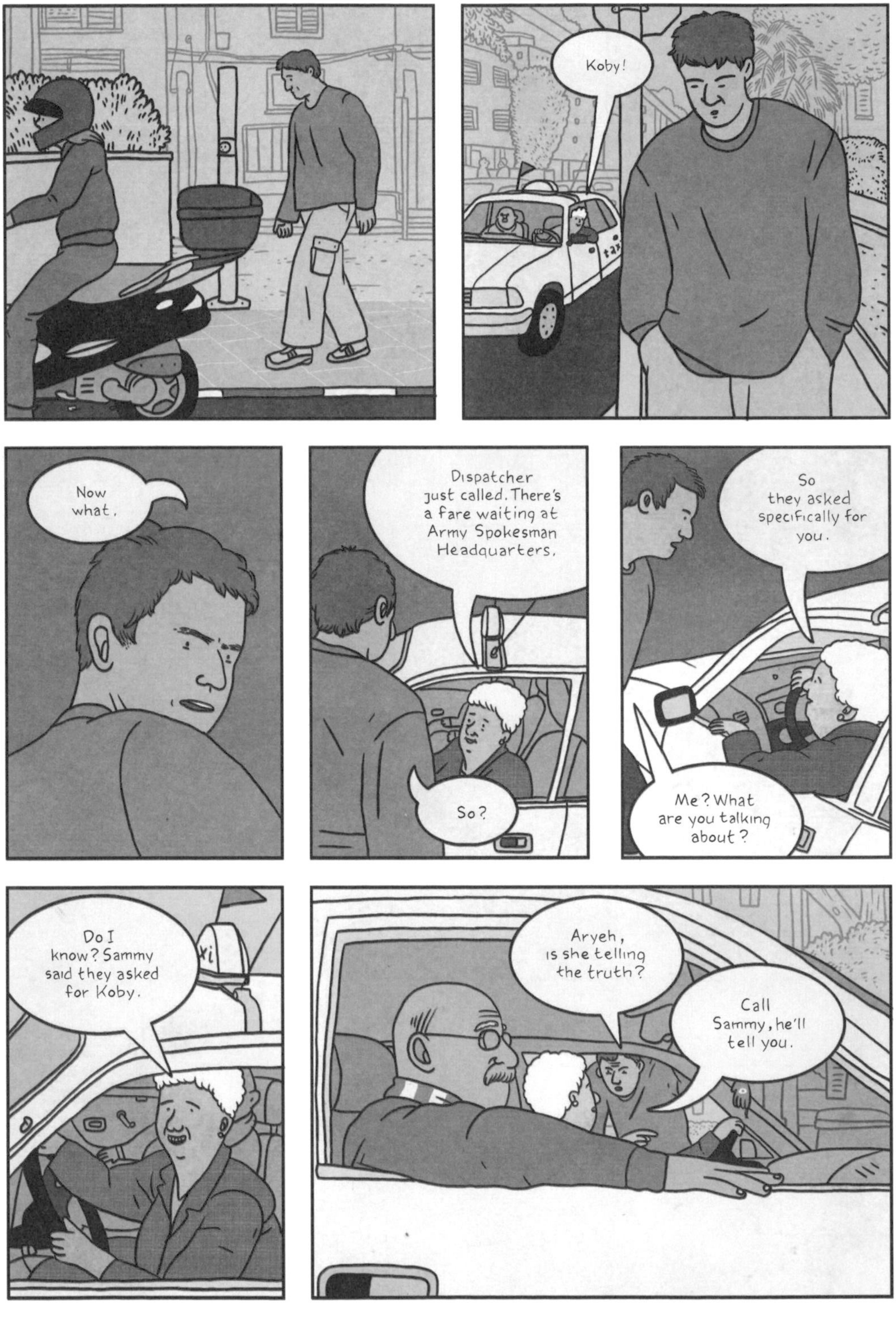
Koby!
Now what.
Dispatcher just called. There's a fare waiting at Army Spokesman Headquarters.
So?
So they asked specifically for you.
Me? What are you talking about?
Do I know? Sammy said they asked for Koby.
Aryeh, is she telling the truth?
Call Sammy, he'll tell you.

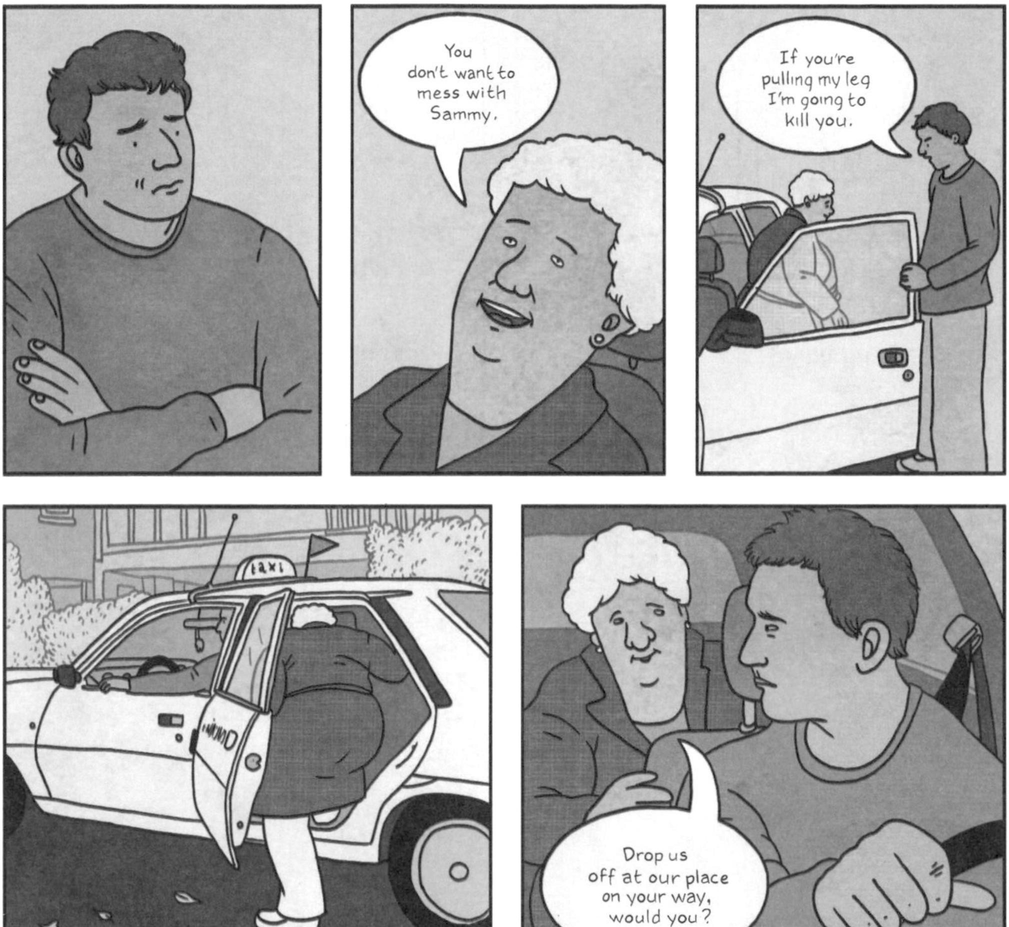
You don't want to mess with Sammy.
If you're pulling my leg I'm going to kill you.
taxi
Drop us off at our place on your way, would you?
How different can twin sisters be? I don't mean physically, it's just that my Mom was such a pushover. I'm sure Aunt Ruthie played her like a pro when they were kids.

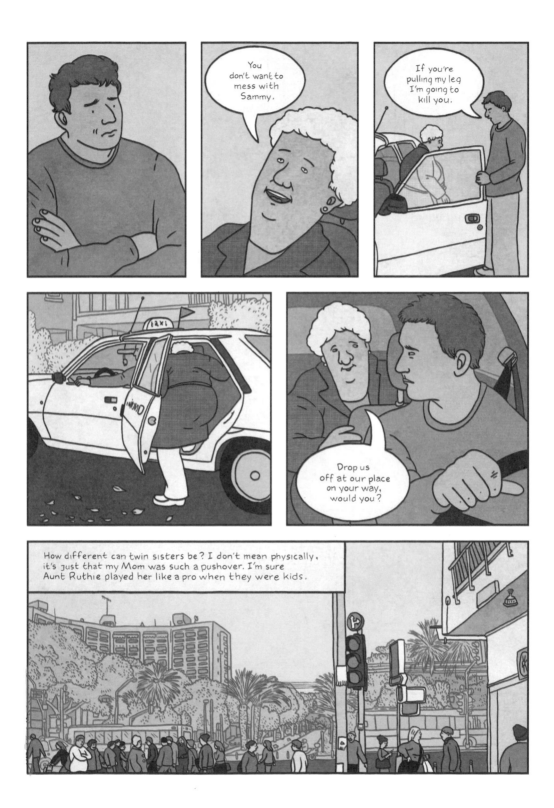

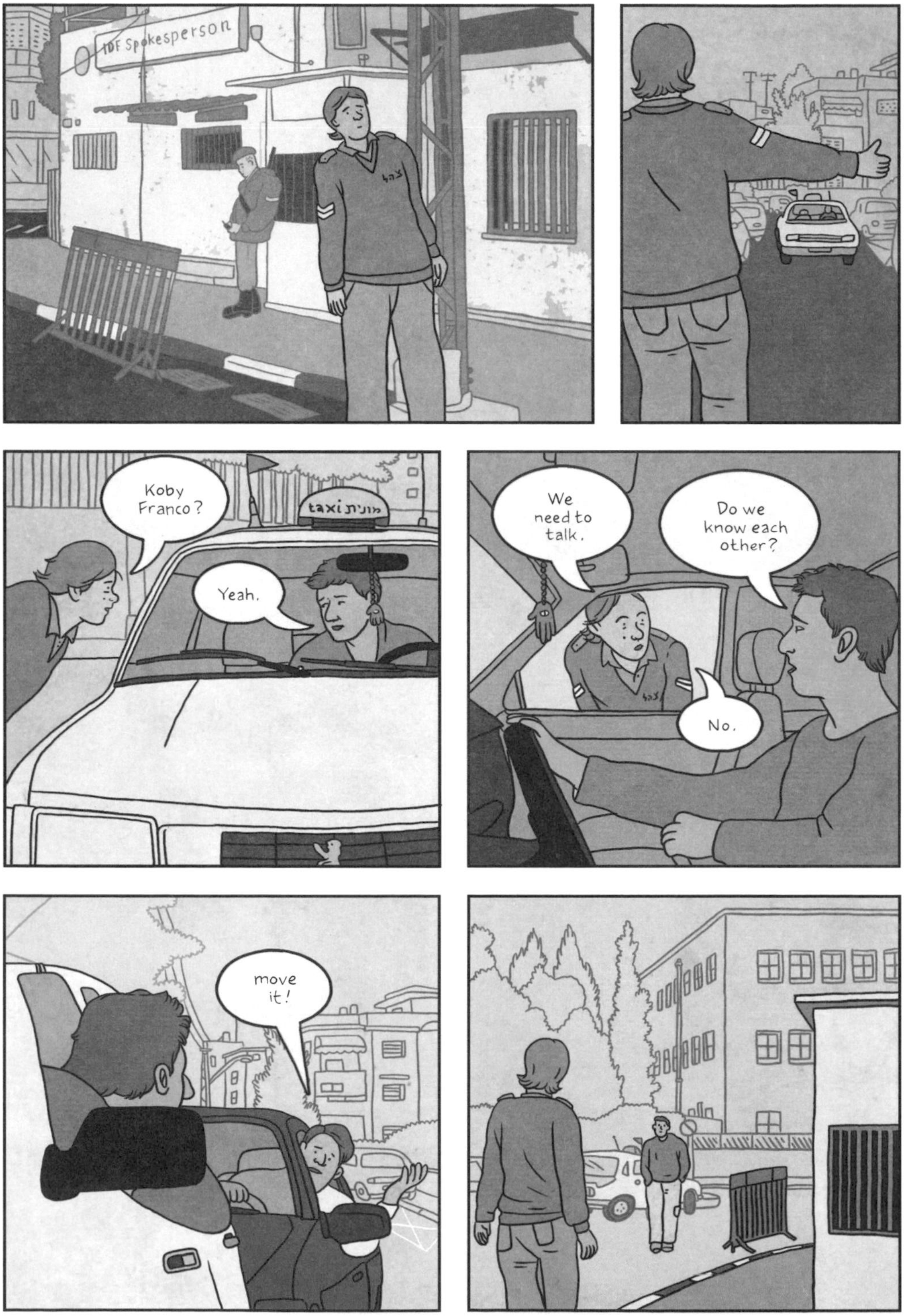
IDF Spokesperson
Koby Franco?
Yeah.
We need to talk.
Do we know each other?
No.
move it!

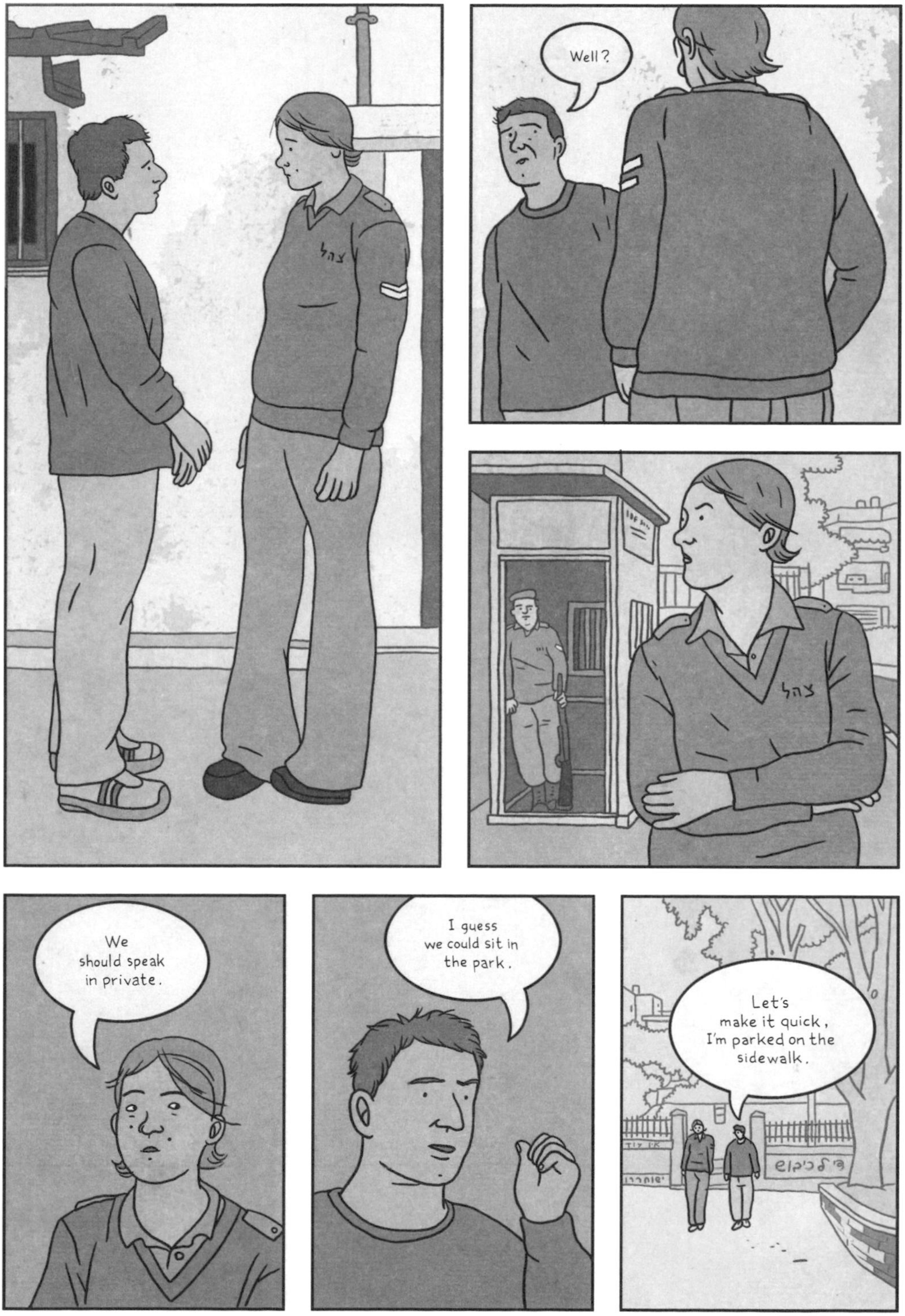
Well?
We should speak in private.
I guess we could sit in the park.
Let's make it quick, I'm parked on the sidewalk.

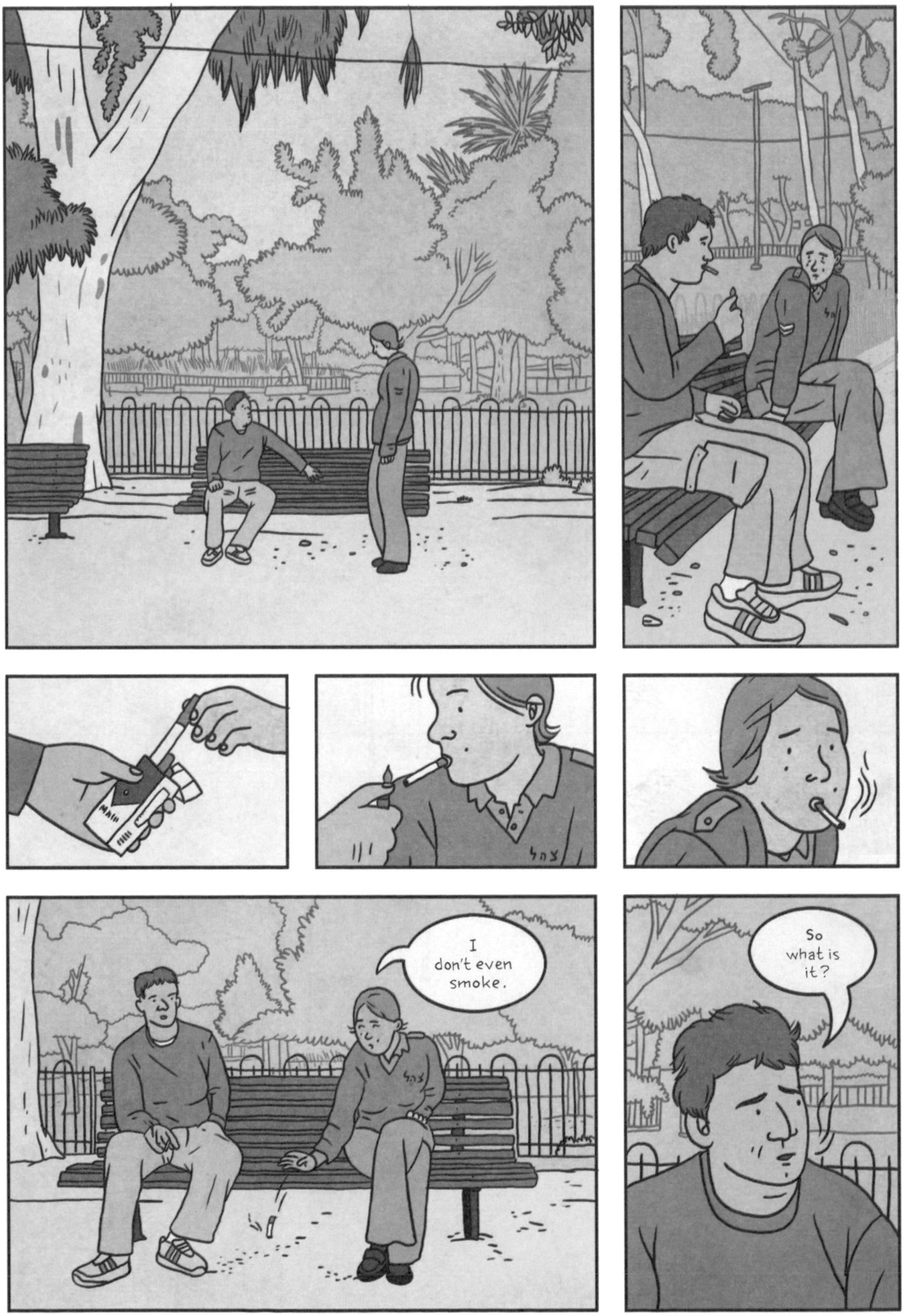
I don't even smoke.
So what is it?

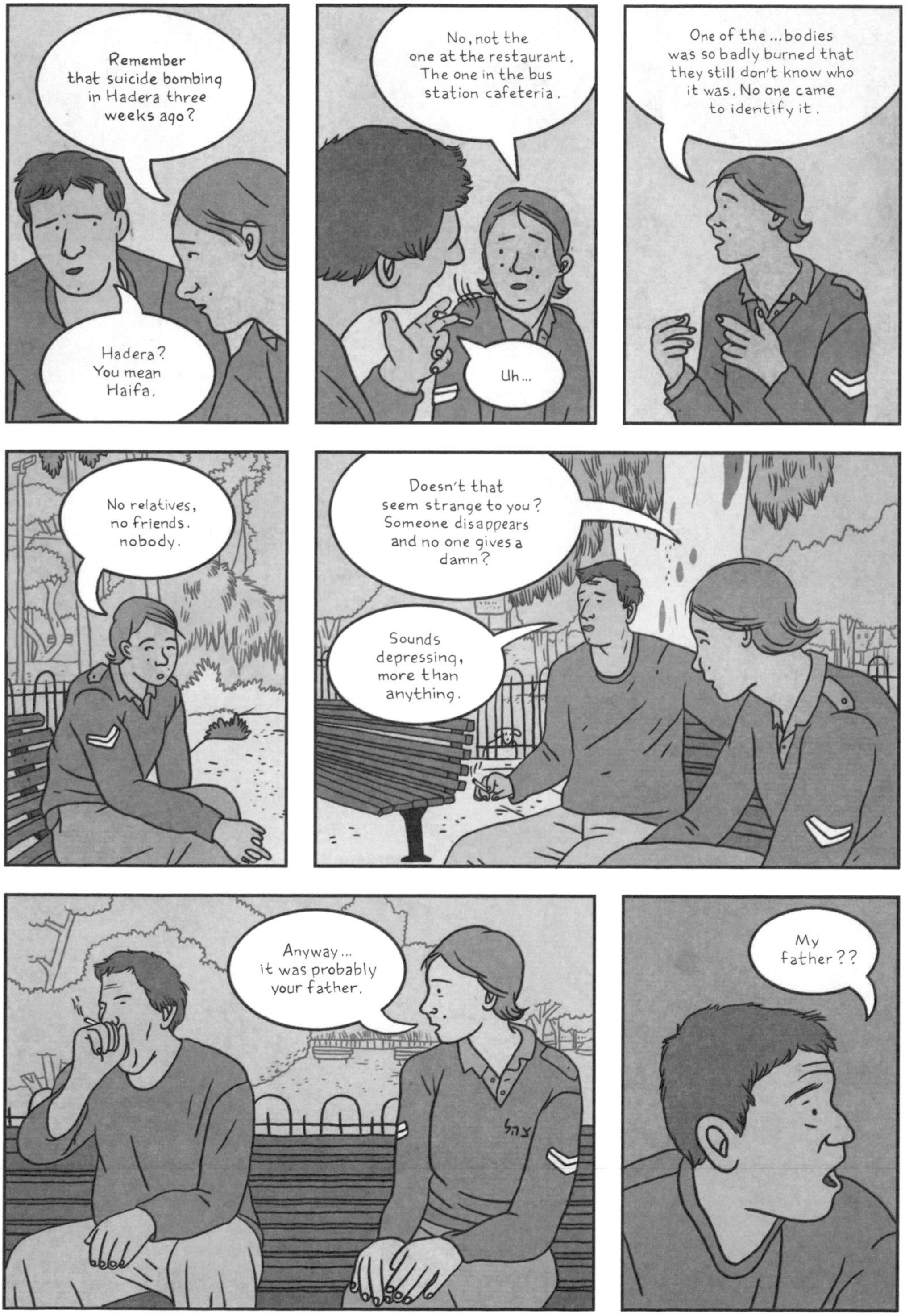
Remember that suicide bombing in Hadera three weeks ago?
Hadera? You mean Haifa.
No, not the one at the restaurant. The one in the bus station cafeteria.
Uh...
One of the ... bodies was so badly burned that they still don't know who it was. No one came to identify it.
No relatives, no friends. nobody.
Doesn't that seem strange to you? Someone disappears and no one gives a damn?
Sounds depressing, more than anything.
Anyway... it was probably your father.
My father??

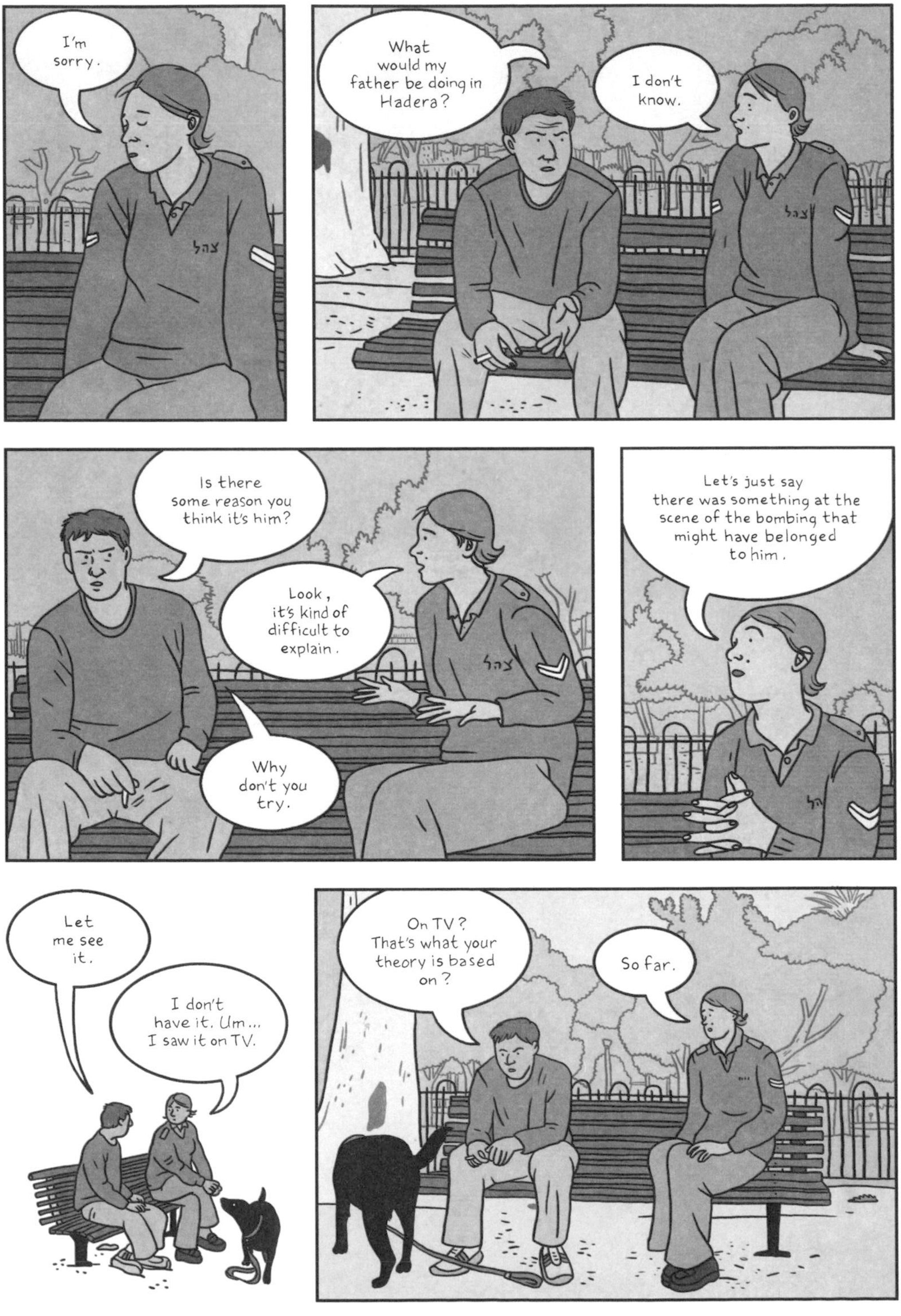
I'm sorry.
What would my father be doing in Hadera?
I don't know.
Is there some reason you think it's him?
Look, it's kind of difficult to explain.
Why don't you try.
Let's just say there was something at the scene of the bombing that might have belonged to him.
Let me see it.
I don't have it. Um... I saw it on TV.
On TV? That's what your theory is based on?
So far.

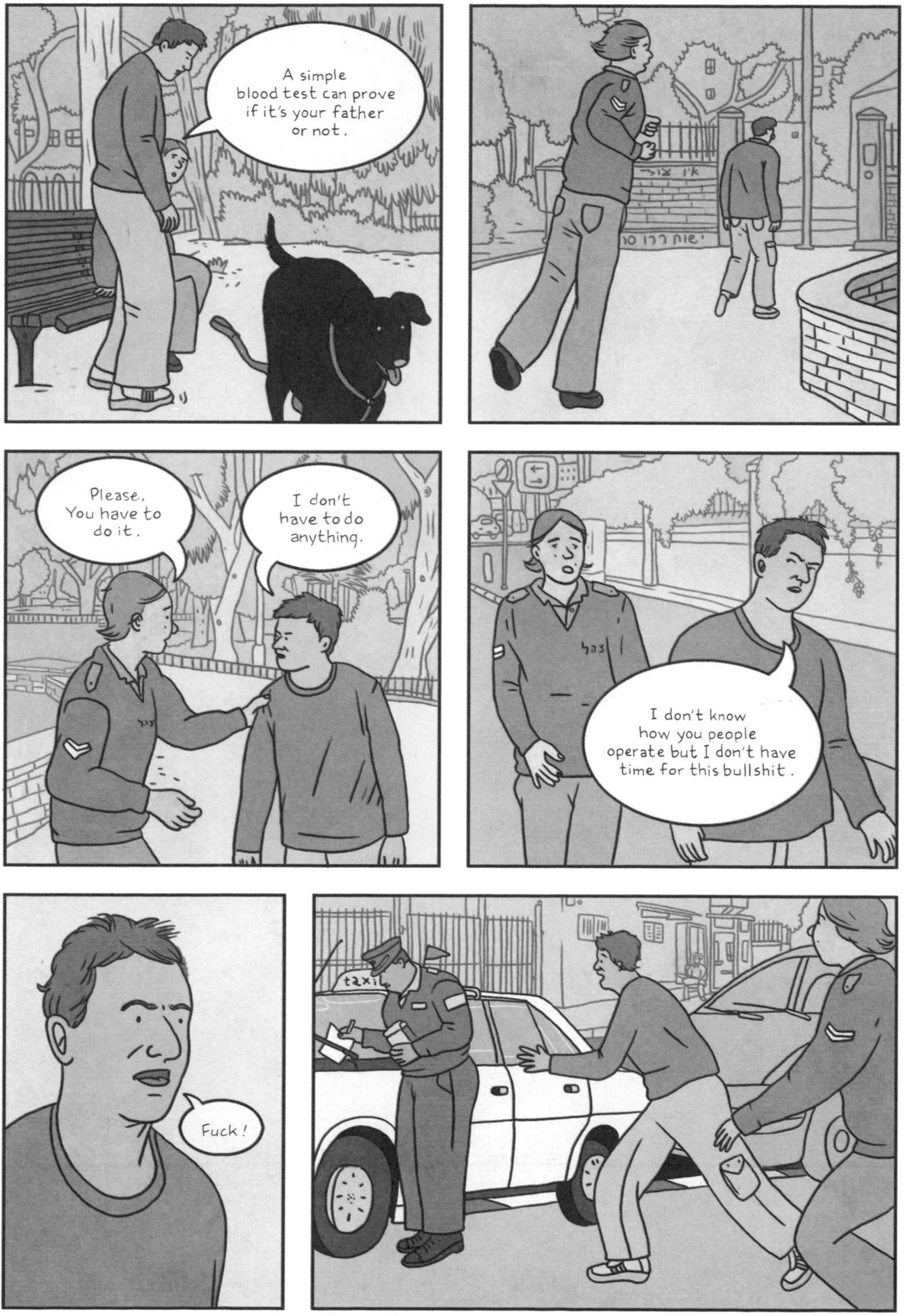
A simple blood test can prove if it's your father or not.
Please, You have to do it.
I don't have to do anything.
I don't know how you people operate but I don't have time for this bullshit.
Fuck!

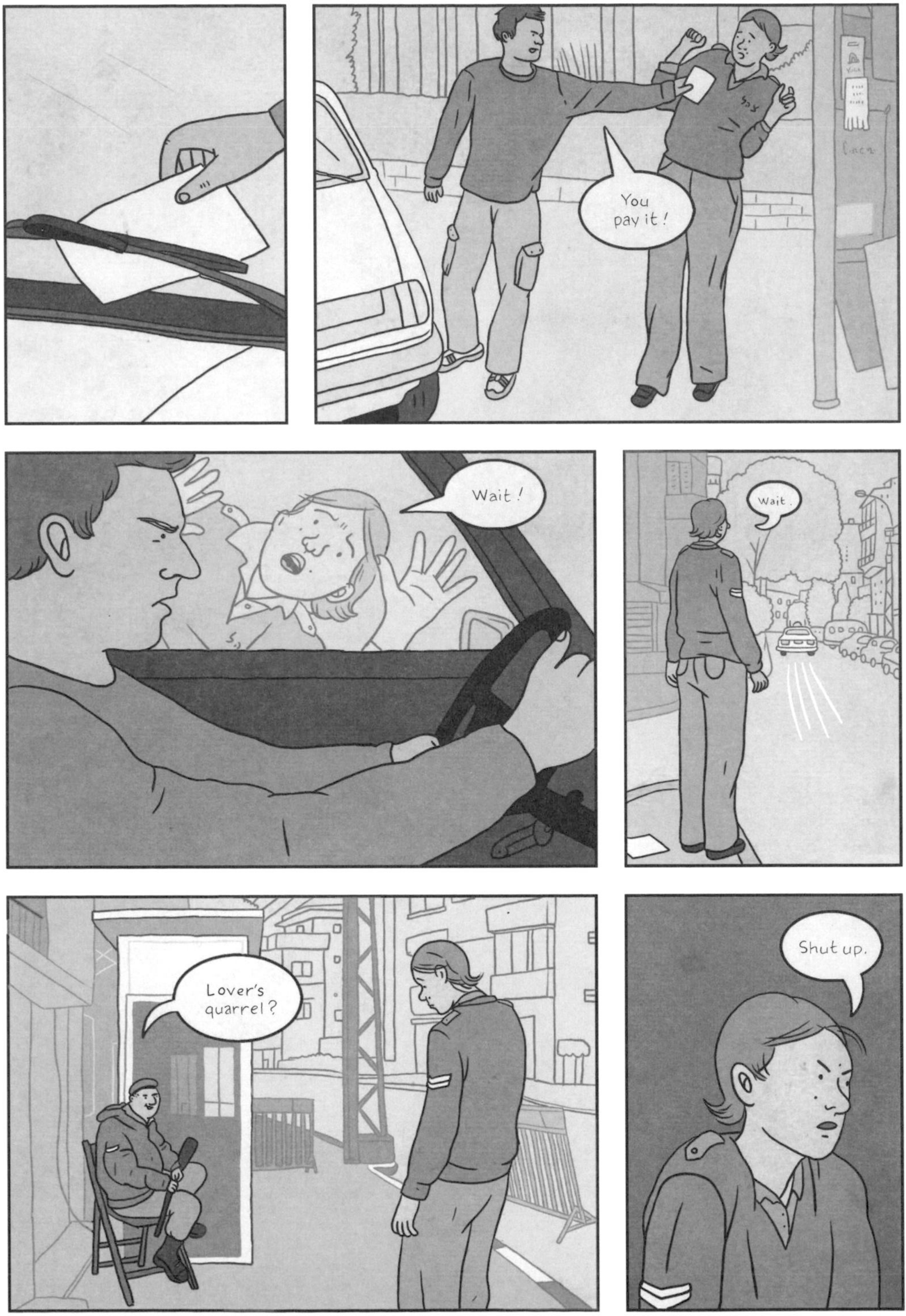
You pay it!
Wait!
Wait.
Lover's quarrel?
Shut up.

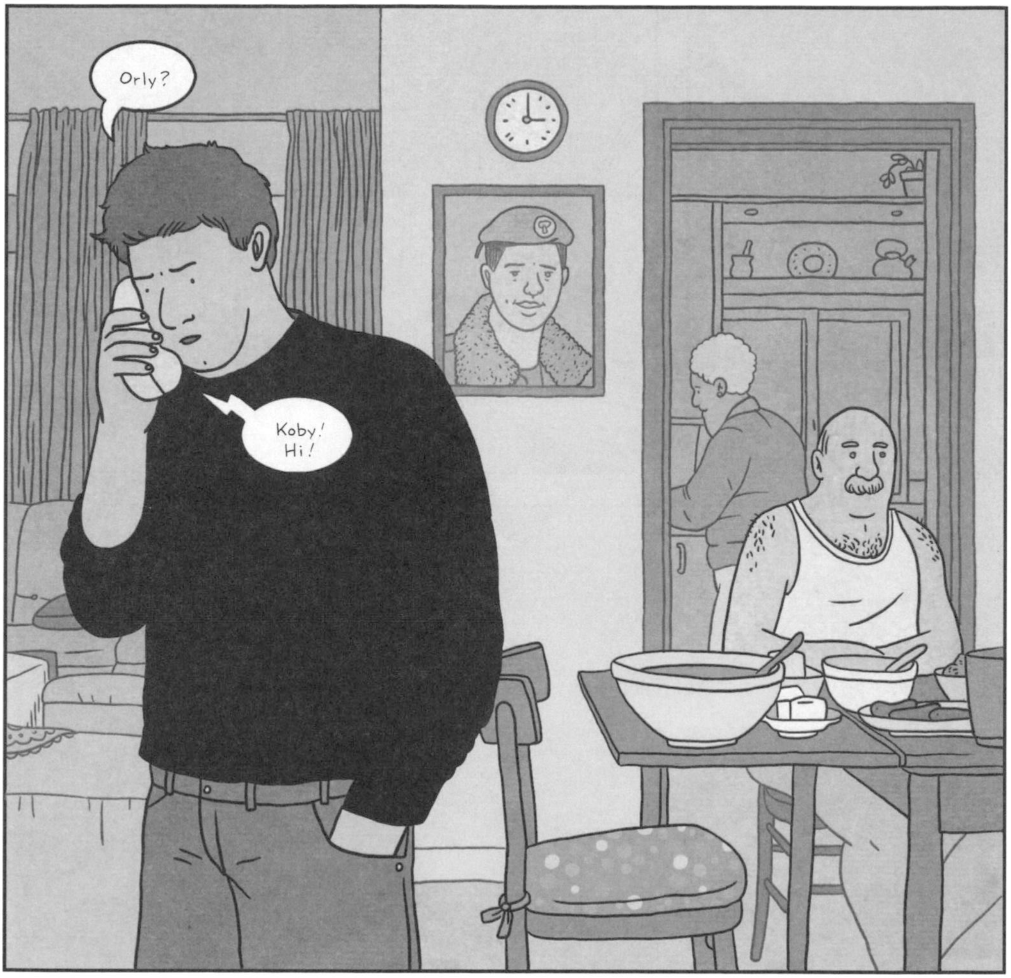
Orly?
Koby! Hi!

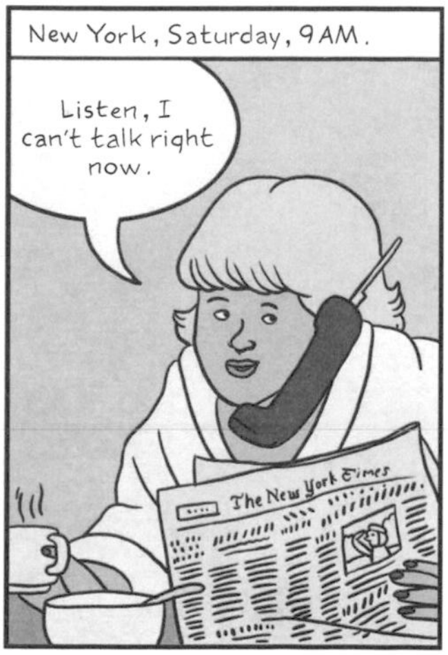
New York, Saturday, 9AM.
Listen, I can't talk right now.
The New York Times

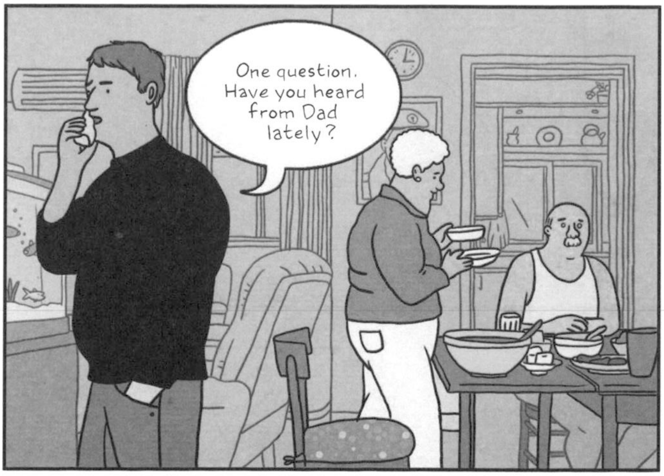
One question. Have you heard from Dad lately?

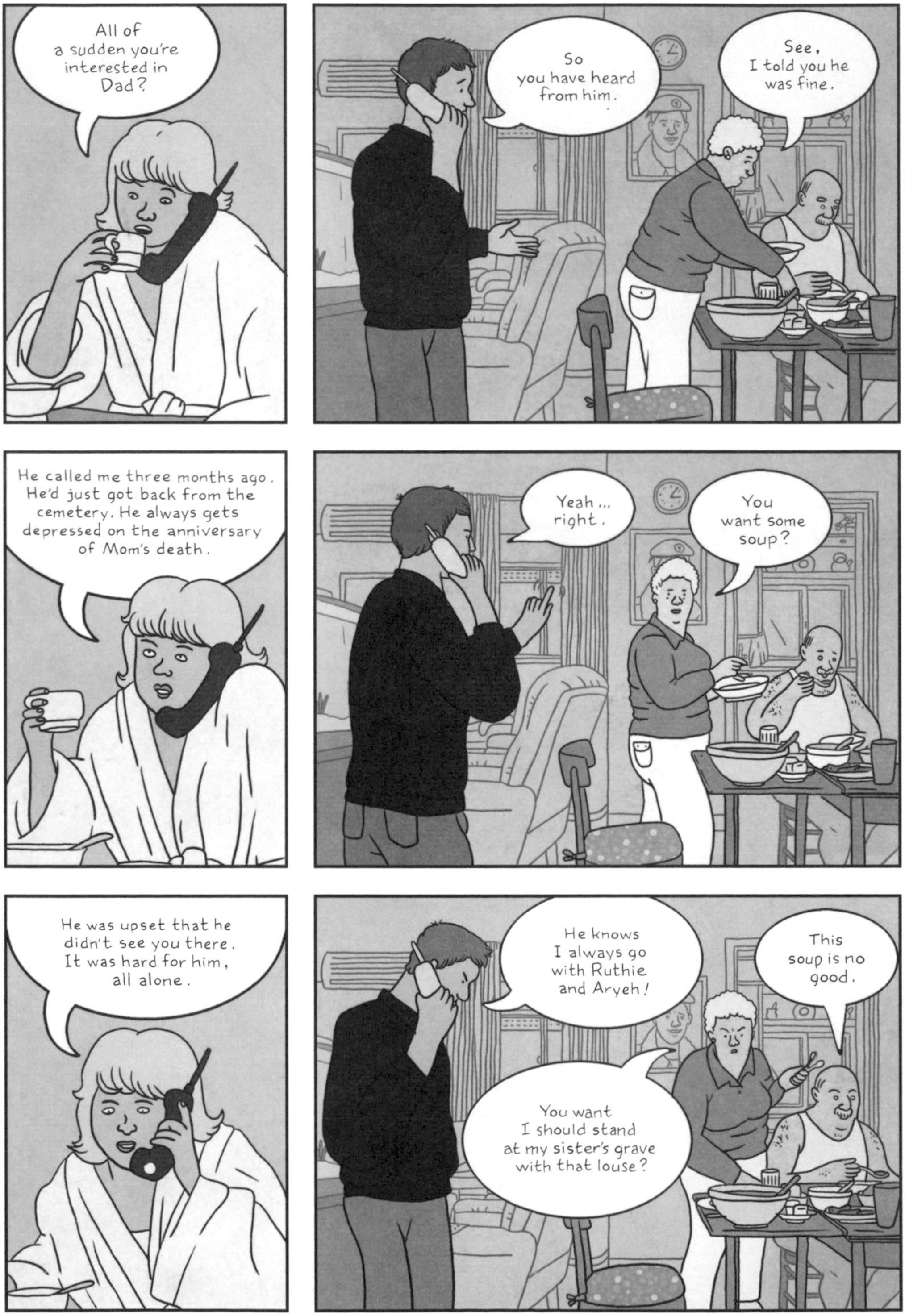
All of a sudden you're interested in Dad?
So you have heard from him.
See, I told you he was fine.
He called me three months ago. He'd just got back from the cemetery. He always gets depressed on the anniversary of Mom's death.
Yeah... right.
You want some soup?
He was upset that he didn't see you there. It was hard for him, all alone.
He knows I always go with Ruthie and Aryeh!
This soup is no good.
You want I should stand at my sister's grave with that louse?

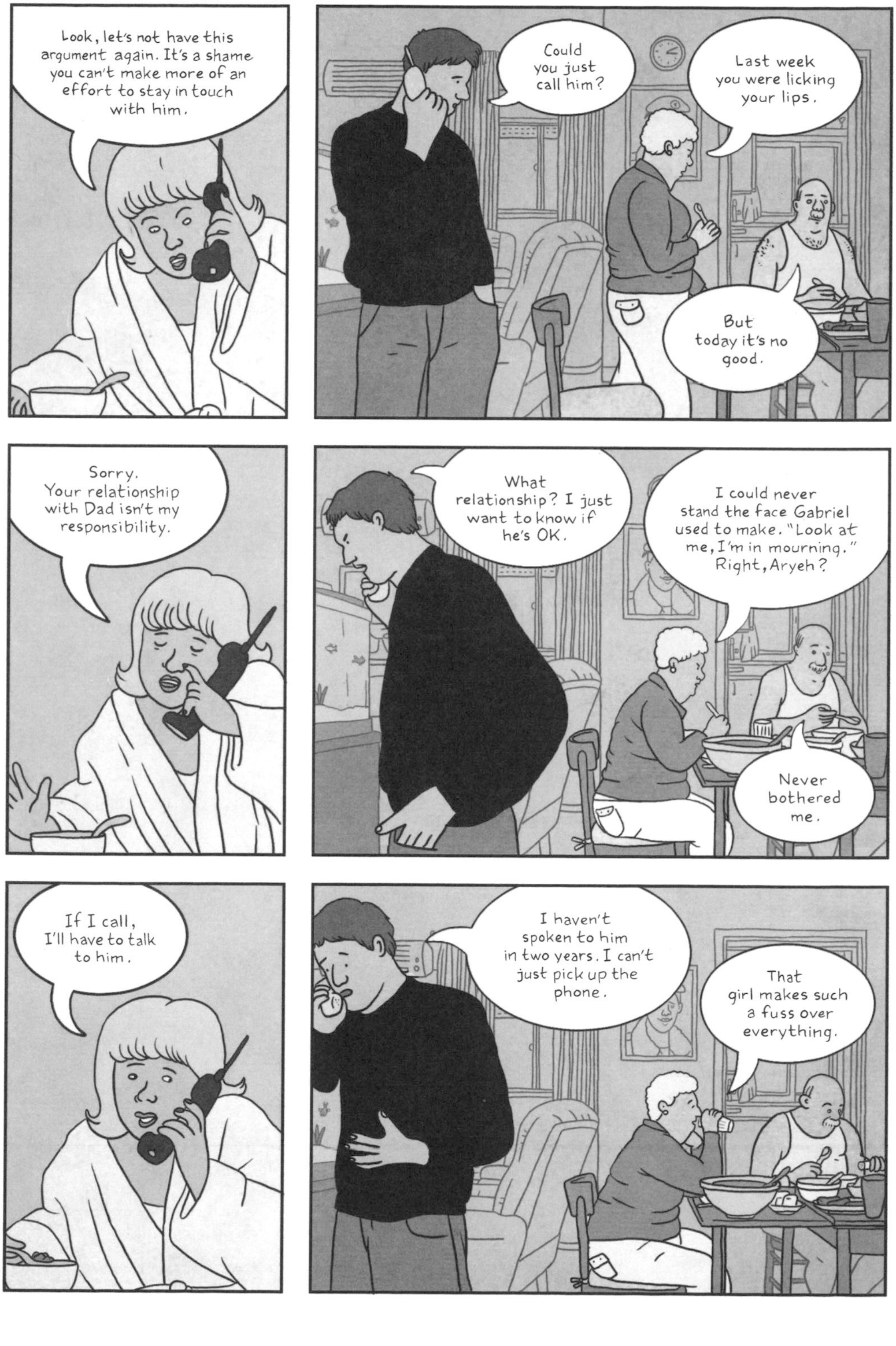

Look, let's not have this argument again. It's a shame you can't make more of an effort to stay in touch with him.
Could you just call him?
Last week you were licking your lips.
But today it's no good.
Sorry. Your relationship with Dad isn't my responsibility.
What relationship? I just want to know if he's OK.
I could never stand the face Gabriel used to make. "Look at me, I'm in mourning." Right, Aryeh?
Never bothered me.
If I call, I'll have to talk to him.
I haven't spoken to him in two years. I can't just pick up the phone.
That girl makes such a fuss over everything.

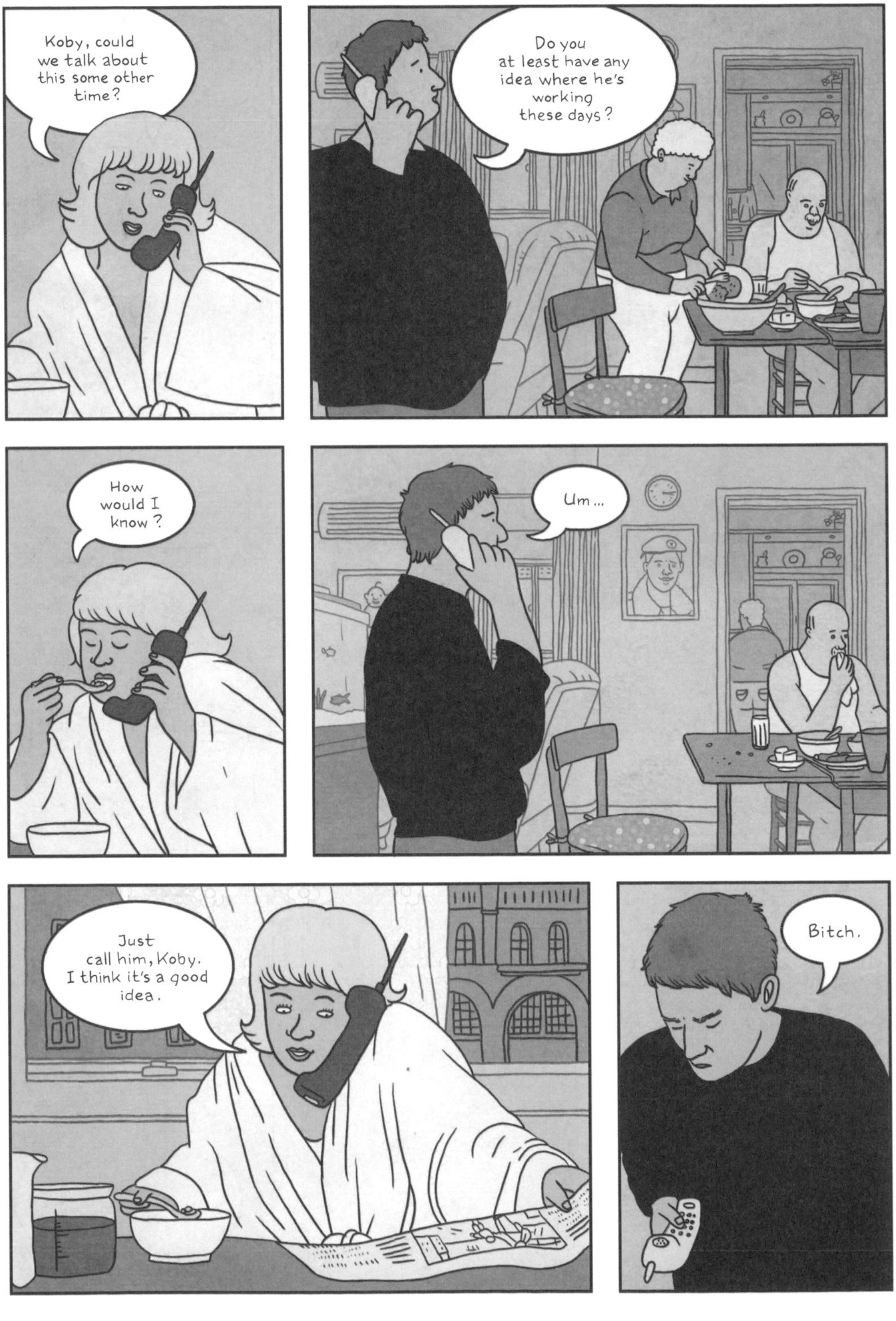

Koby, could we talk about this some other time?
Do you at least have any idea where he's working these days?
How would I know?
Um...
Just call him, Koby. I think it's a good idea.
Bitch.

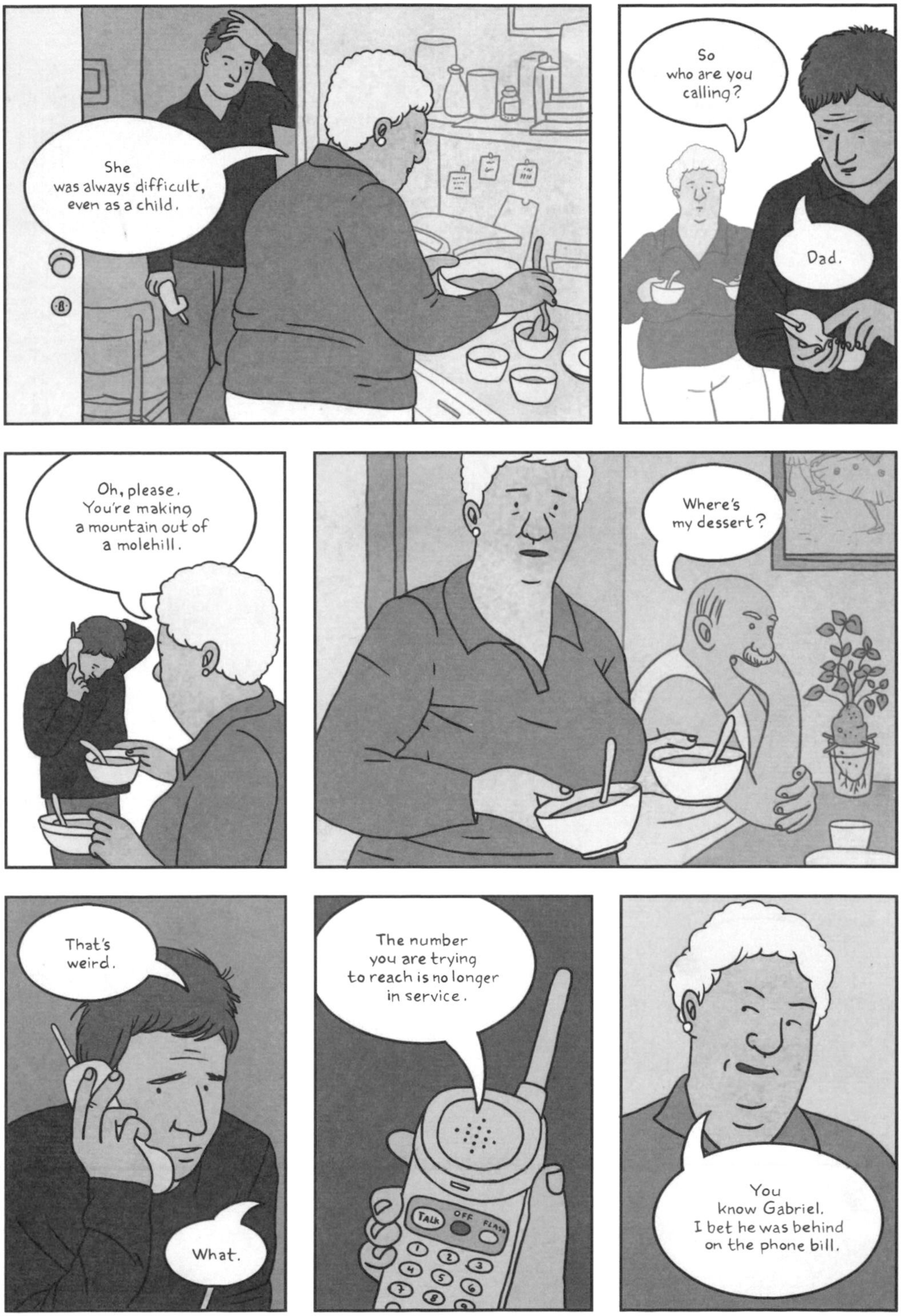
She was always difficult, even as a child.
So who are you calling?
Dad.
Oh, please. You're making a mountain out of a molehill.
Where's my dessert?
That's weird.
What.
The number you are trying to reach is no longer in service.
TALK
OFF
FLASH
You know Gabriel. I bet he was behind on the phone bill.

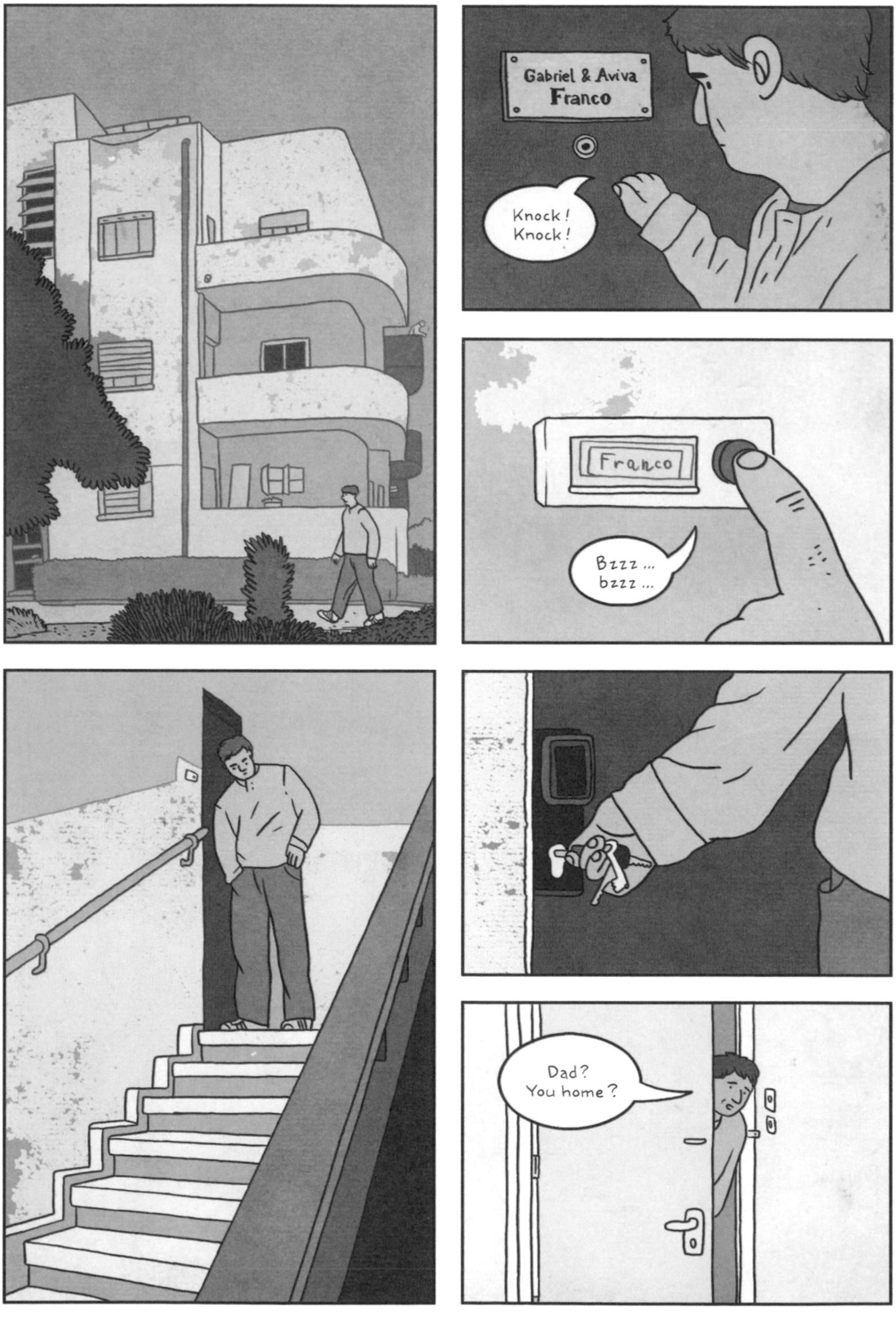
Gabriel & Aviva
Franco
Knock! Knock!
Franco
Bzzz... bzzz...
Dad? You home?

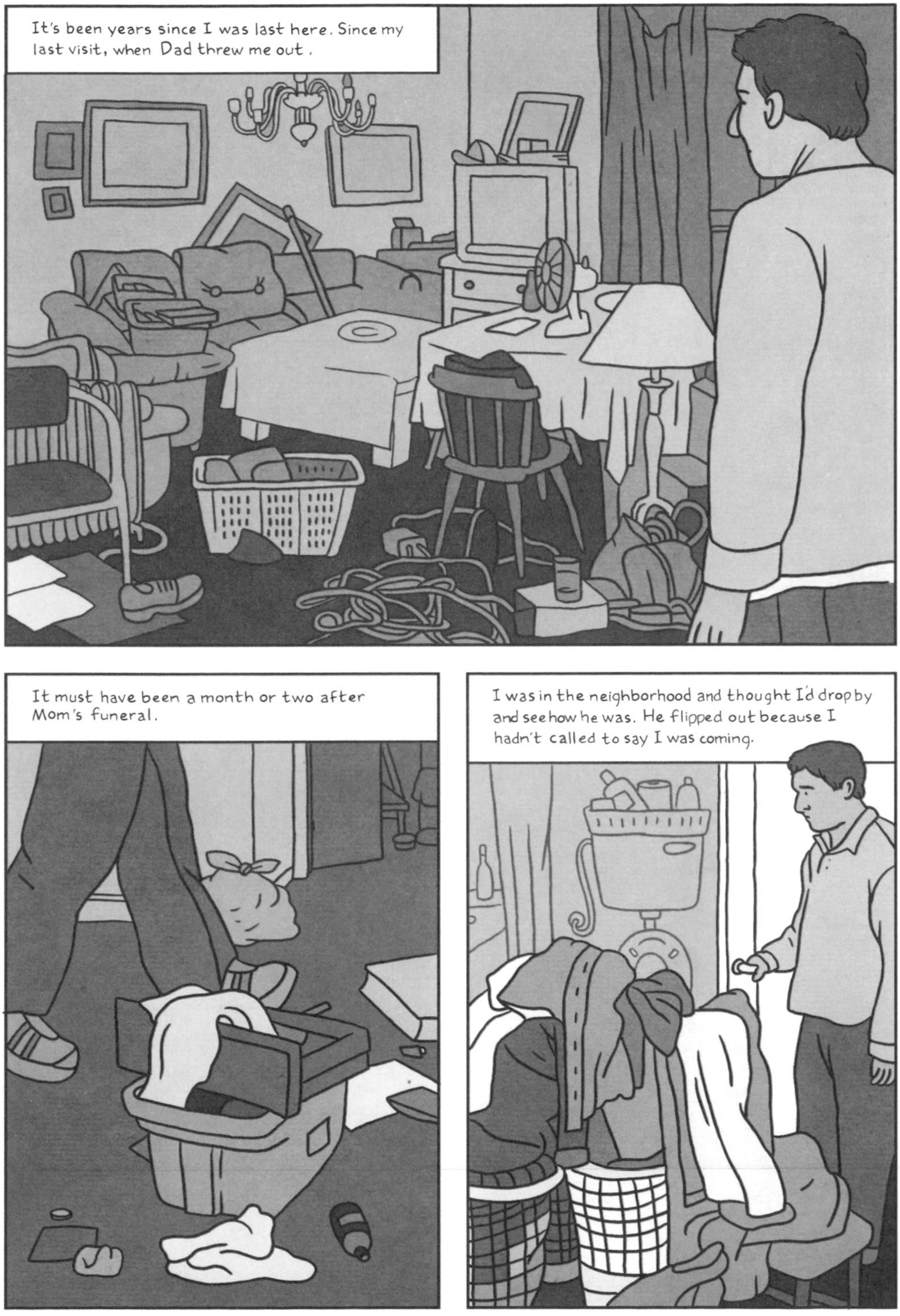
It's been years since I was last here. Since my last visit, when Dad threw me out.
It must have been a month or two after Mom's funeral.
I was in the neighborhood and thought I'd drop by and see how he was. He flipped out because I hadn't called to say I was coming.

Aunt Ruthie was here, she tried to calm him down but he went on and on. I need my privacy, he said. I need my goddamn privacy.

Later he kind of apologized, but from then on I wouldn't see him at home. Only in cafes, or in the park.

Five times in three years.

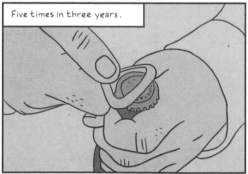

And then not even that.

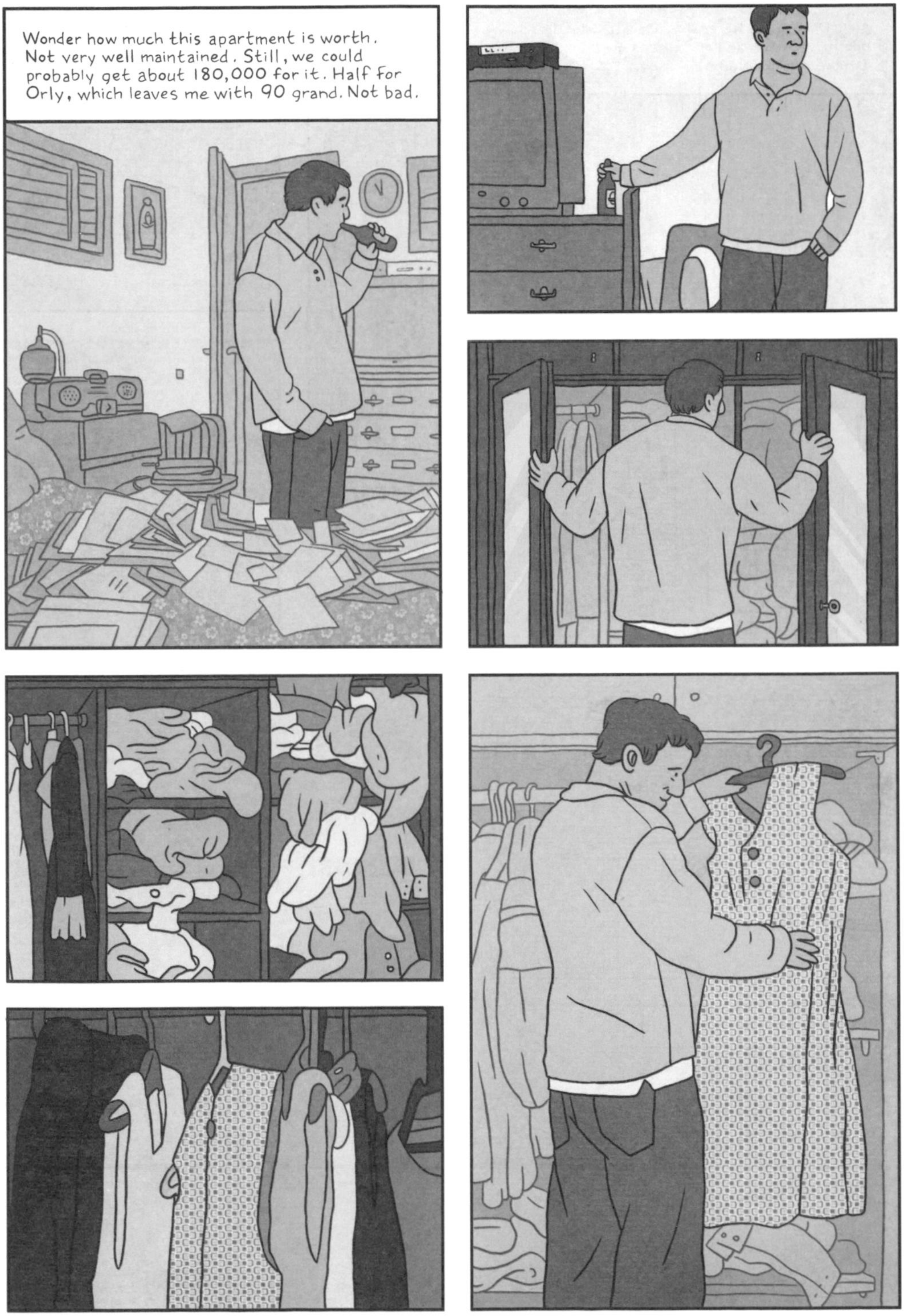
Wonder how much this apartment is worth. Not very well maintained. Still, we could probably get about 180,000 for it. Half for Orly, which leaves me with 90 grand. Not bad.

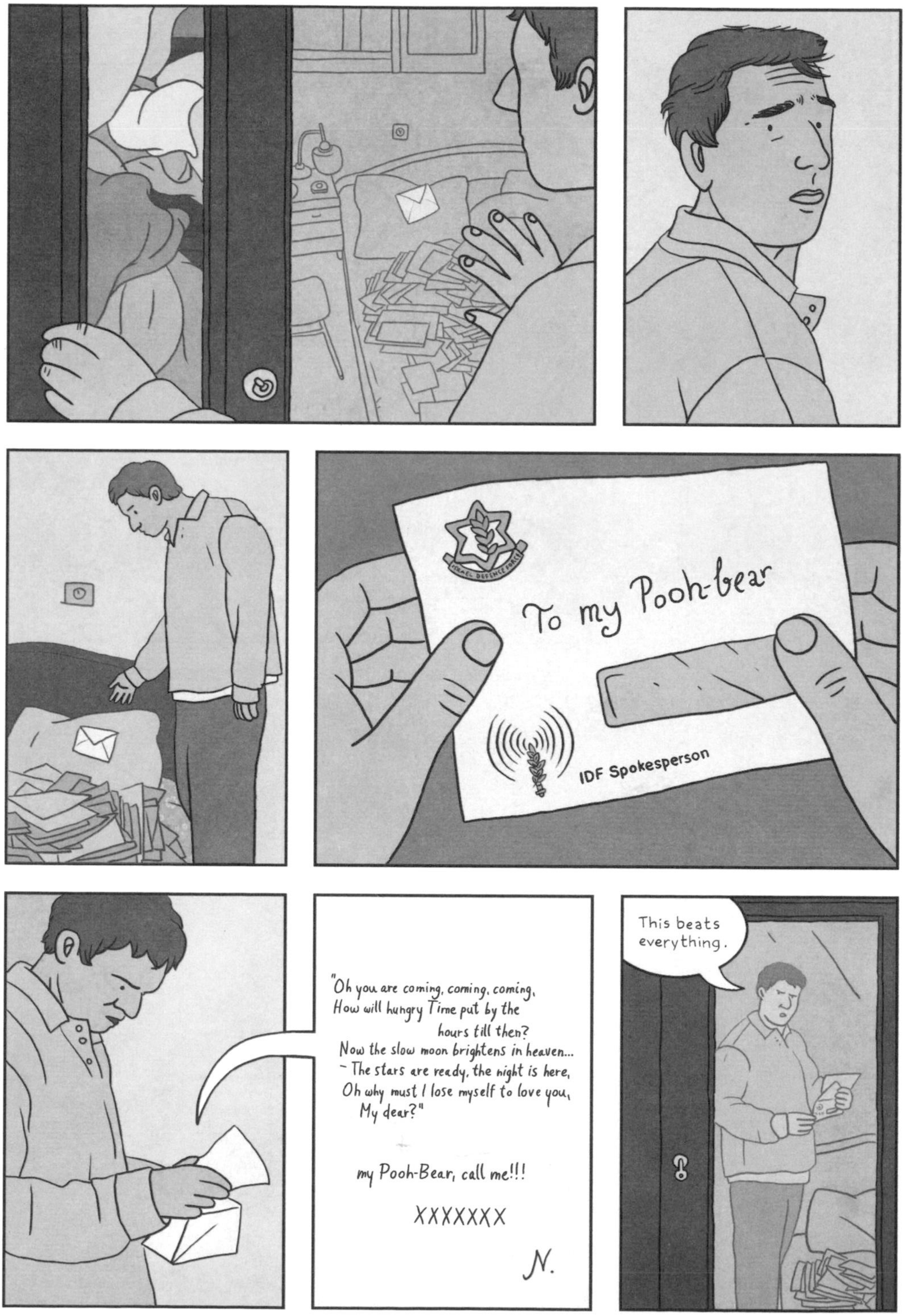

ISRAEL DEFENCE FORCES
To my Pooh-bear
IDF Spokesperson
"Oh you are coming, coming, coming,
How will hungry Time put by the
hours till then?
Now the slow moon brightens in heaven...
- The stars are ready, the night is here,
Oh why must I lose myself to love you,
My dear?"
my Pooh-Bear, call me!!!
XXXXXXX
N.
This beats everything.

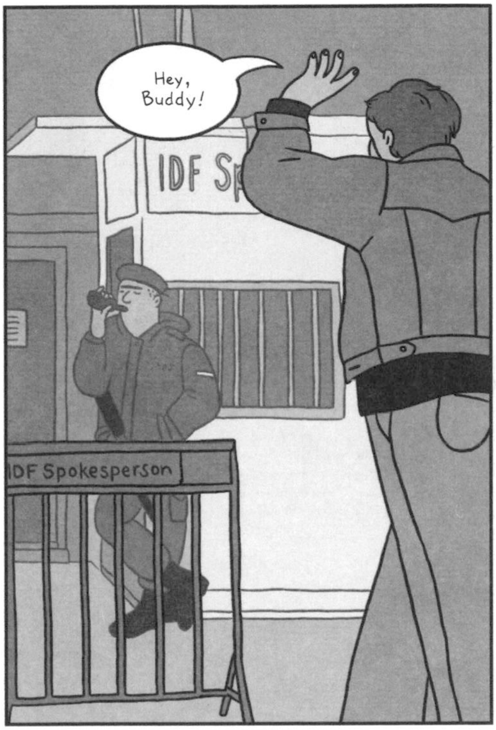
Hey, Buddy!
IDF Sp
IDF Spokesperson

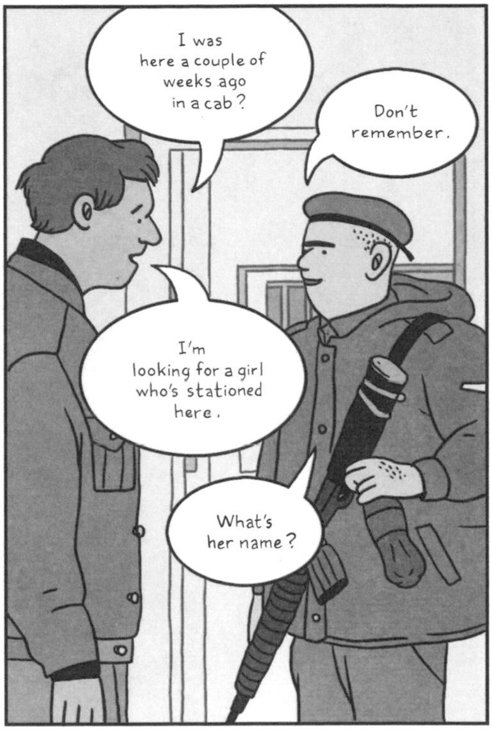
I was here a couple of weeks ago in a cab?
Don't remember.
I'm looking for a girl who's stationed here.
What's her name?

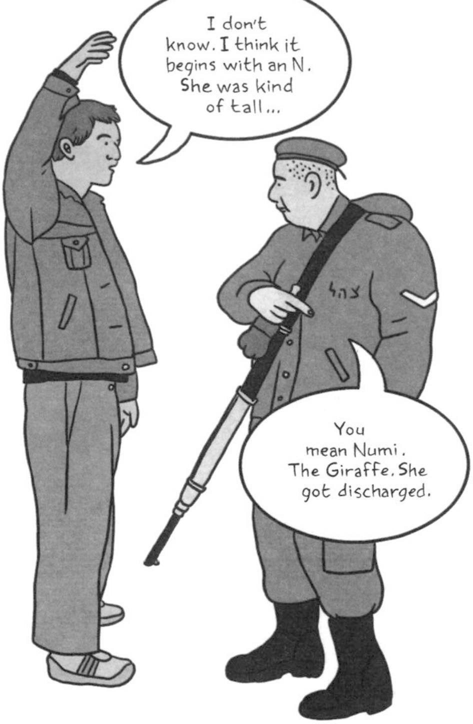
I don't know. I think it begins with an N. She was kind of tall...
You mean Numi. The Giraffe. She got discharged.

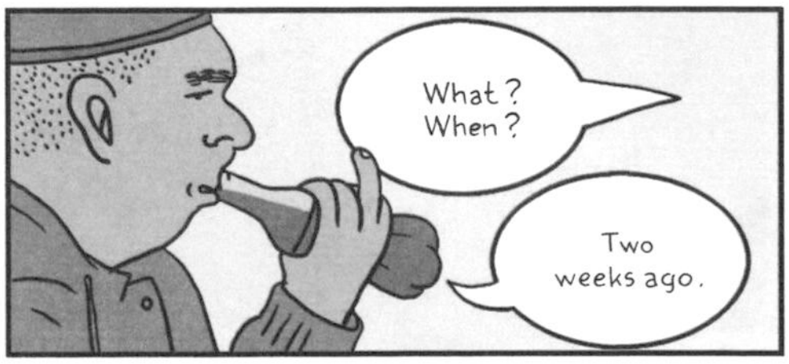
What? When?
Two weeks ago.

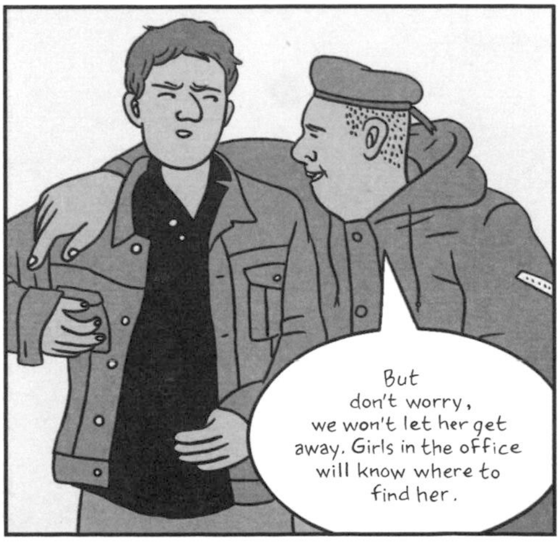
But don't worry, we won't let her get away. Girls in the office will know where to find her.

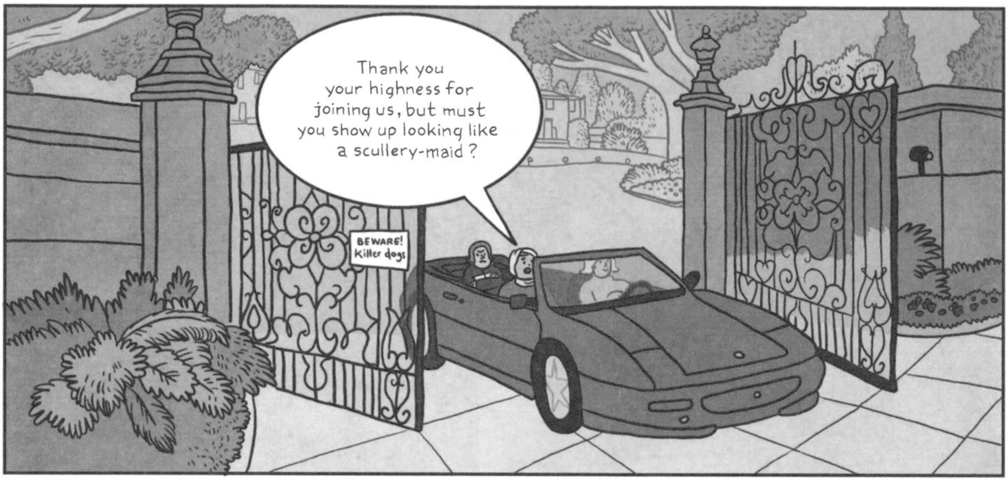
BEWARE! Killer dogs
Thank you your highness for joining us, but must you show up looking like a scullery-maid?

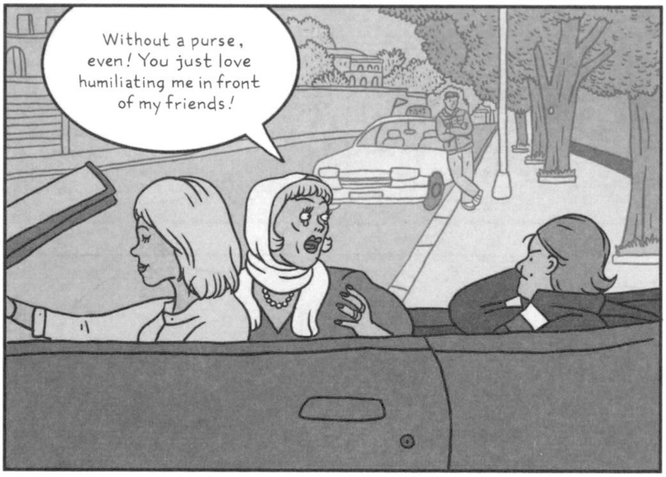
Without a purse, even! You just love humiliating me in front of my friends!

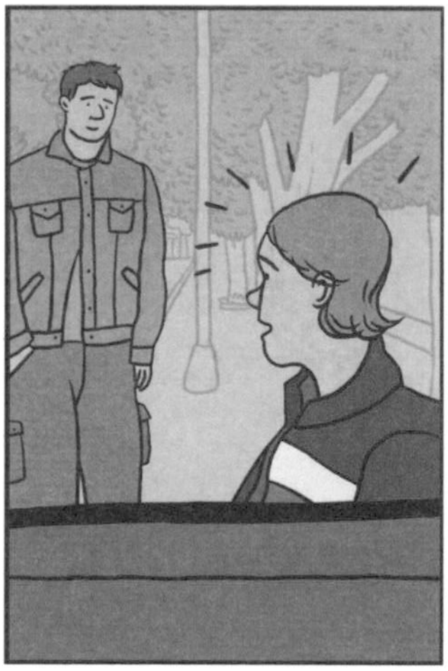

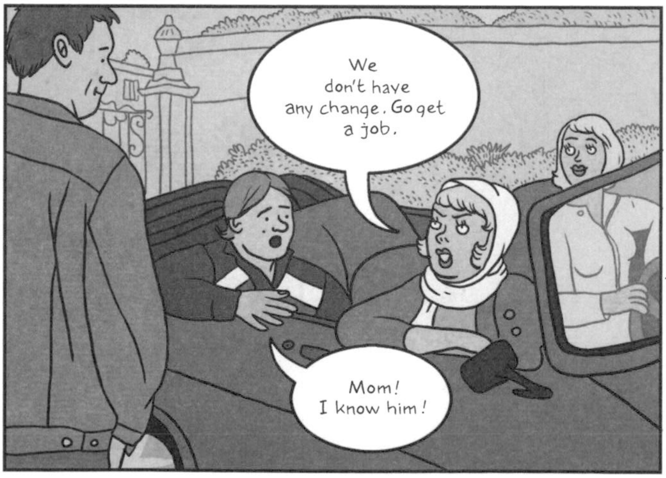
We don't have any change. Go get a job.
Mom! I know him!

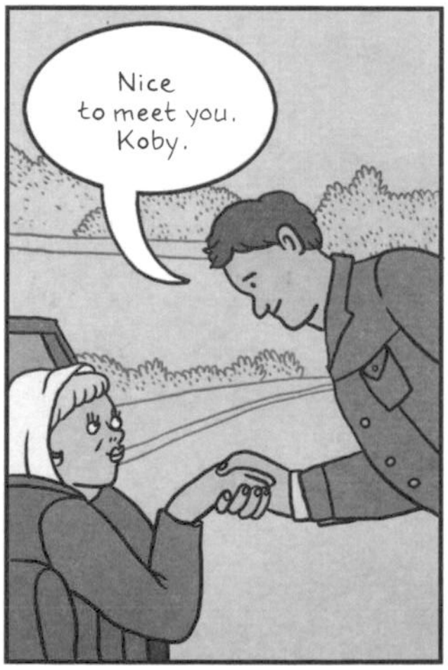
Nice to meet you. Koby.

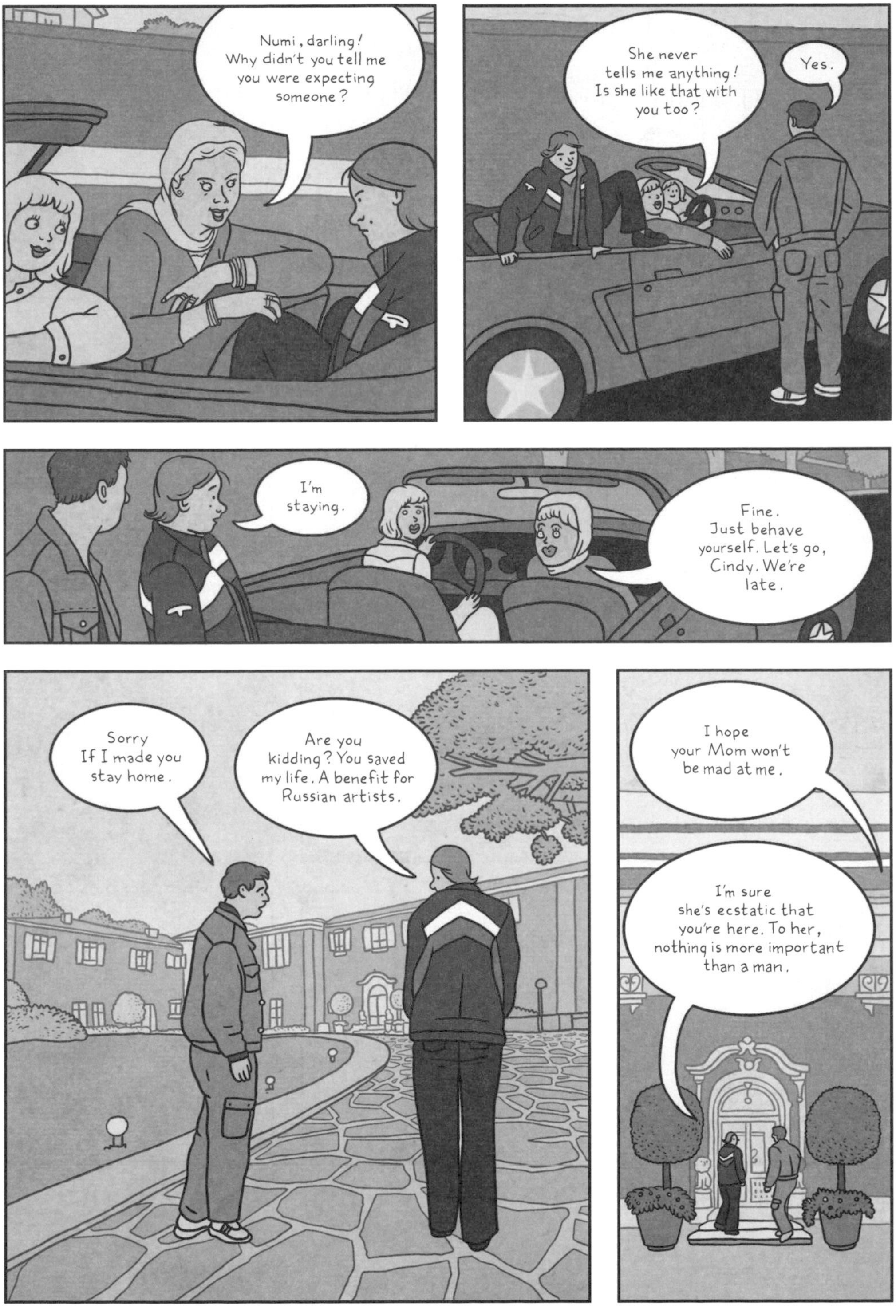
Numi, darling! Why didn't you tell me you were expecting someone?
She never tells me anything! Is she like that with you too?
Yes.
I'm staying.
Fine. Just behave yourself. Let's go, Cindy. We're late.
Sorry If I made you stay home.
Are you kidding? You saved my life. A benefit for Russian artists.
I hope your Mom won't be mad at me.
I'm sure she's ecstatic that you're here. To her, nothing is more important than a man.

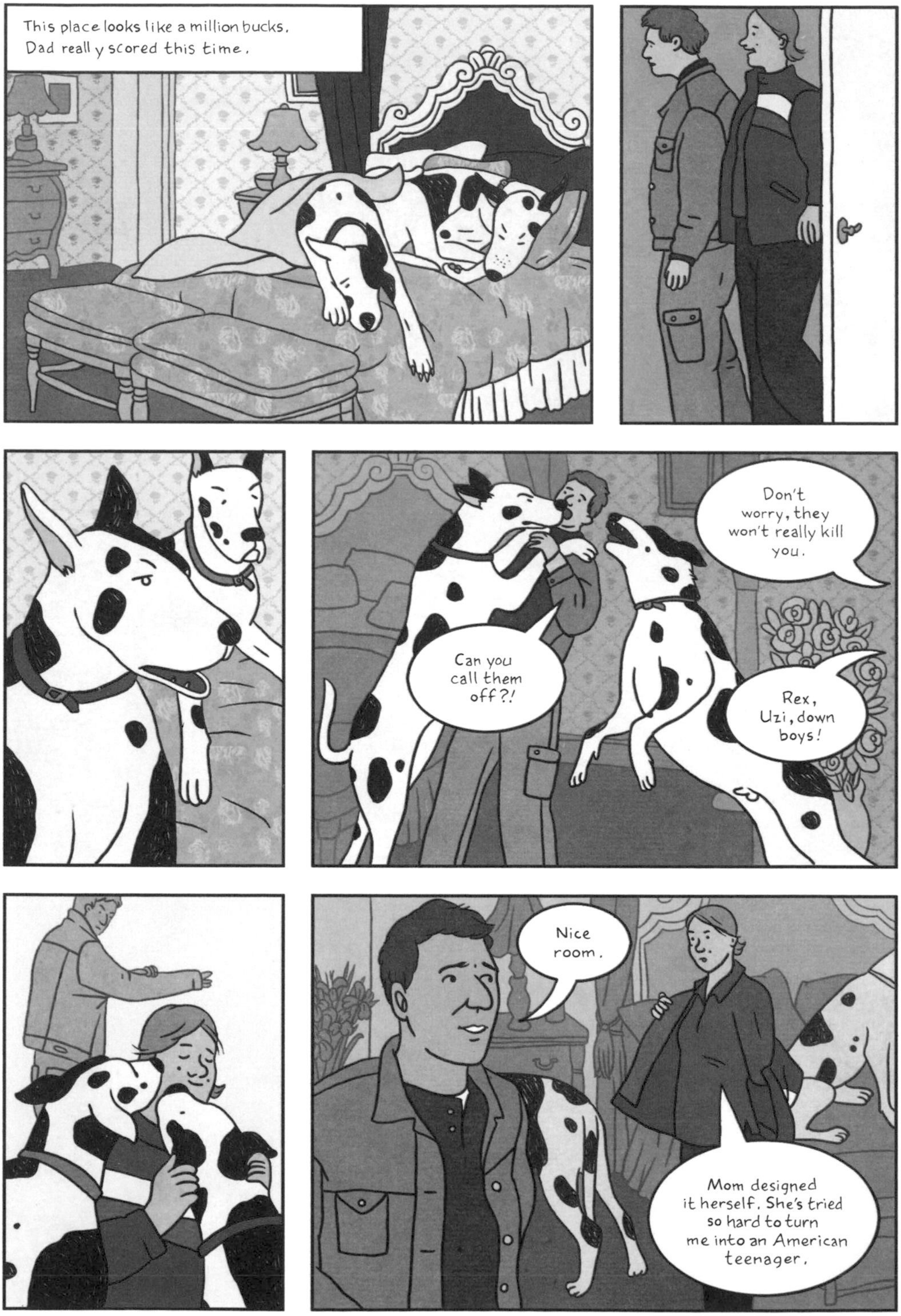
This place looks like a million bucks. Dad really scored this time.
Don't worry, they won't really kill you.
Can you call them off?!
Rex, Uzi, down boys!
Nice room.
Mom designed it herself. She's tried so hard to turn me into an American teenager.

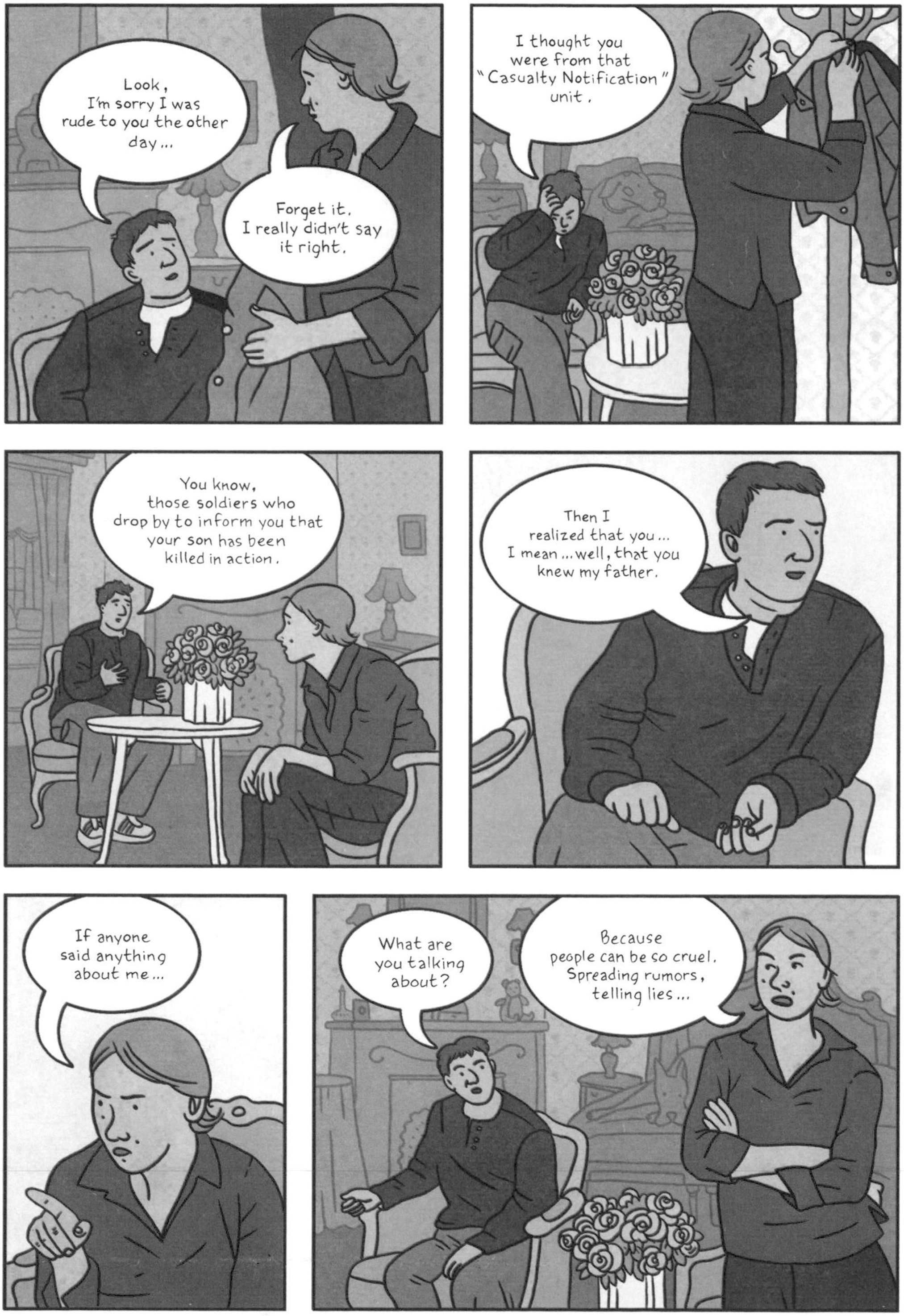
Look, I'm sorry I was rude to you the other day...
Forget it. I really didn't say it right.
I thought you were from that "Casualty Notification" unit.
You know, those soldiers who drop by to inform you that your son has been killed in action.
Then I realized that you... I mean... well, that you knew my father.
If anyone said anything about me...
What are you talking about?
Because people can be so cruel. Spreading rumors, telling lies...

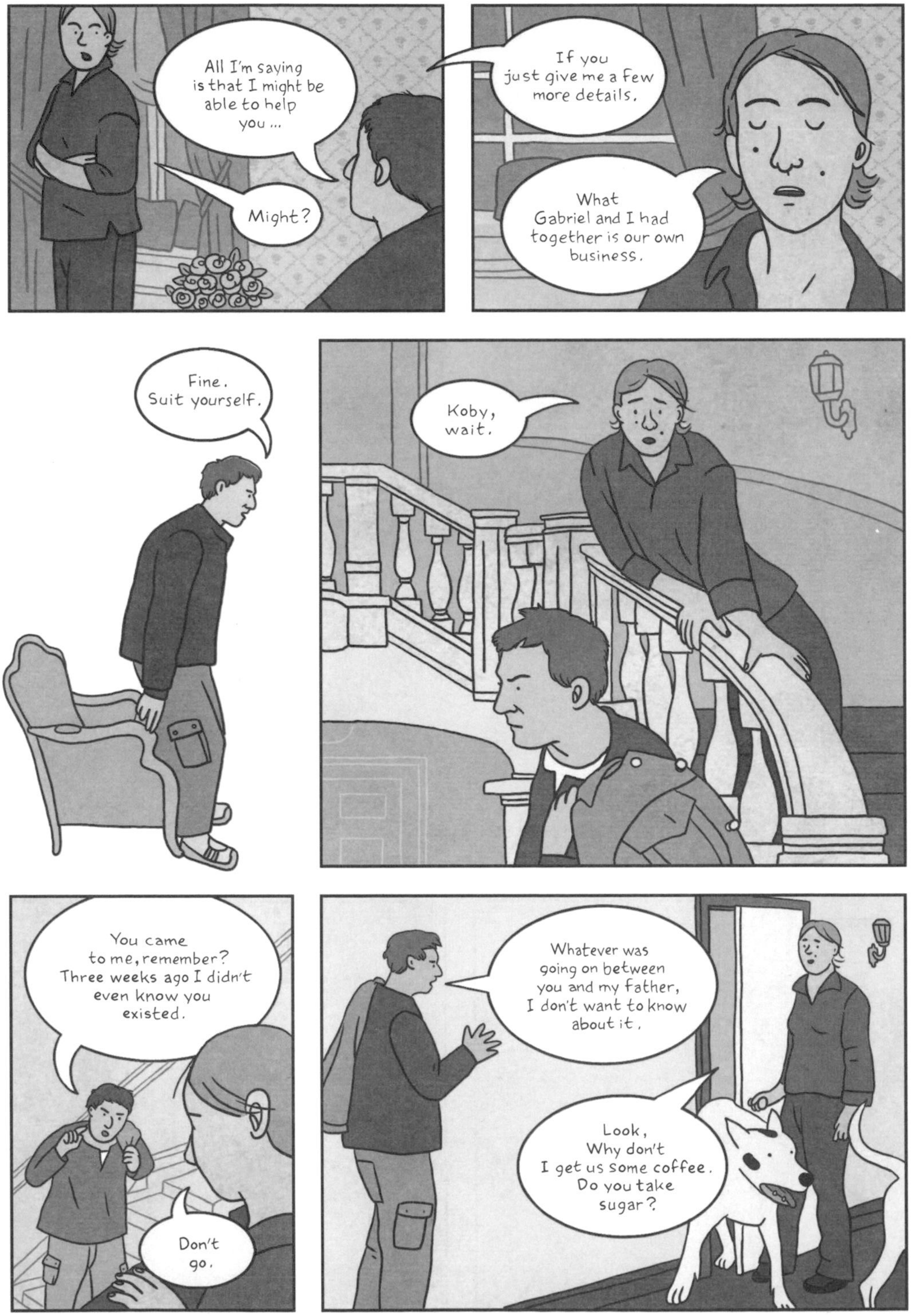
All I'm saying is that I might be able to help you ...
Might?
If you just give me a few more details.
What Gabriel and I had together is our own business.
Fine. Suit yourself.
Koby, wait.
You came to me, remember? Three weeks ago I didn't even know you existed.
Don't go.
Whatever was going on between you and my father, I don't want to know about it.
Look, Why don't I get us some coffee. Do you take sugar?

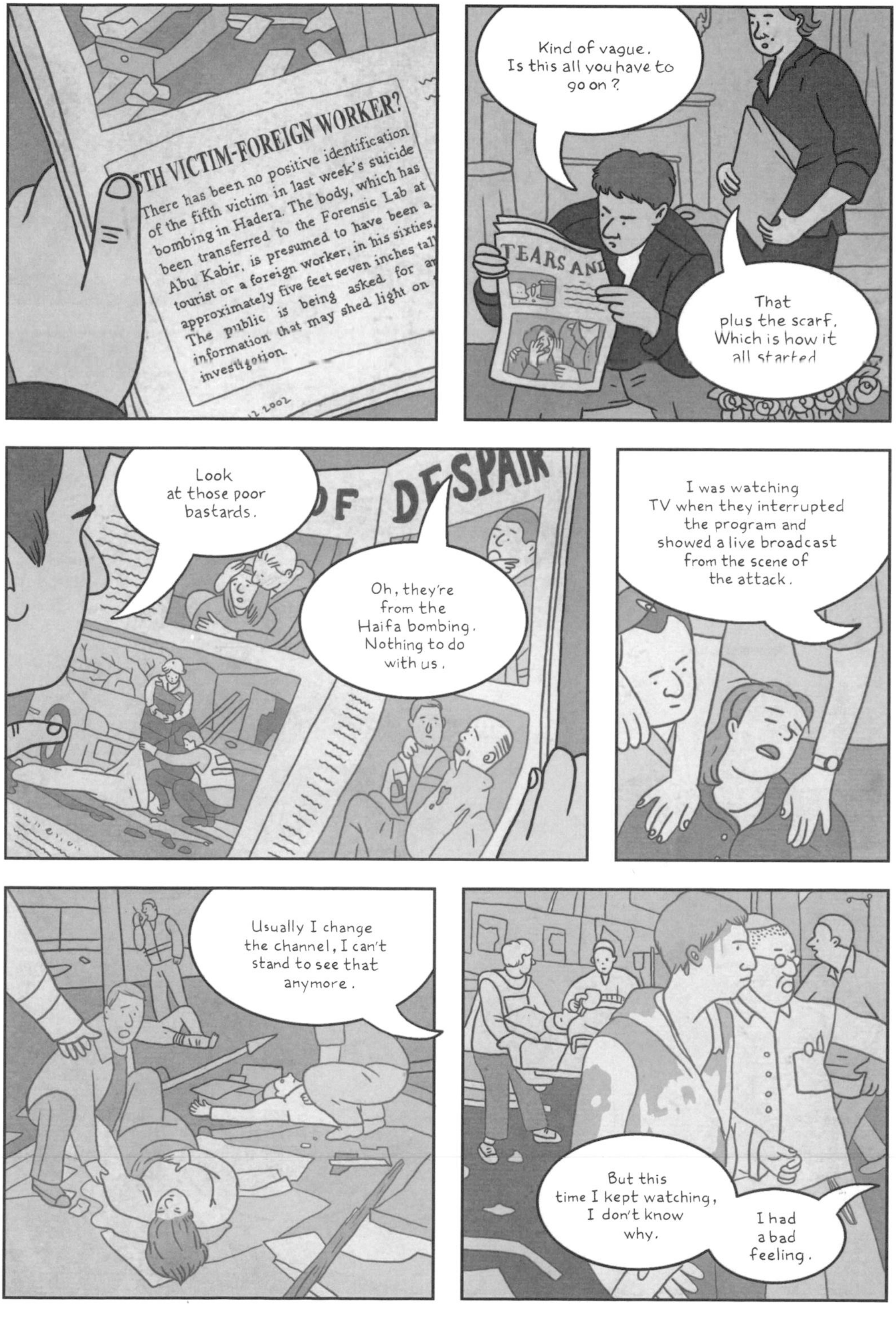
5TH VICTIM-FOREIGN WORKER?
There has been no positive identification of the fifth victim in last week's suicide bombing in Hadera. The body, which has been transferred to the Forensic Lab at Abu Kabir, is presumed to have been a tourist or a foreign worker, in his sixties, approximately five feet seven inches tal
The public is being asked for a
information that may shed light on
investigation.
Kind of vague. Is this all you have to go on?
TEARS AN
That plus the scarf. Which is how it all started.
Look at those poor bastards.
DESPAIR
Oh, they're from the Haifa bombing. Nothing to do with us.
I was watching TV when they interrupted the program and showed a live broadcast from the scene of the attack.
Usually I change the channel, I can't stand to see that anymore.
But this time I kept watching, I don't know why.
I had a bad feeling.

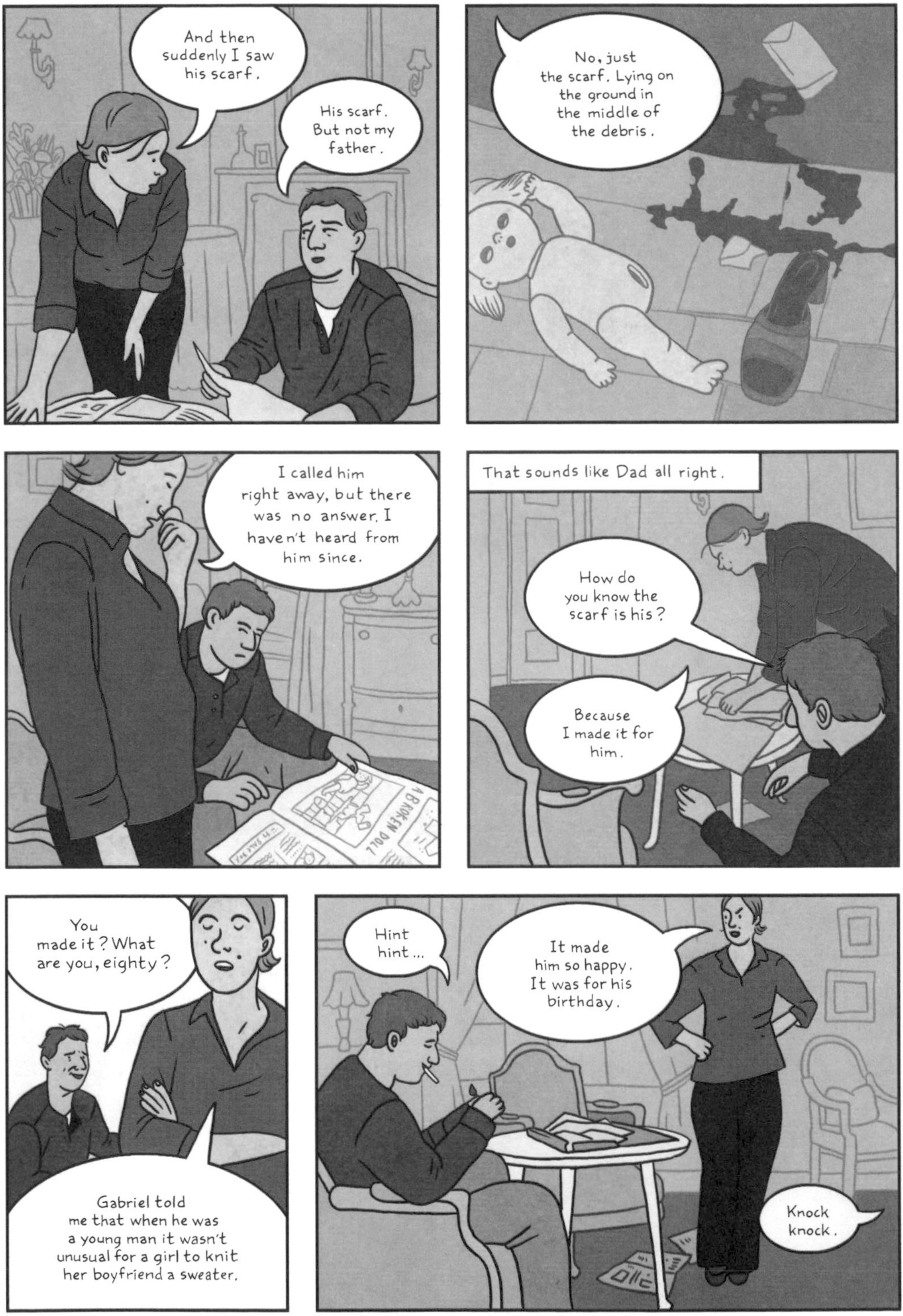

And then suddenly I saw his scarf.
His scarf. But not my father.
No, just the scarf. Lying on the ground in the middle of the debris.
I called him right away, but there was no answer. I haven't heard from him since.
That sounds like Dad all right.
How do you know the scarf is his?
Because I made it for him.
You made it? What are you, eighty?
Gabriel told me that when he was a young man it wasn't unusual for a girl to knit her boyfriend a sweater.
Hint hint...
It made him so happy. It was for his birthday.
Knock knock.

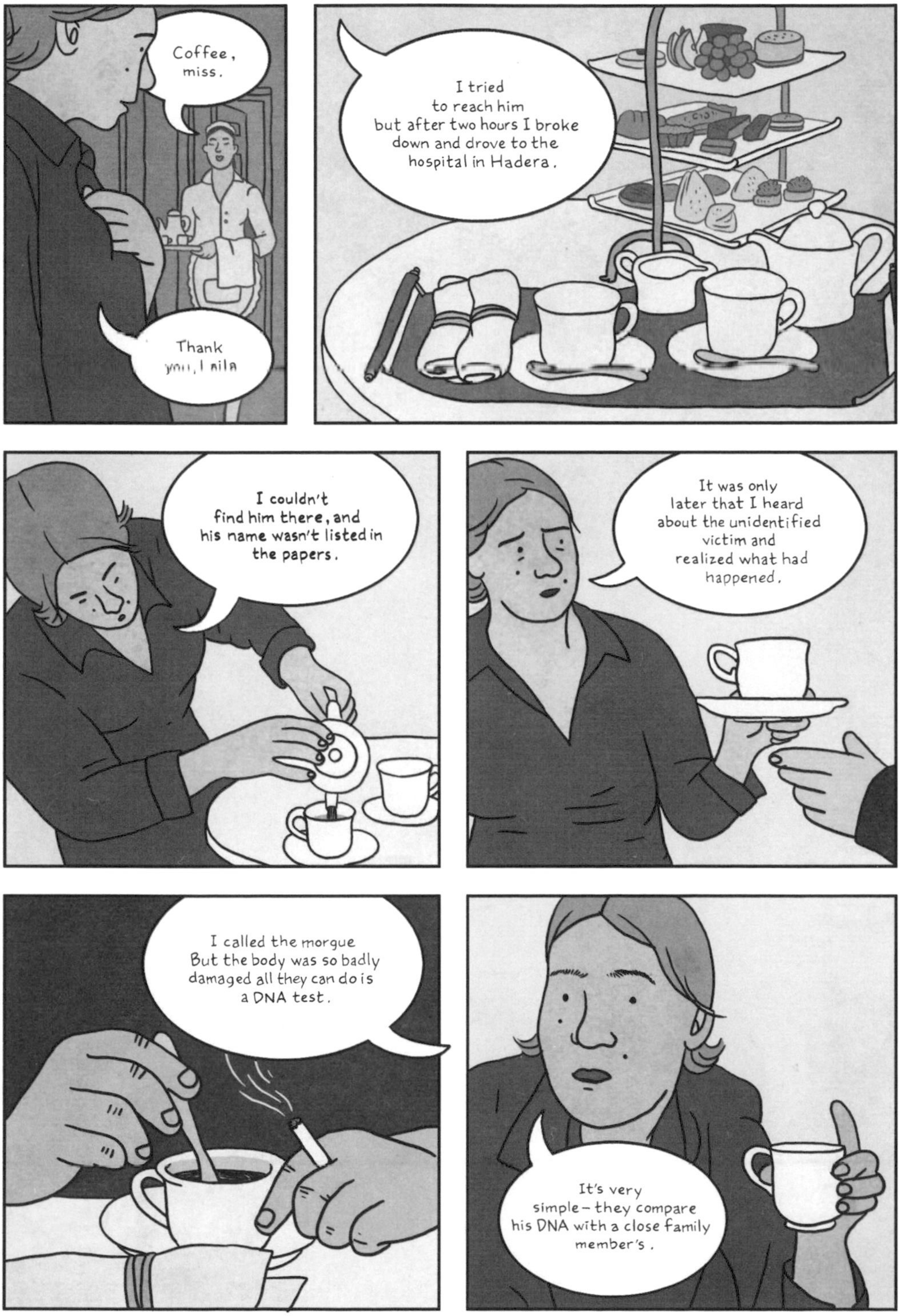
Coffee, miss.
Thank you, Laila
I tried to reach him but after two hours I broke down and drove to the hospital in Hadera.
I couldn't find him there, and his name wasn't listed in the papers.
It was only later that I heard about the unidentified victim and realized what had happened.
I called the morgue But the body was so badly damaged all they can do is a DNA test.
It's very simple – they compare his DNA with a close family member's.

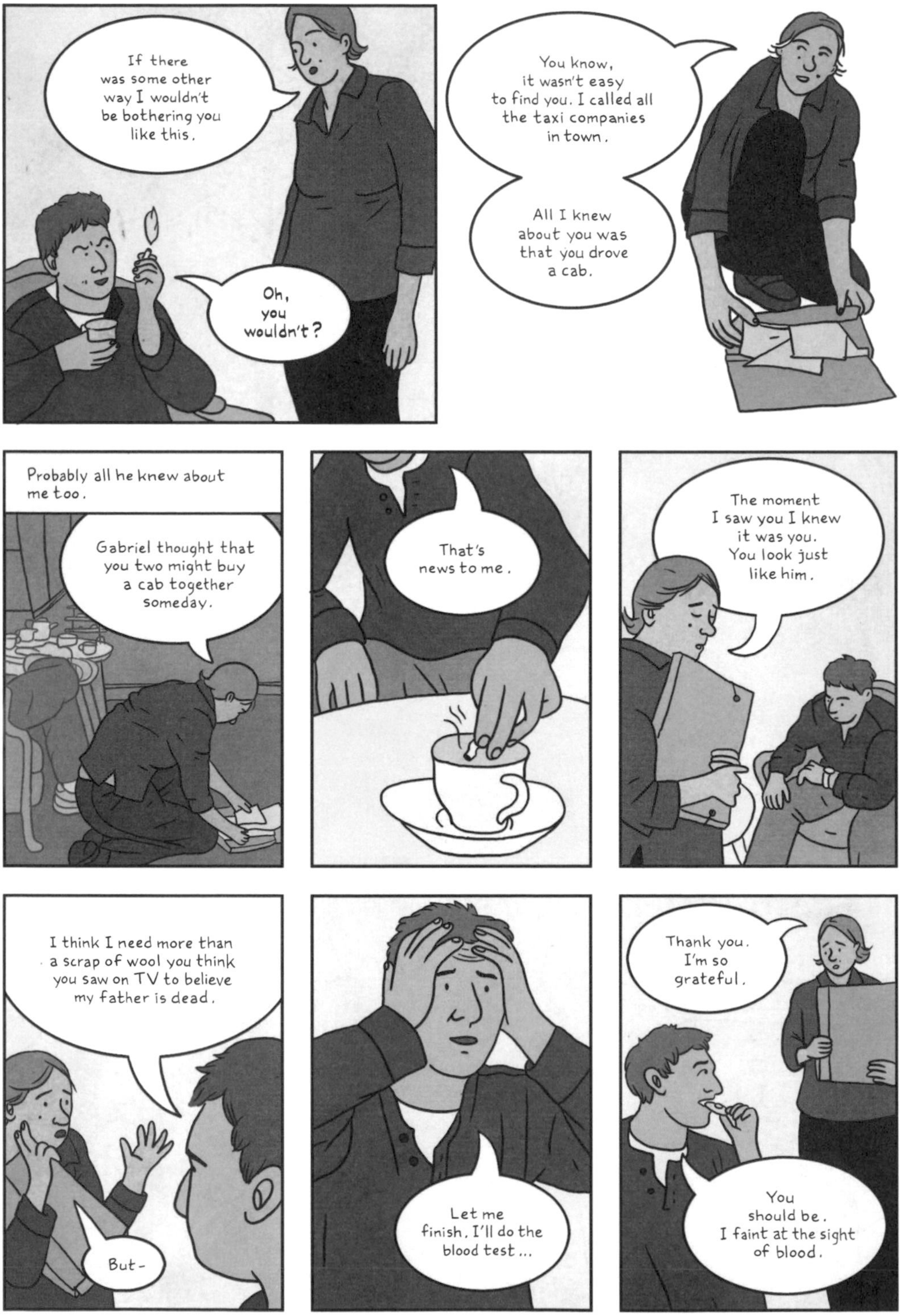
If there was some other way I wouldn't be bothering you like this.
Oh, you wouldn't?
You know, it wasn't easy to find you. I called all the taxi companies in town.
All I knew about you was that you drove a cab.
Probably all he knew about me too.
Gabriel thought that you two might buy a cab together someday.
That's news to me.
The moment I saw you I knew it was you. You look just like him.
I think I need more than a scrap of wool you think you saw on TV to believe my father is dead.
But-
Let me finish. I'll do the blood test...
Thank you. I'm so grateful.
You should be. I faint at the sight of blood.

chapter two
my travels with the giraffe

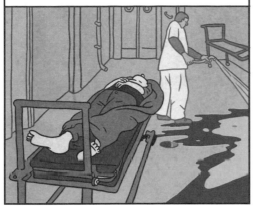

Pathological Institute for Forensic Medicine, Abu Kabir.

Any thoughts on lunch?

How about Chinese?

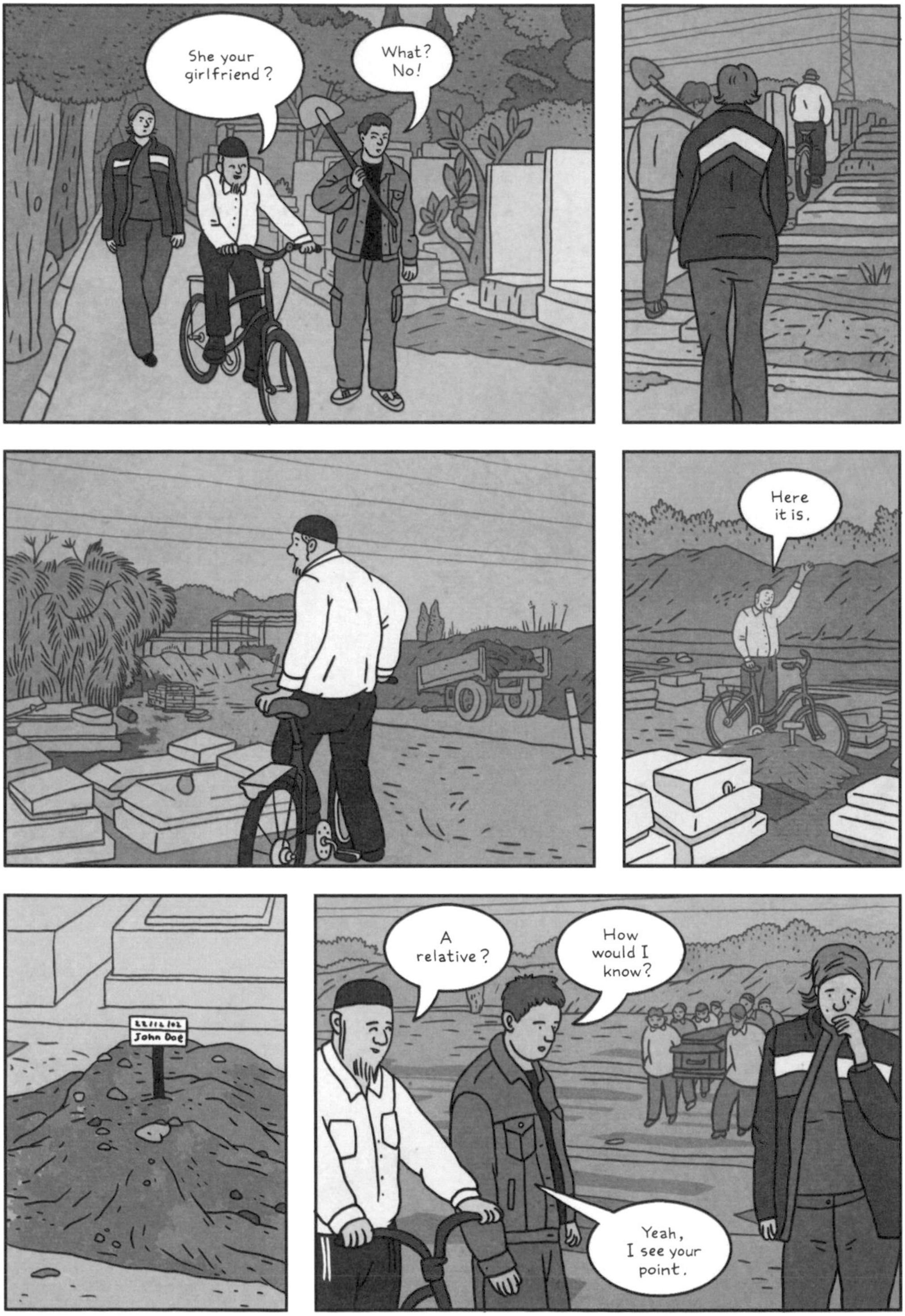
She your girlfriend?
What? No!
Here it is.
22/12/02
John Doe
A relative?
How would I know?
Yeah, I see your point.

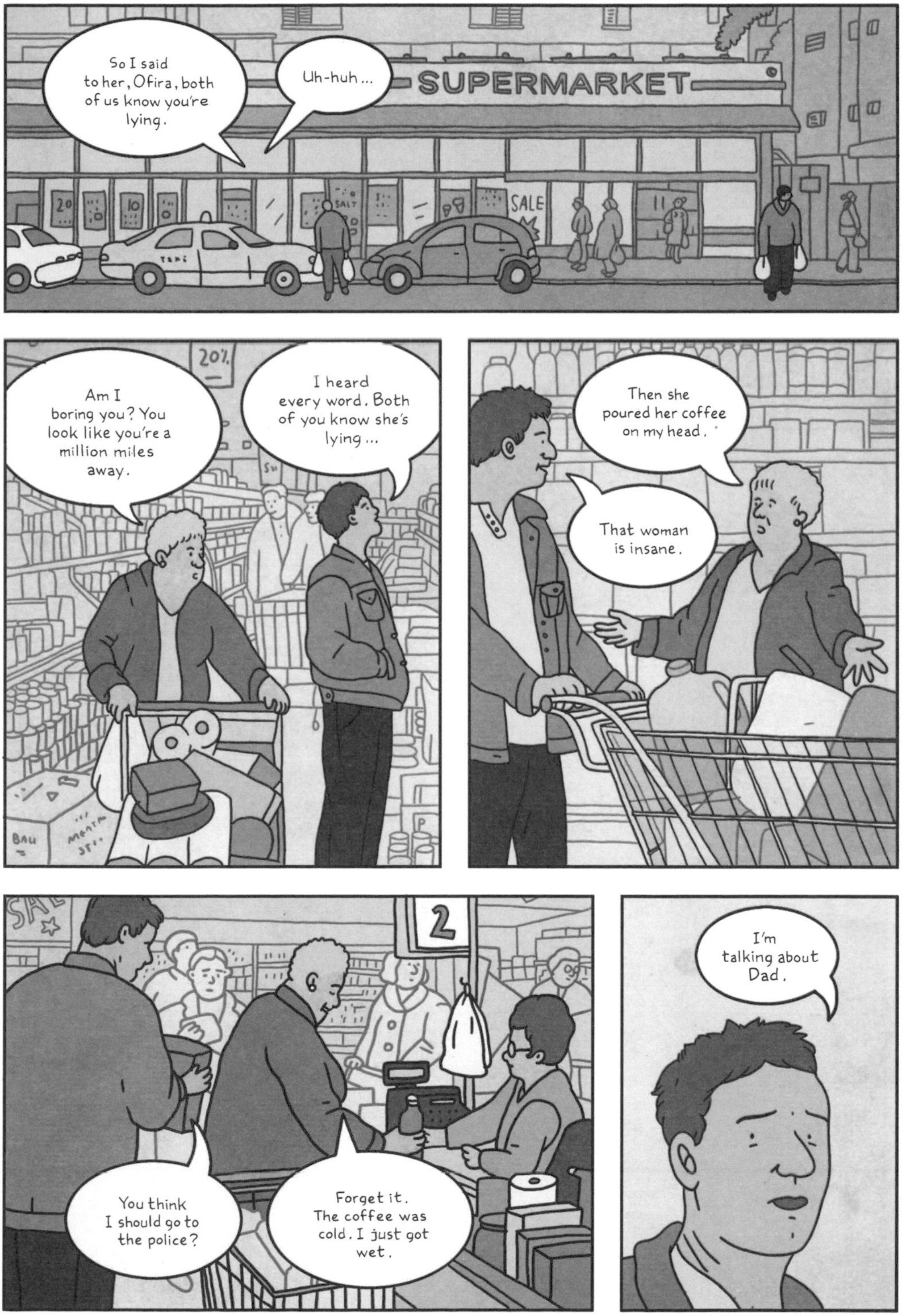
SUPERMARKET
So I said to her, Ofira, both of us know you're lying.
Uh-huh ...
SALE
Am I boring you? You look like you're a million miles away.
I heard every word. Both of you know she's lying ...
20%
Then she poured her coffee on my head.
That woman is insane.
You think I should go to the police?
Forget it. The coffee was cold. I just got wet.
2
I'm talking about Dad.

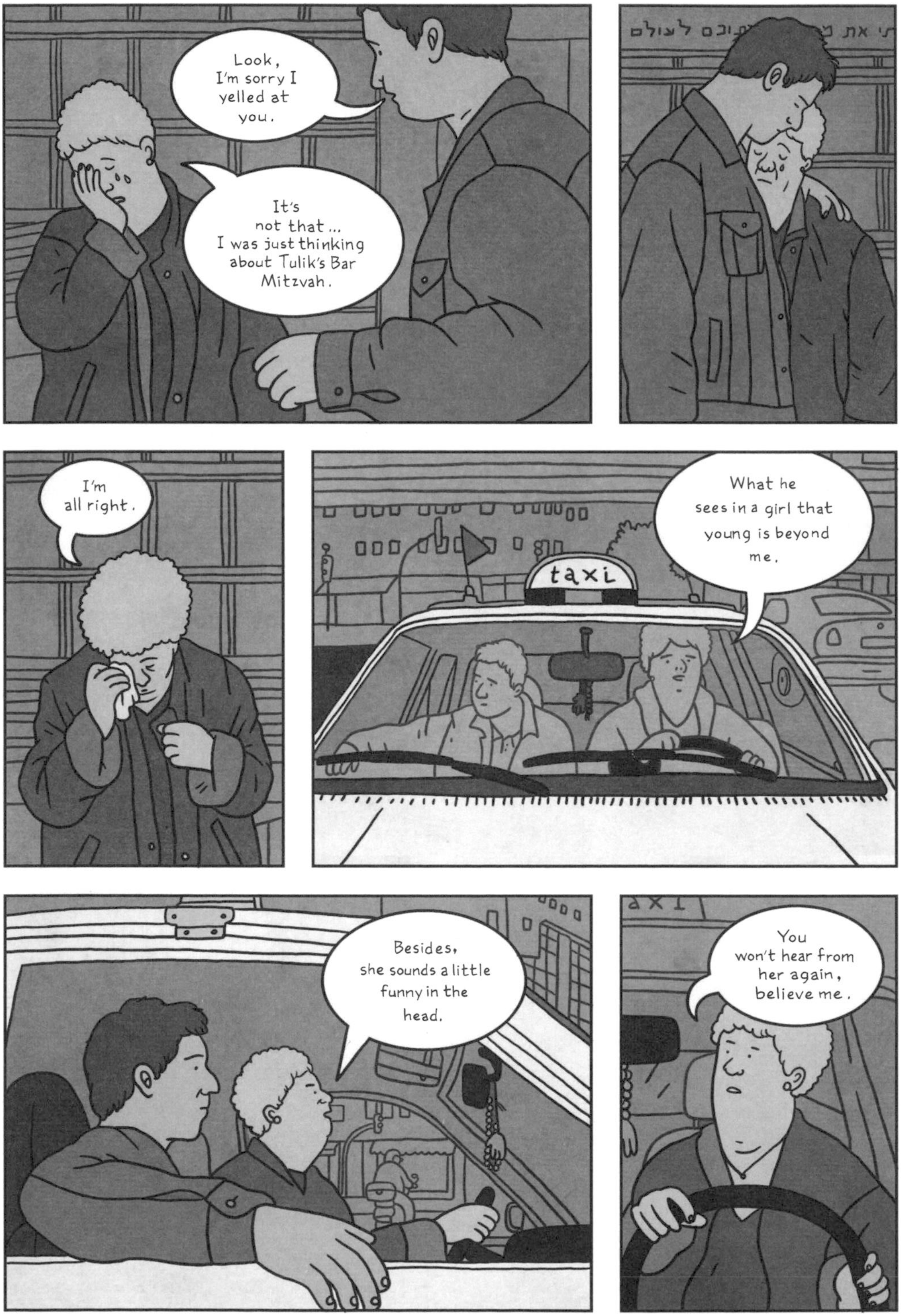
Look, I'm sorry I yelled at you.
It's not that... I was just thinking about Tulik's Bar Mitzvah.
I'm all right.
taxi
What he sees in a girl that young is beyond me.
Besides, she sounds a little funny in the head.
You won't hear from her again, believe me.

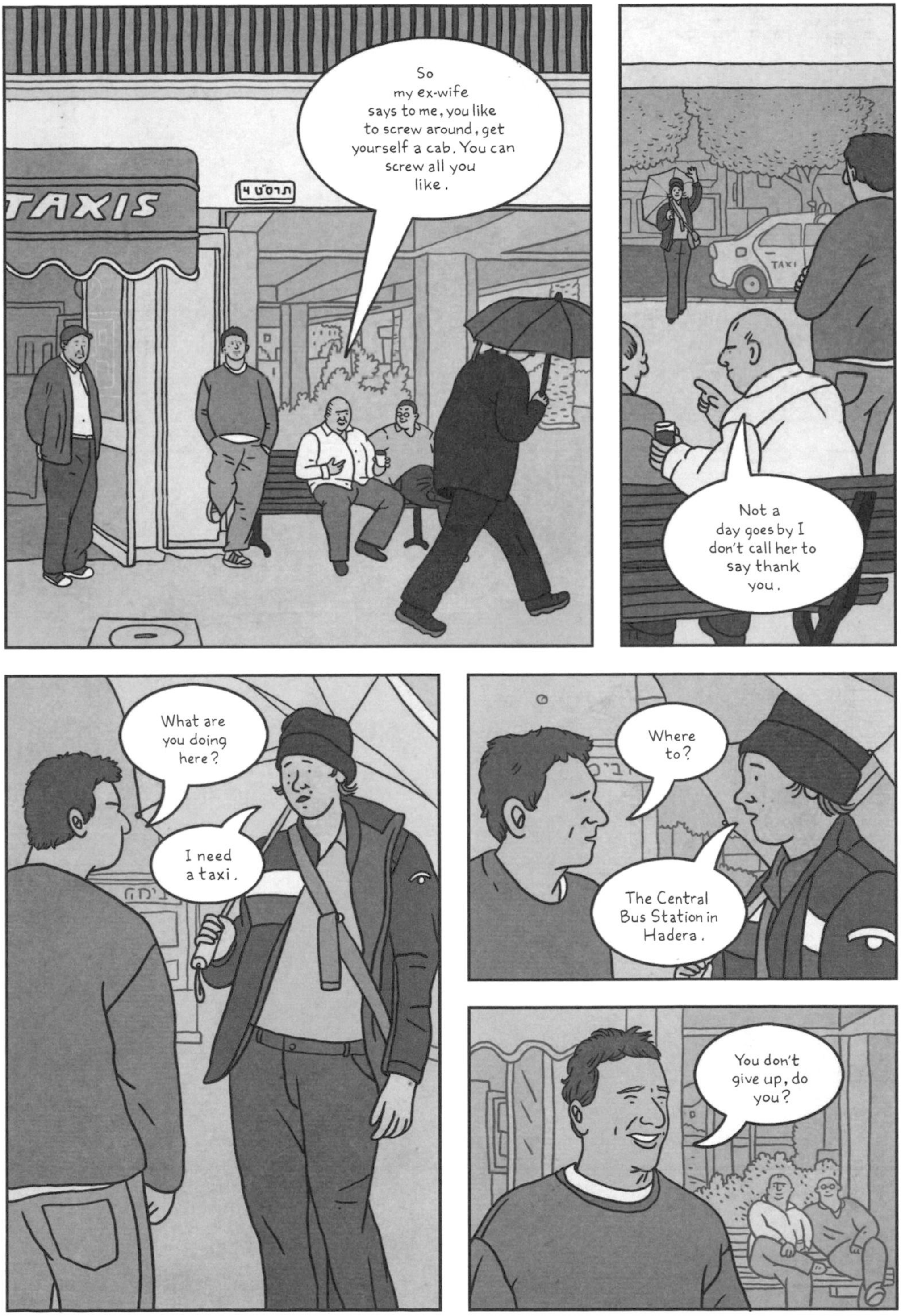
TAXIS
So my ex-wife says to me, you like to screw around, get yourself a cab. You can screw all you like.
TAXI
Not a day goes by I don't call her to say thank you.
What are you doing here?
I need a taxi.
Where to?
The Central Bus Station in Hadera.
You don't give up, do you?

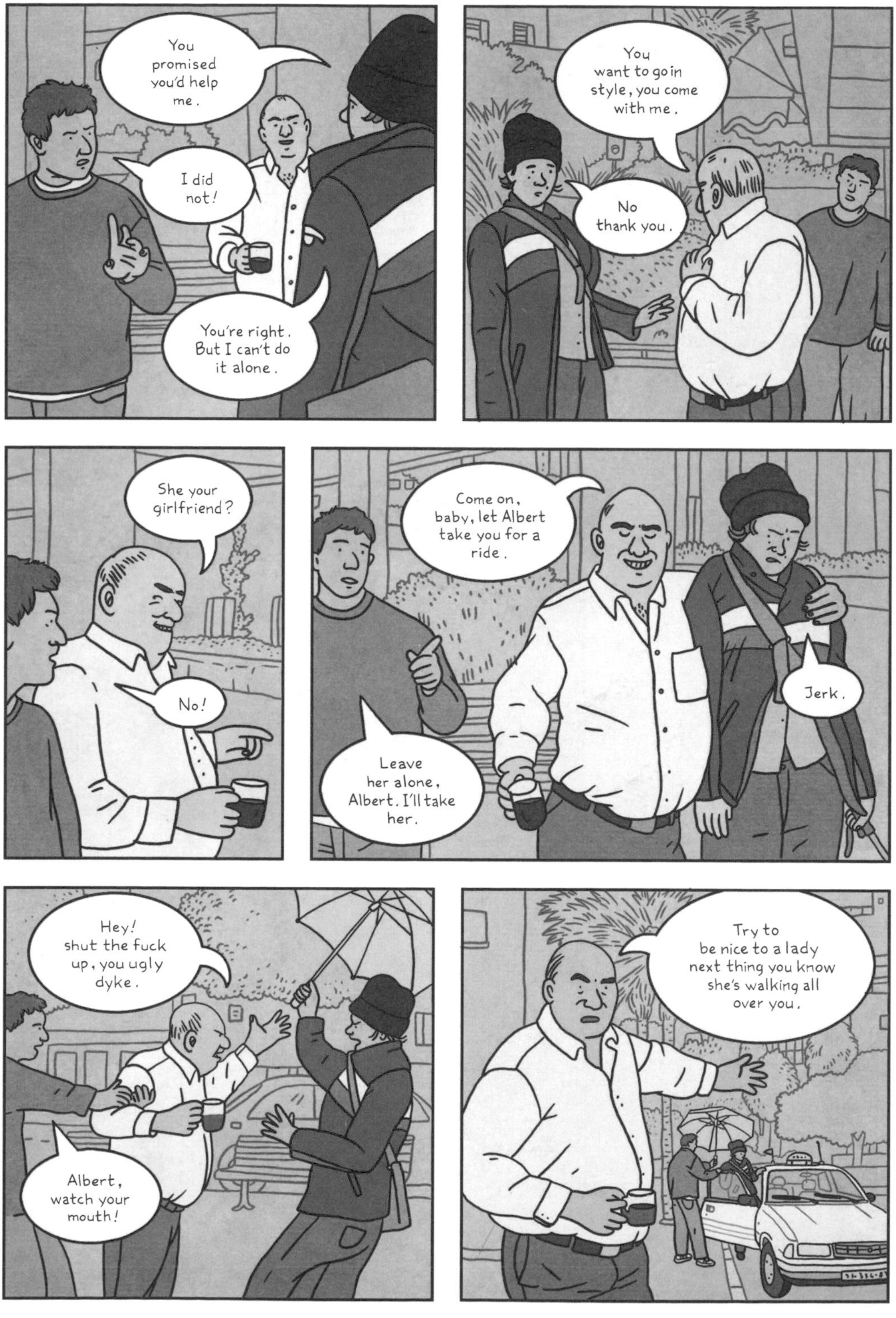
You promised you'd help me.
I did not!
You're right. But I can't do it alone.
You want to go in style, you come with me.
No thank you.
She your girlfriend?
No!
Come on, baby, let Albert take you for a ride.
Jerk.
Leave her alone, Albert. I'll take her.
Hey! shut the fuck up, you ugly dyke.
Albert, watch your mouth!
Try to be nice to a lady next thing you know she's walking all over you.

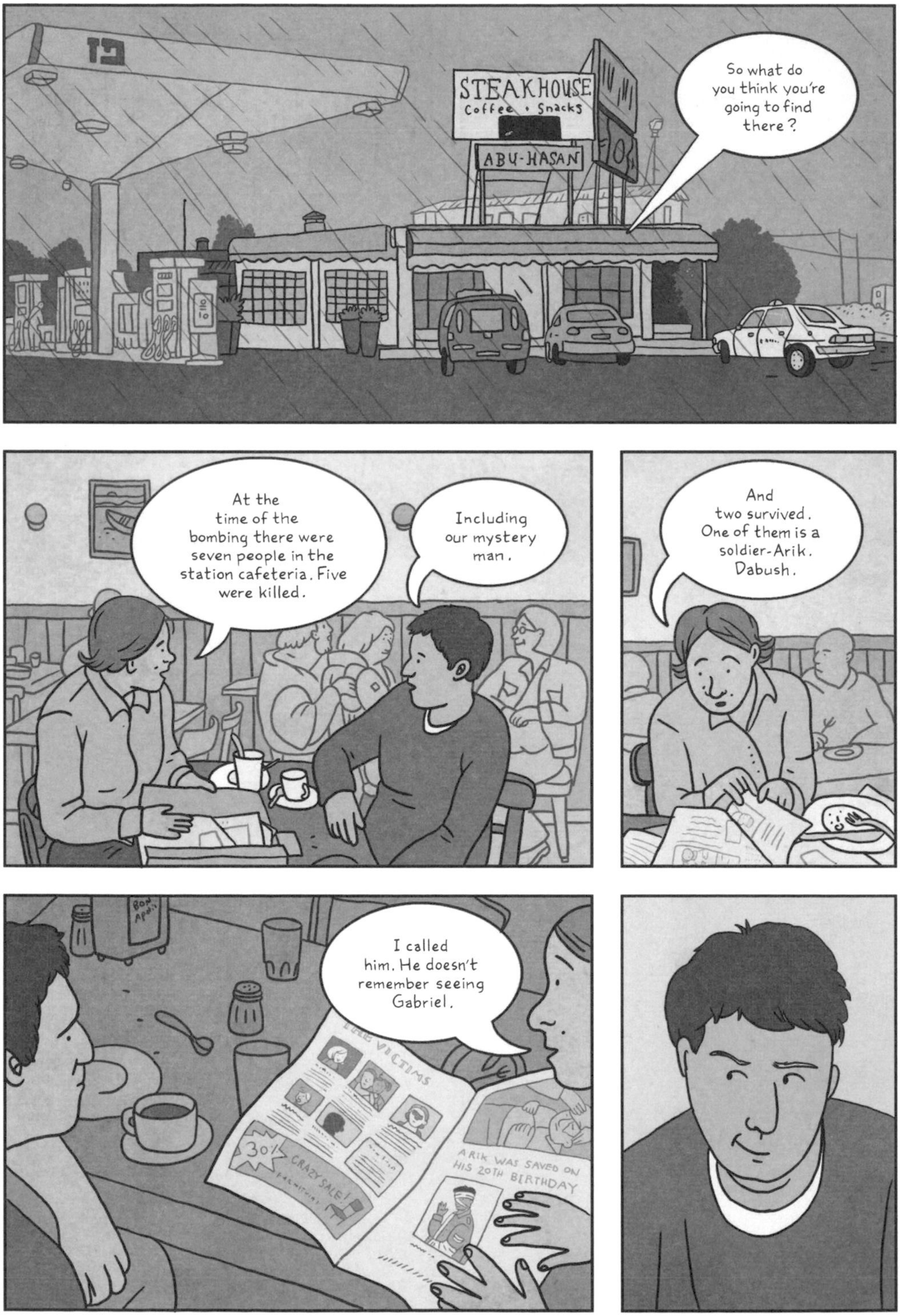
STEAKHOUSE
Coffee + Snacks
ABU-HASAN
So what do you think you're going to find there?
At the time of the bombing there were seven people in the station cafeteria. Five were killed.
Including our mystery man.
And two survived. One of them is a soldier-Arik. Dabush.
I called him. He doesn't remember seeing Gabriel.
THE VICTIMS
30%
CRAZY SALE!
ARIK WAS SAVED ON HIS 20TH BIRTHDAY

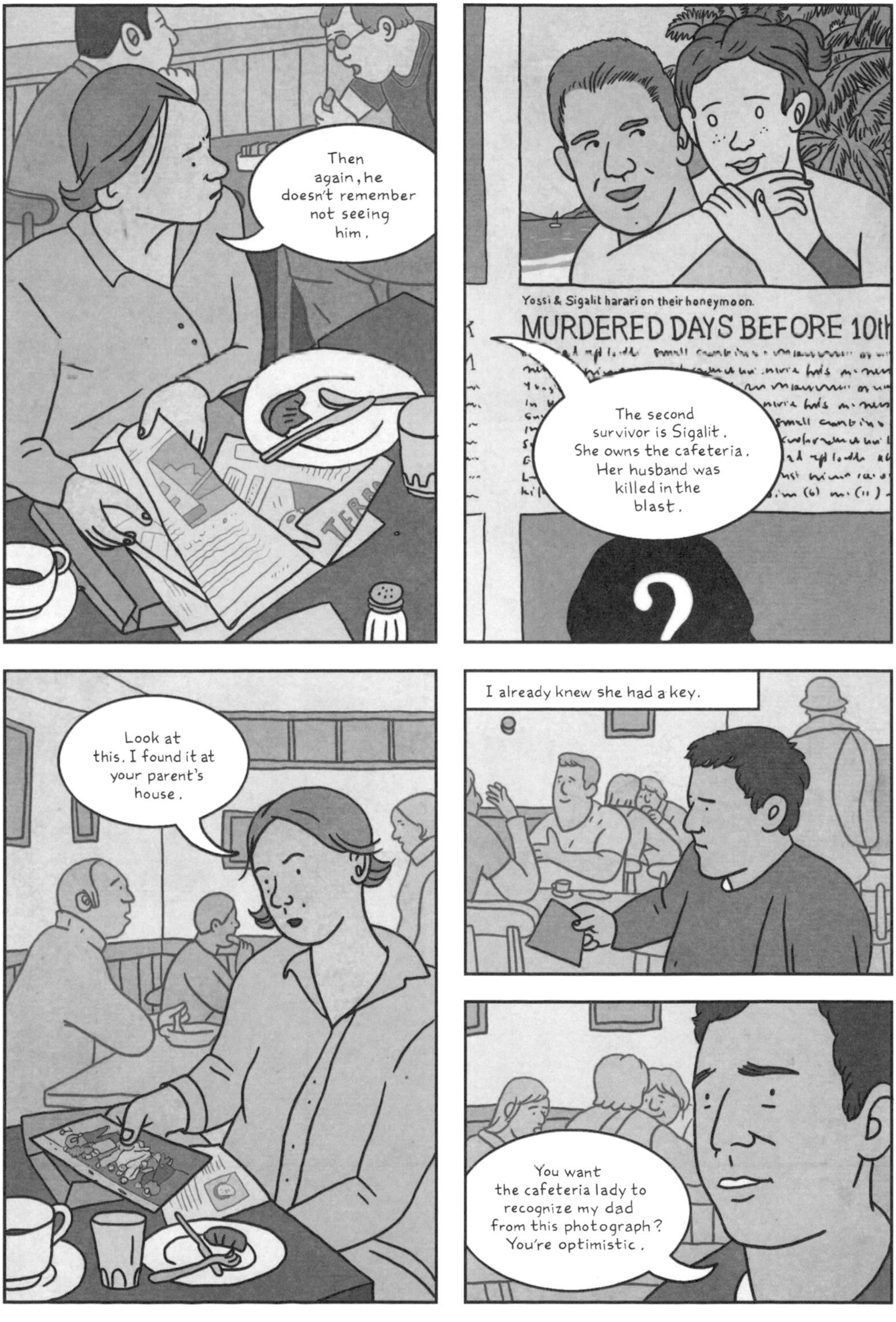

Then again, he doesn't remember not seeing him.
Yossi & Sigalit harari on their honeymoon.
MURDERED DAYS BEFORE 10th
The second survivor is Sigalit. She owns the cafeteria. Her husband was killed in the blast.
Look at this. I found it at your parent's house.
I already knew she had a key.
You want the cafeteria lady to recognize my dad from this photograph? You're optimistic.

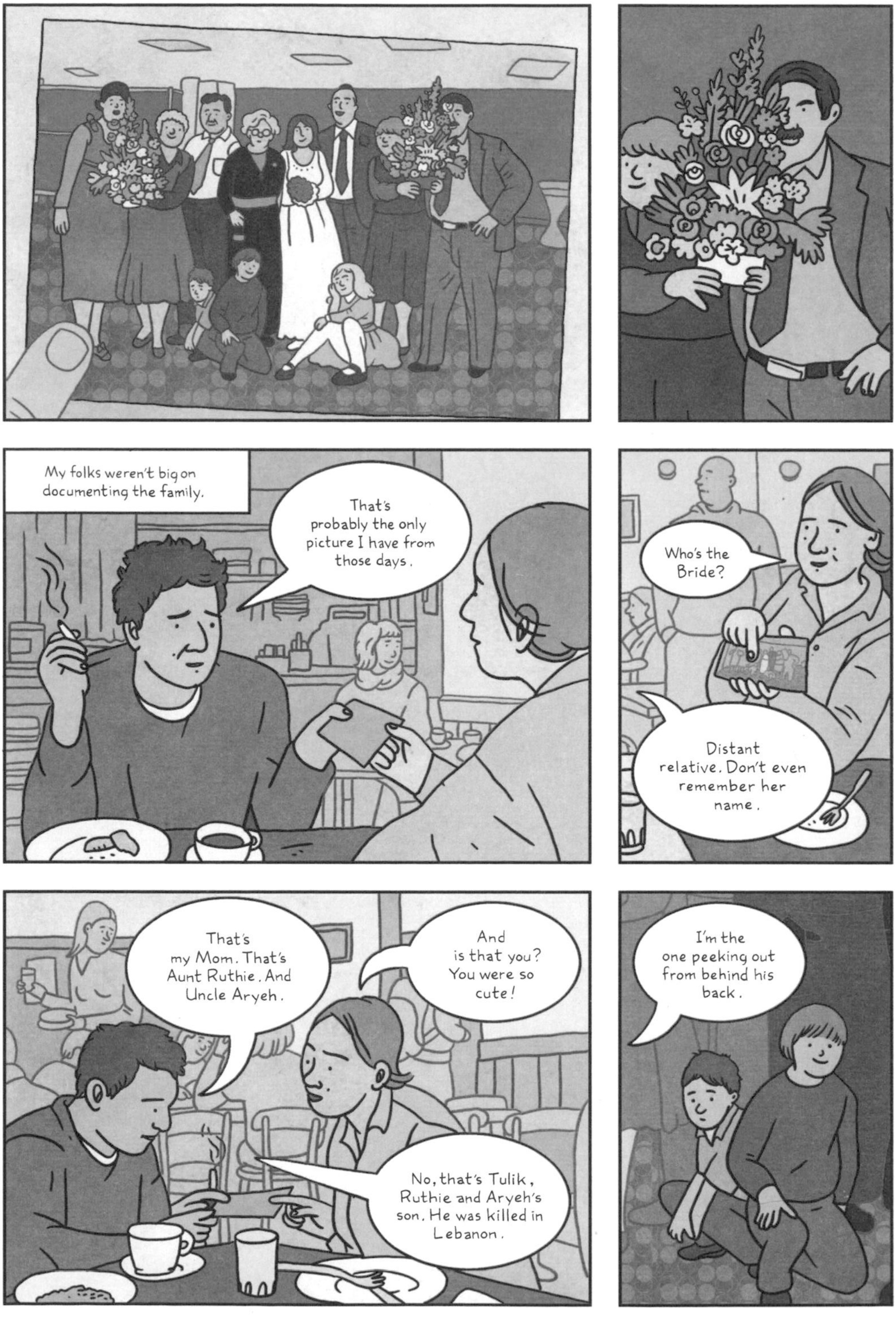
My folks weren't big on documenting the family.
That's probably the only picture I have from those days.
Who's the Bride?
Distant relative. Don't even remember her name.
That's my Mom. That's Aunt Ruthie. And Uncle Aryeh.
And is that you? You were so cute!
No, that's Tulik, Ruthie and Aryeh's son. He was killed in Lebanon.
I'm the one peeking out from behind his back.

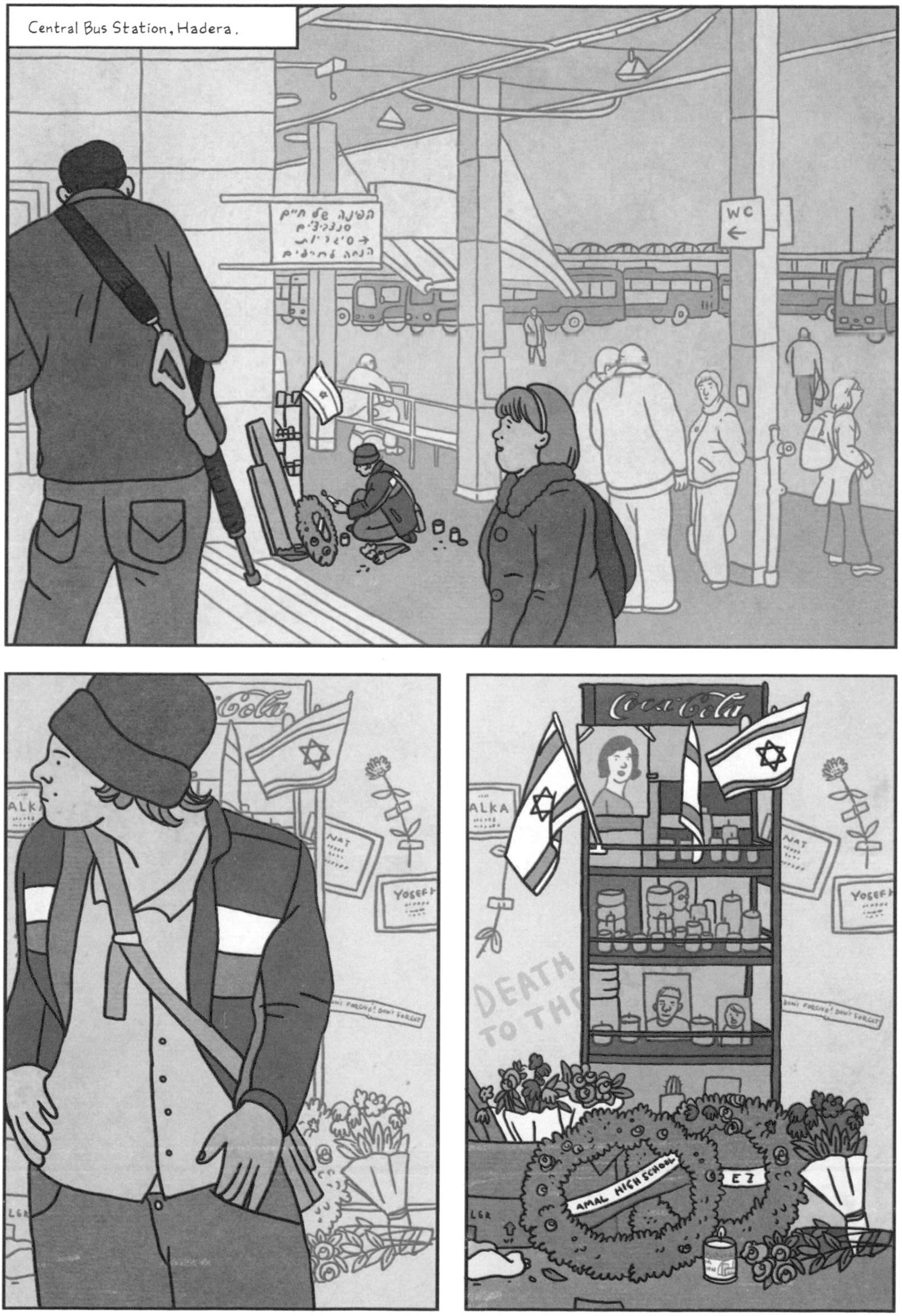
Central Bus Station, Hadera.
WC
Coca-Cola
ALKA
NAT
YOSEFH
DON'T FORGET! DON'T FORGET
DEATH
TO THO
AMAL HIGH SCHOOL
EZ

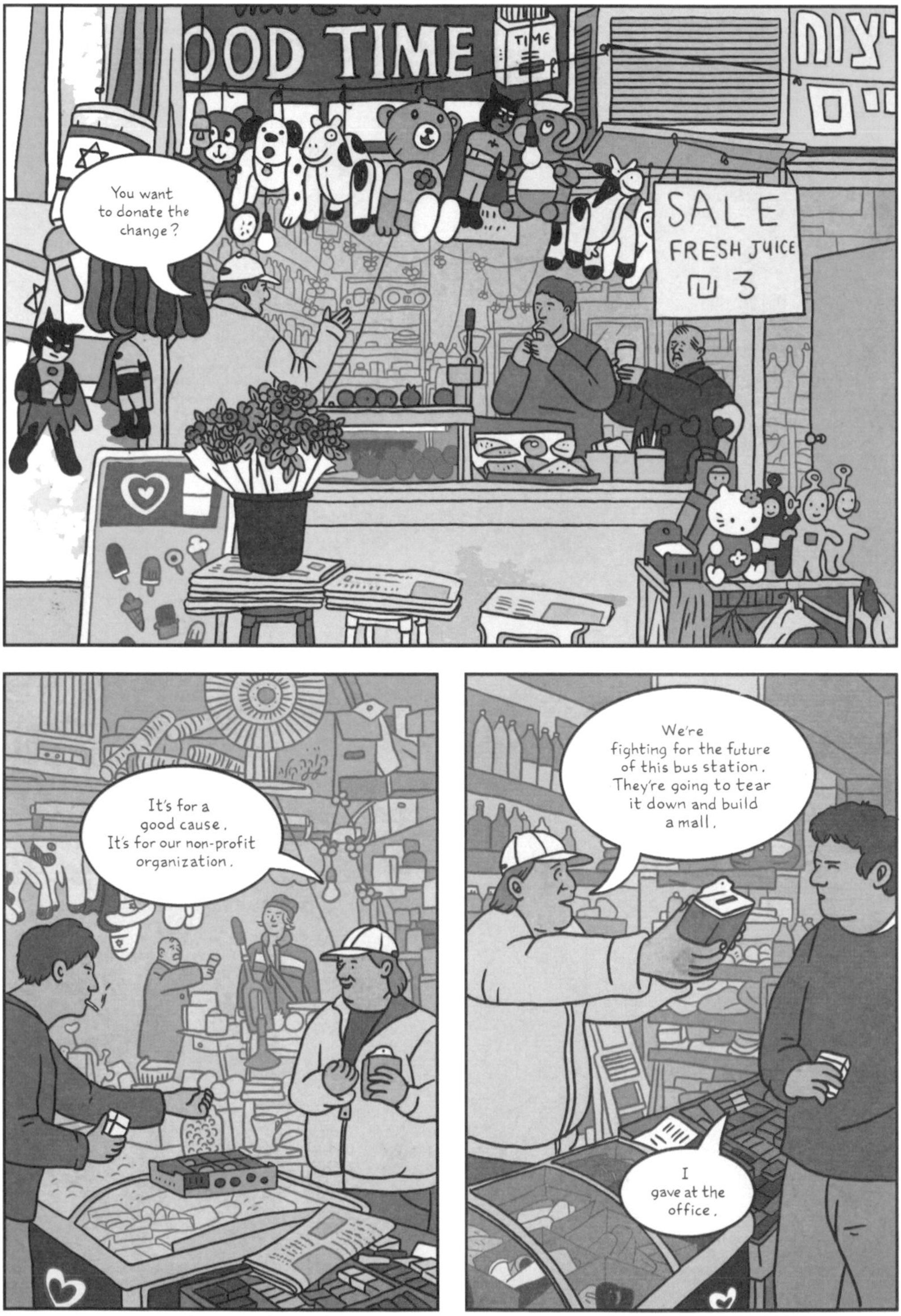

OOD TIME
TIME
SALE
FRESH JUICE
₪ 3
You want to donate the change?
It's for a good cause. It's for our non-profit organization.
We're fighting for the future of this bus station. They're going to tear it down and build a mall.
I gave at the office.

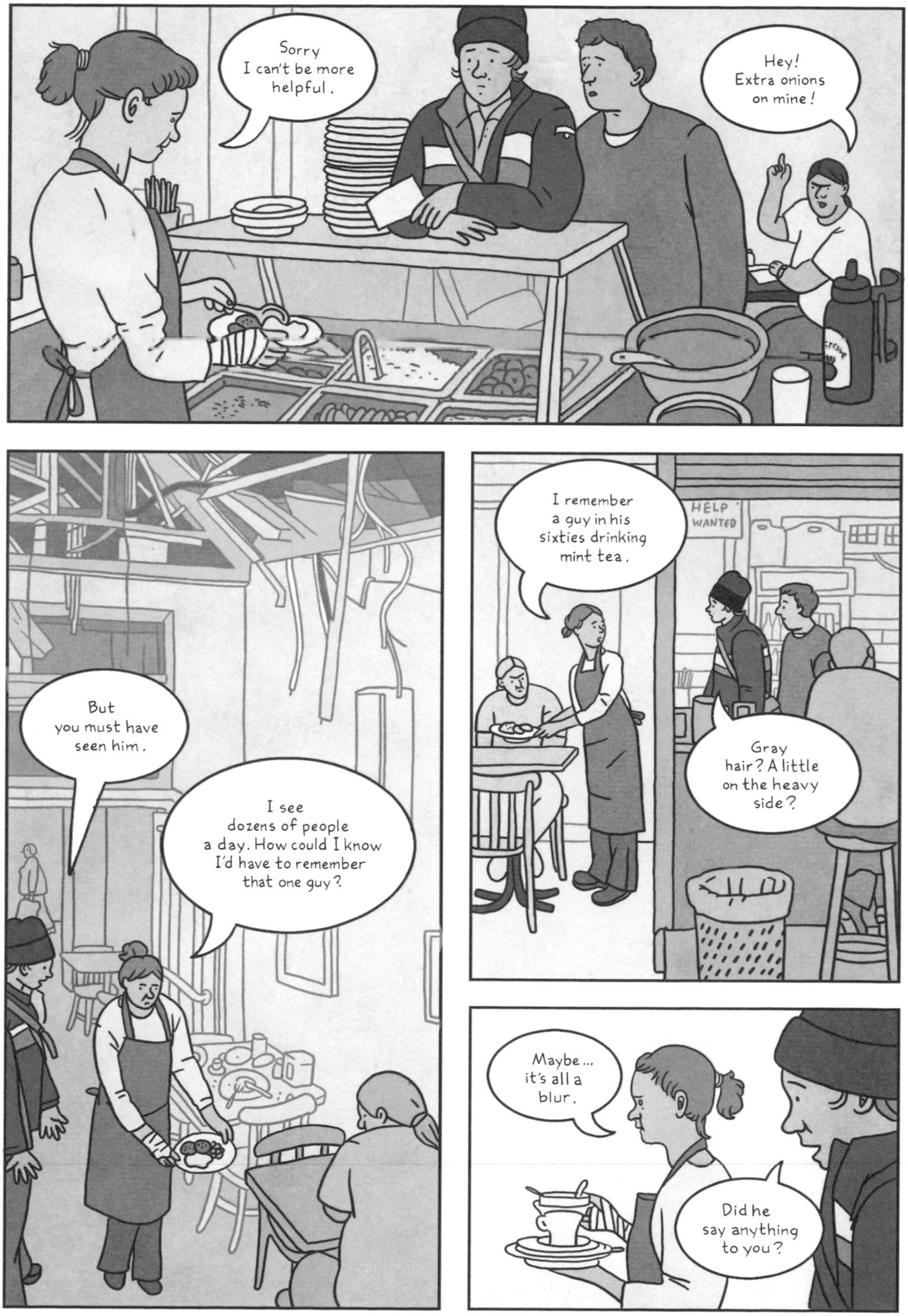
Sorry I can't be more helpful.
Hey! Extra onions on mine!
But you must have seen him.
I see dozens of people a day. How could I know I'd have to remember that one guy?
I remember a guy in his sixties drinking mint tea.
HELP WANTED
Gray hair? A little on the heavy side?
Maybe... it's all a blur.
Did he say anything to you?

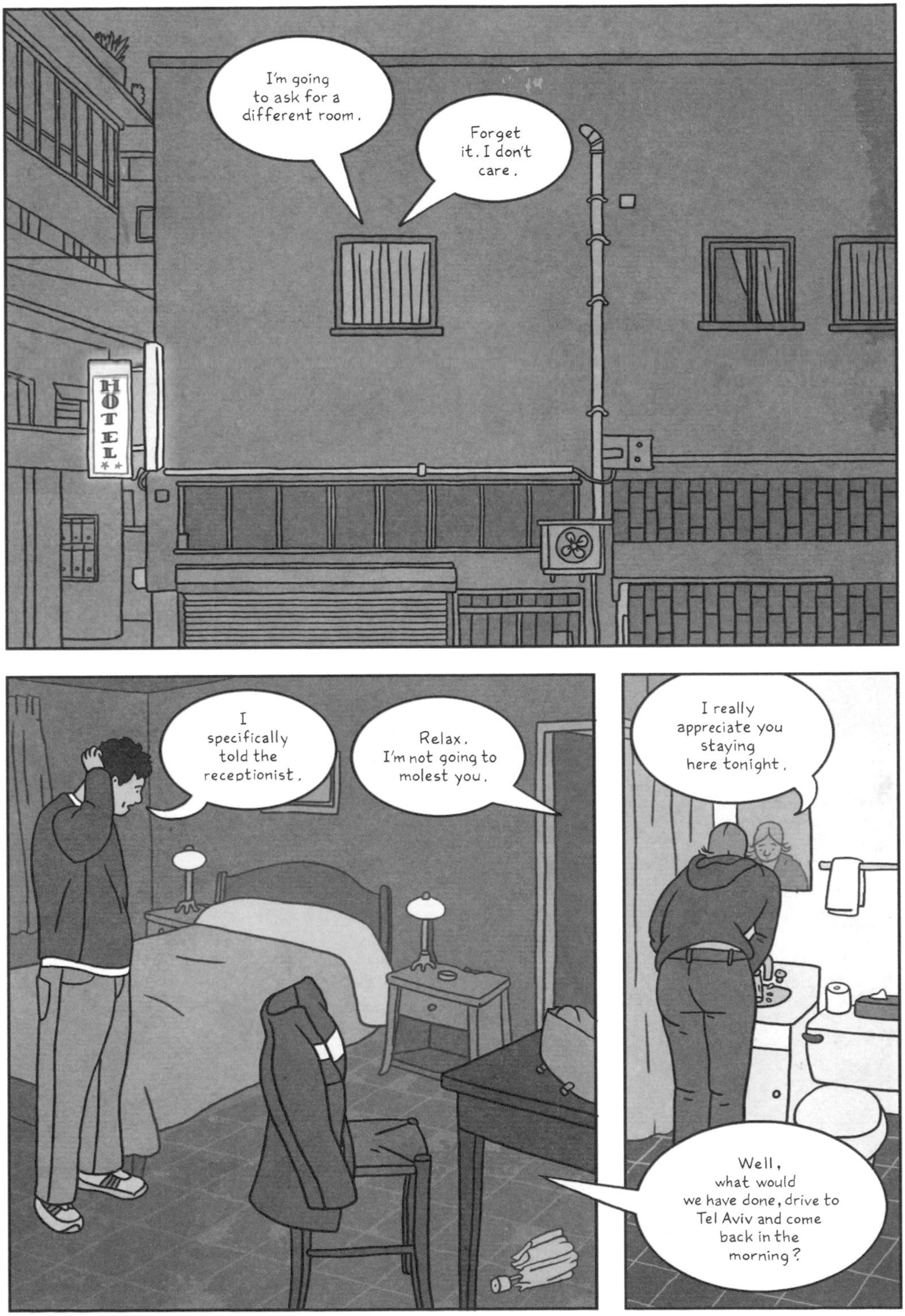
HOTEL
I'm going to ask for a different room.
Forget it. I don't care.
I specifically told the receptionist.
Relax. I'm not going to molest you.
I really appreciate you staying here tonight.
Well, what would we have done, drive to Tel Aviv and come back in the morning?

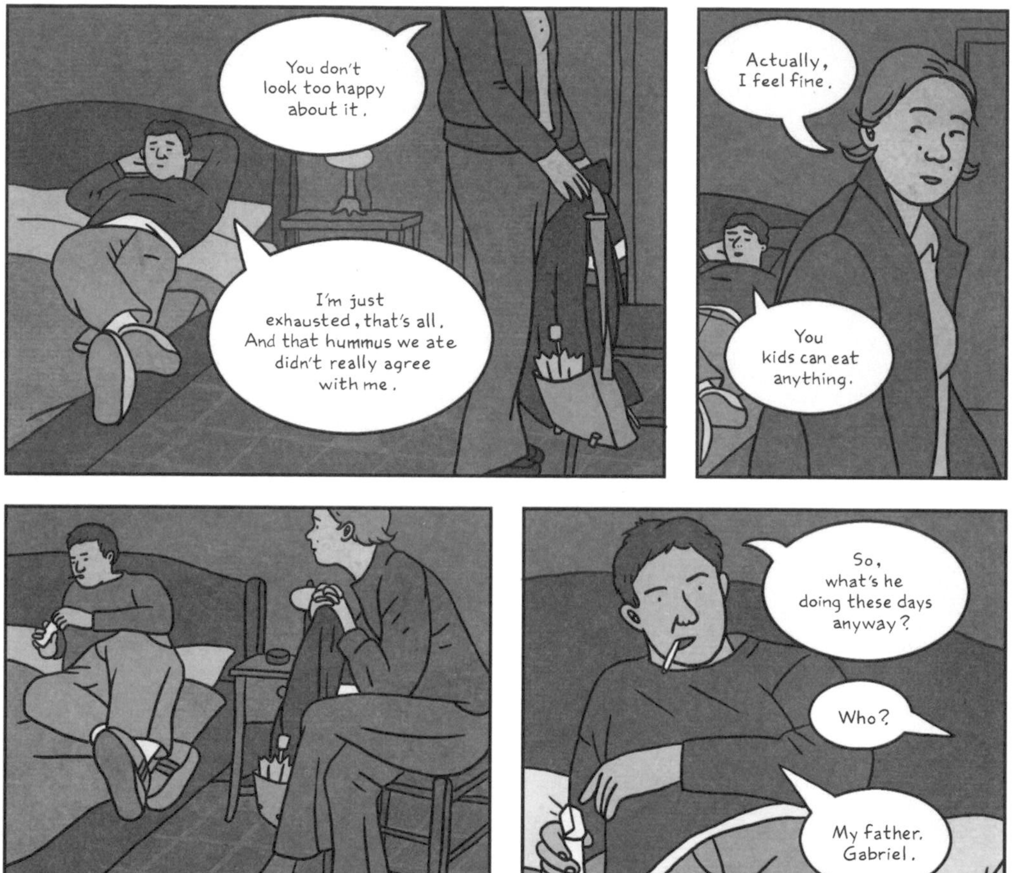
You don't look too happy about it.
I'm just exhausted, that's all. And that hummus we ate didn't really agree with me.
Actually, I feel fine.
You kids can eat anything.
So, what's he doing these days anyway?
Who?
My father. Gabriel.
Last job he had, he was a parking attendant.
You know what I hated most when I was a kid? Filling in "father's occupation". Usually I just made something up.
But I don't think I ever used "parking attendant".

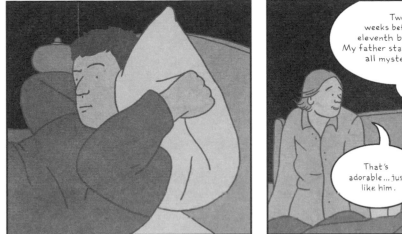

Two weeks before my eleventh birthday. My father starts getting all mysterious.

That's adorable... just like him.

It's the day of my birthday. He takes out a box, tells me to close my eyes. My mother was watching too, all excited.

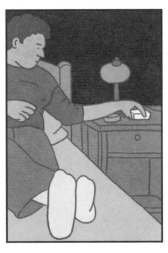

So? What did he get you?

A Maccabi Tel-Aviv soccer outfit. With the whole team's signatures on the jersey.

That's wonderful!

Right. Only I'm a Ha'Poel fan.

Oh, no! But it's funny, isn't it?

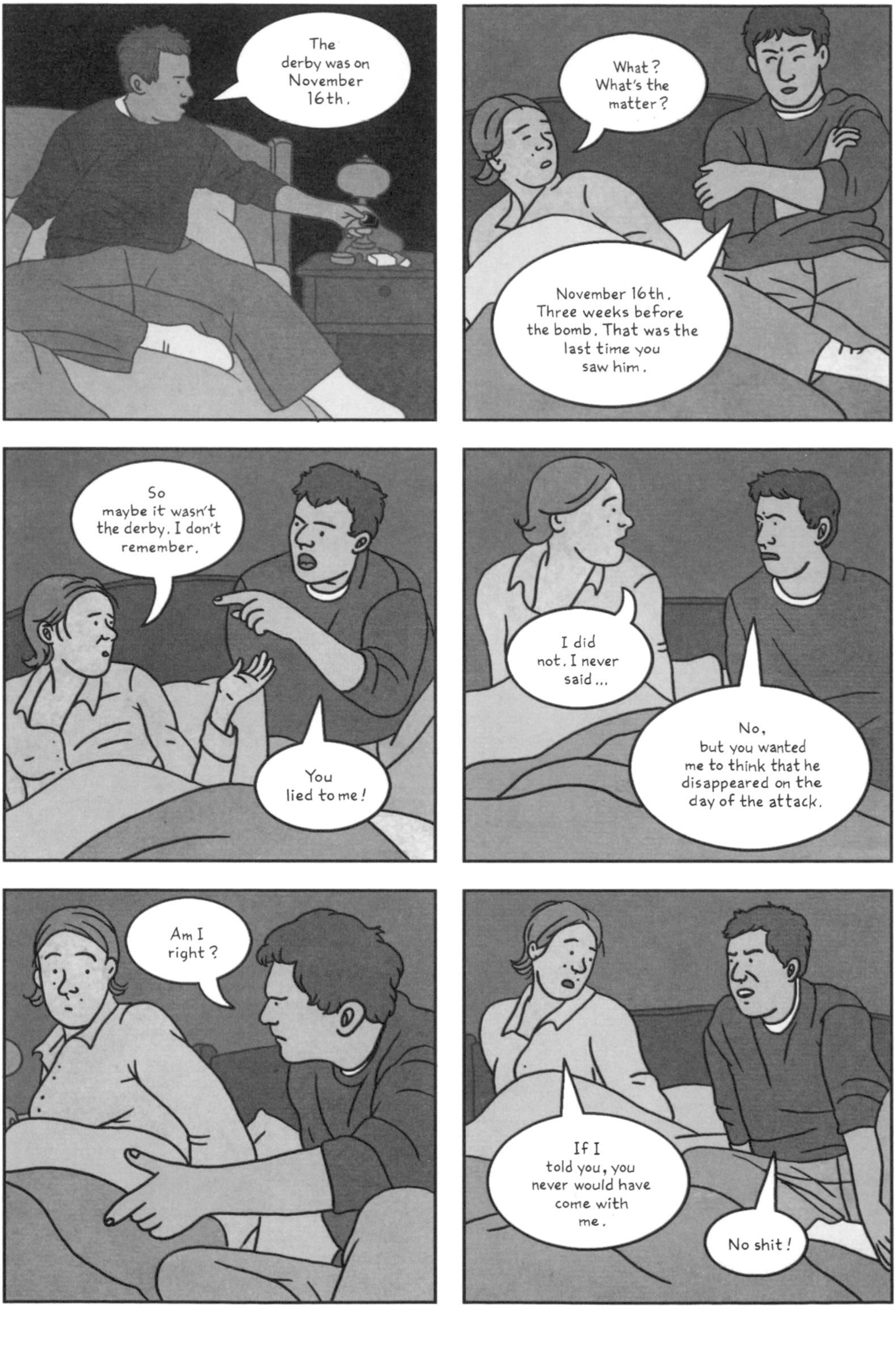
The derby was on November 16th.
What? What's the matter?
November 16th. Three weeks before the bomb. That was the last time you saw him.
So maybe it wasn't the derby. I don't remember.
You lied to me!
I did not. I never said...
No, but you wanted me to think that he disappeared on the day of the attack.
Am I right?
If I told you, you never would have come with me.
No shit!

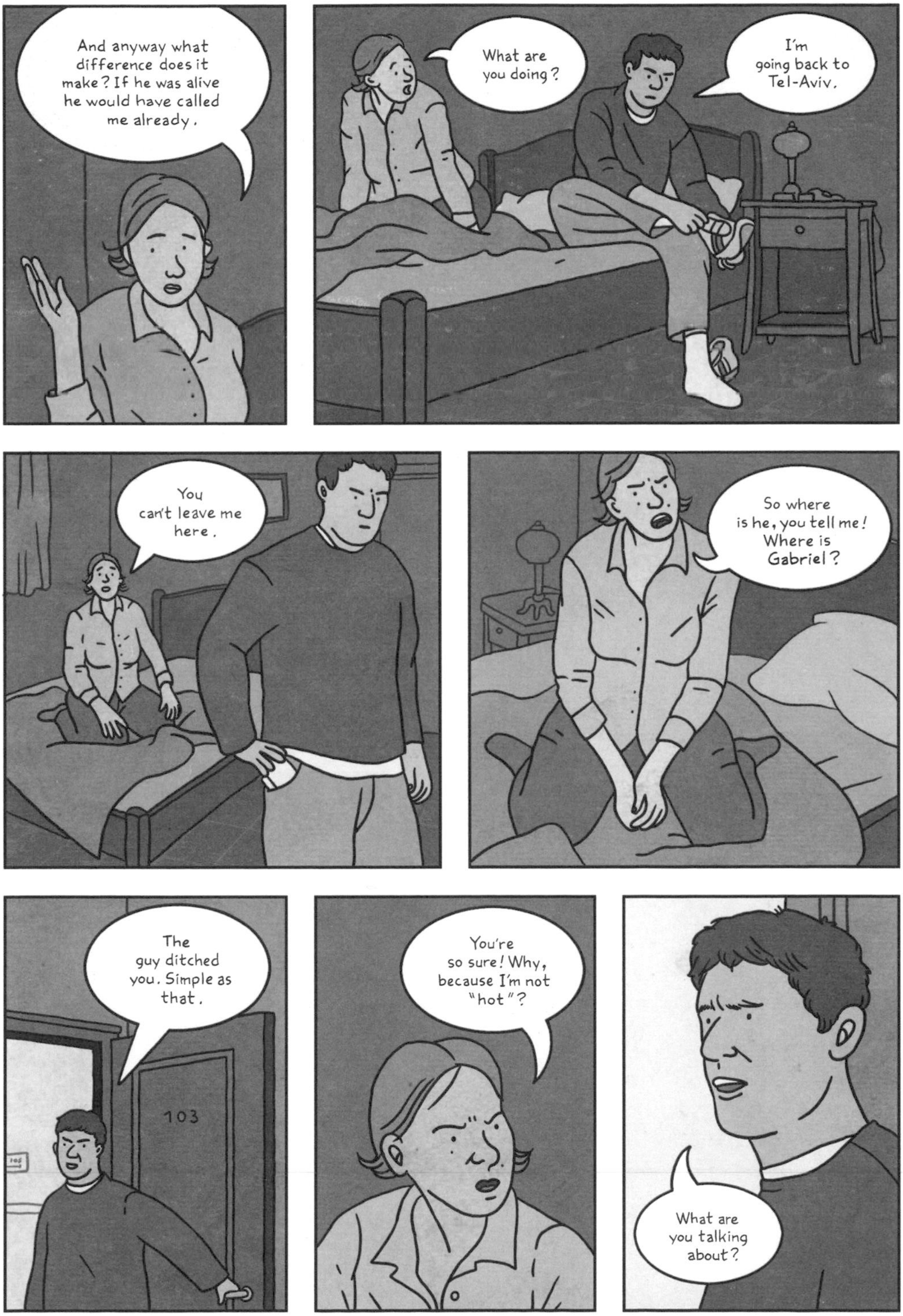
And anyway what difference does it make? If he was alive he would have called me already.
What are you doing?
I'm going back to Tel-Aviv.
You can't leave me here.
So where is he, you tell me! Where is Gabriel?
The guy ditched you. Simple as that.
103
You're so sure! Why, because I'm not "hot"?
What are you talking about?

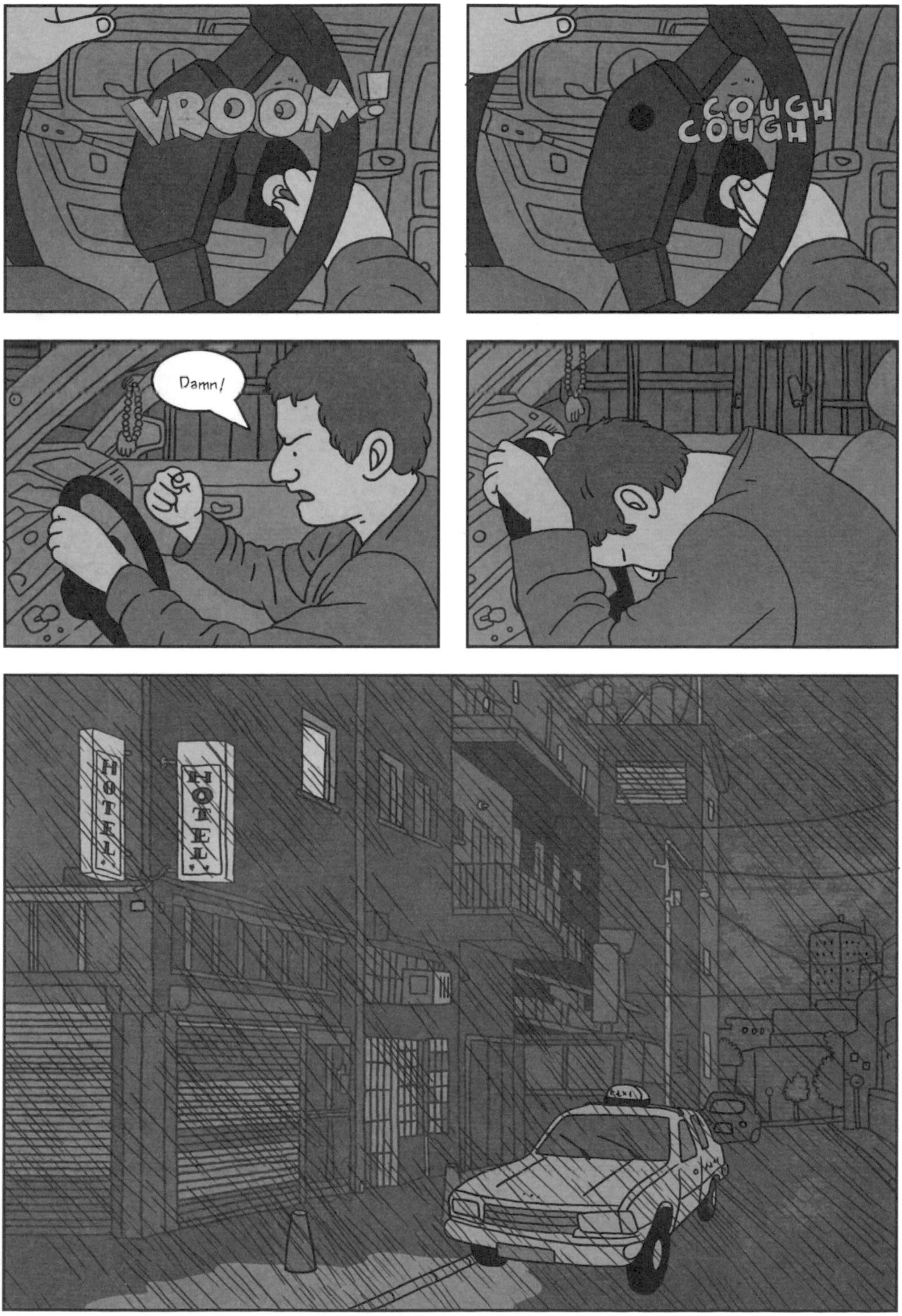
VROOM!
COUGH
COUGH
Damn!
HOTEL
HOTEL

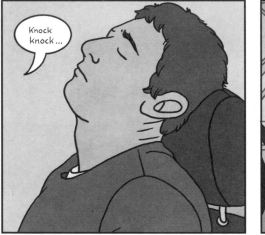

Knock knock...

What time is it?

Almost eight o'clock.

Ugh...

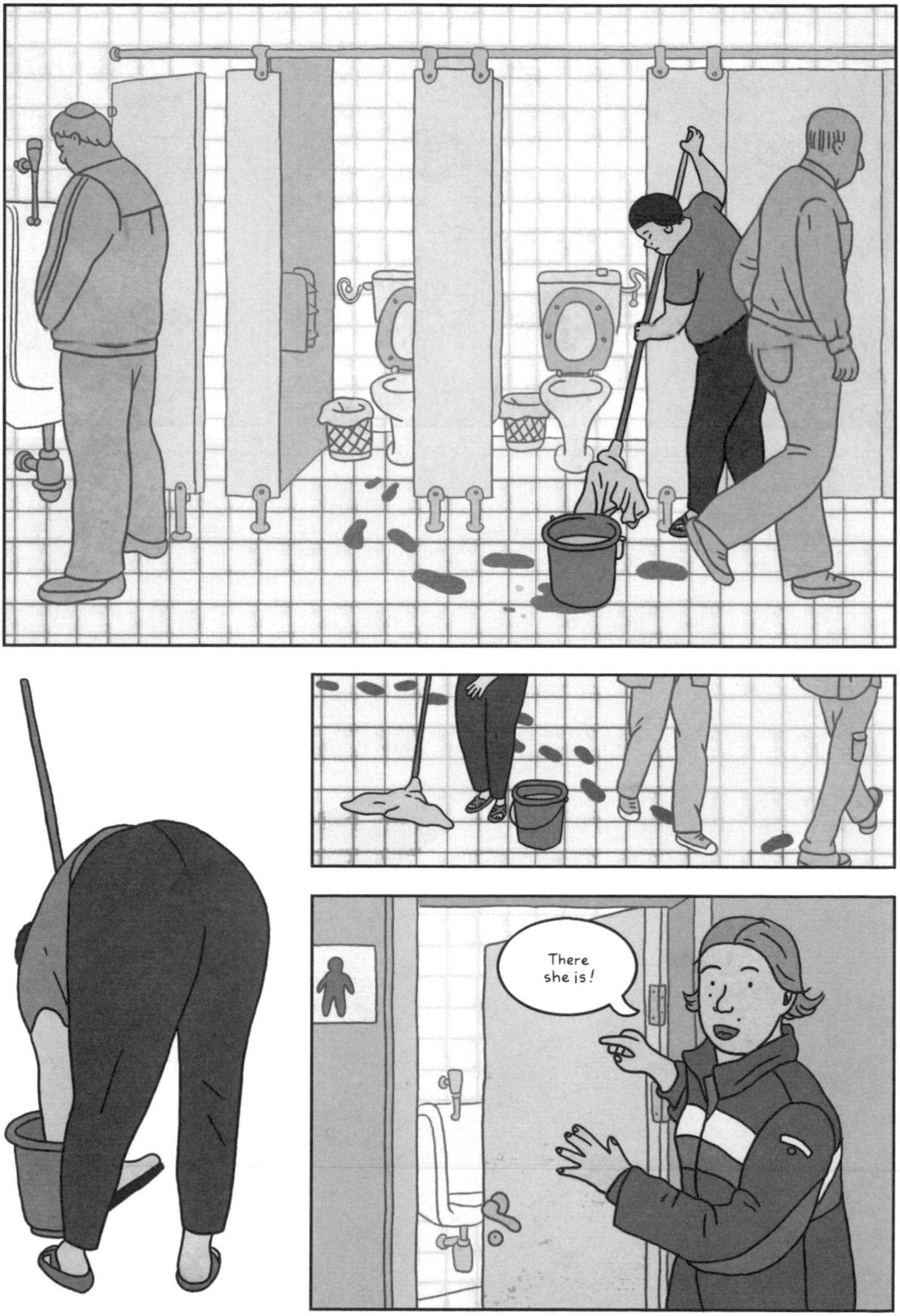
There she is!

Del?

Can we talk to you?

I not Del. I Nora.

Where is Del?

She go back to Philippines.

When?

After the bomb. She has a baby... She got scared.

But the guy from the shop...he said she still works here.

We switch. He not notice.

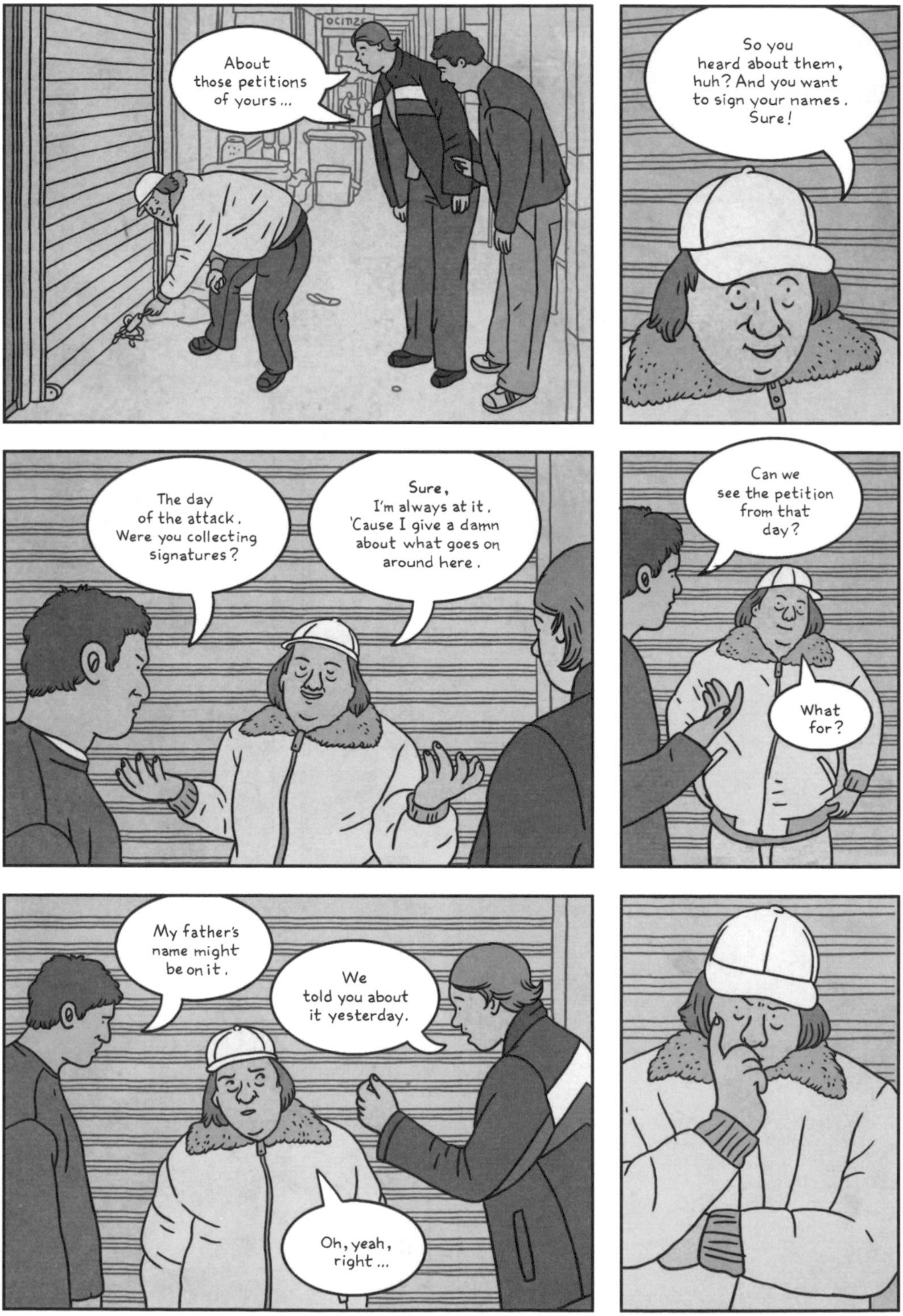
About those petitions of yours ...
So you heard about them, huh? And you want to sign your names. Sure!
The day of the attack. Were you collecting signatures?
Sure, I'm always at it. 'Cause I give a damn about what goes on around here.
Can we see the petition from that day?
What for?
My father's name might be on it.
We told you about it yesterday.
Oh, yeah, right ...

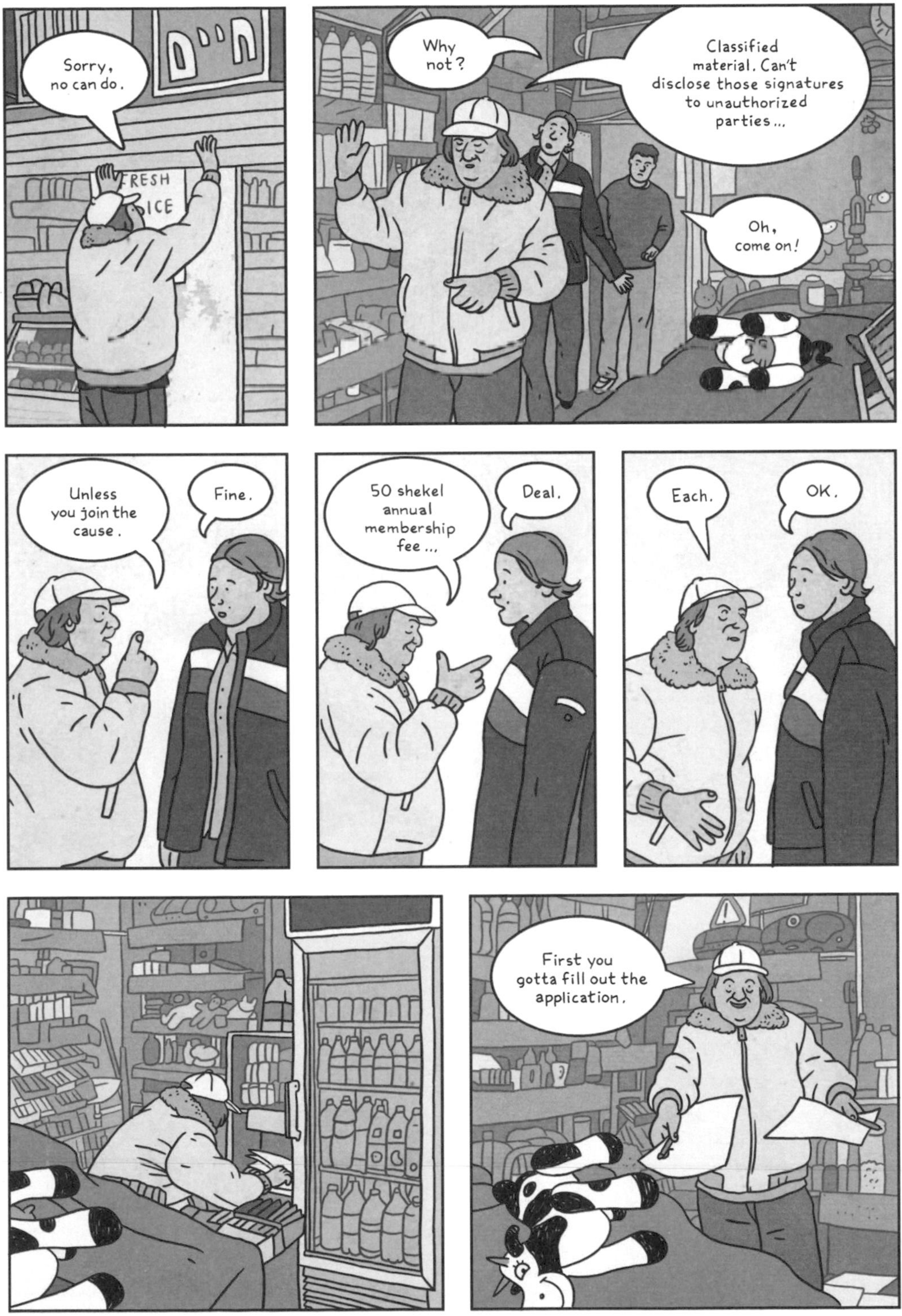
Sorry, no can do.
Why not?
Classified material. Can't disclose those signatures to unauthorized parties...
Oh, come on!
Unless you join the cause.
Fine.
50 shekel annual membership fee...
Deal.
Each.
OK.
First you gotta fill out the application.

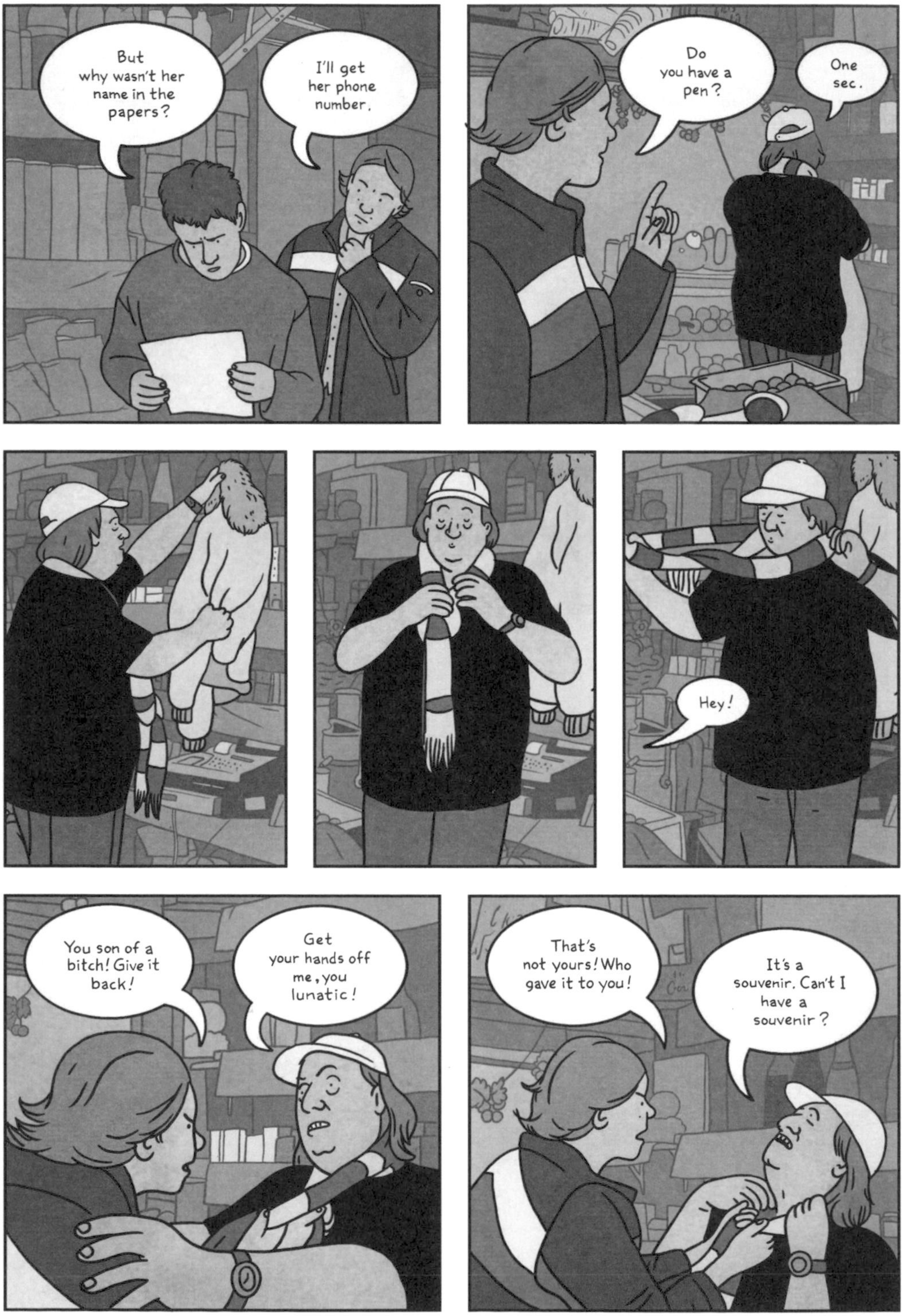
But why wasn't her name in the papers?
I'll get her phone number.
Do you have a pen?
One sec.
Hey!
You son of a bitch! Give it back!
Get your hands off me, you lunatic!
That's not yours! Who gave it to you!
It's a souvenir. Can't I have a souvenir?

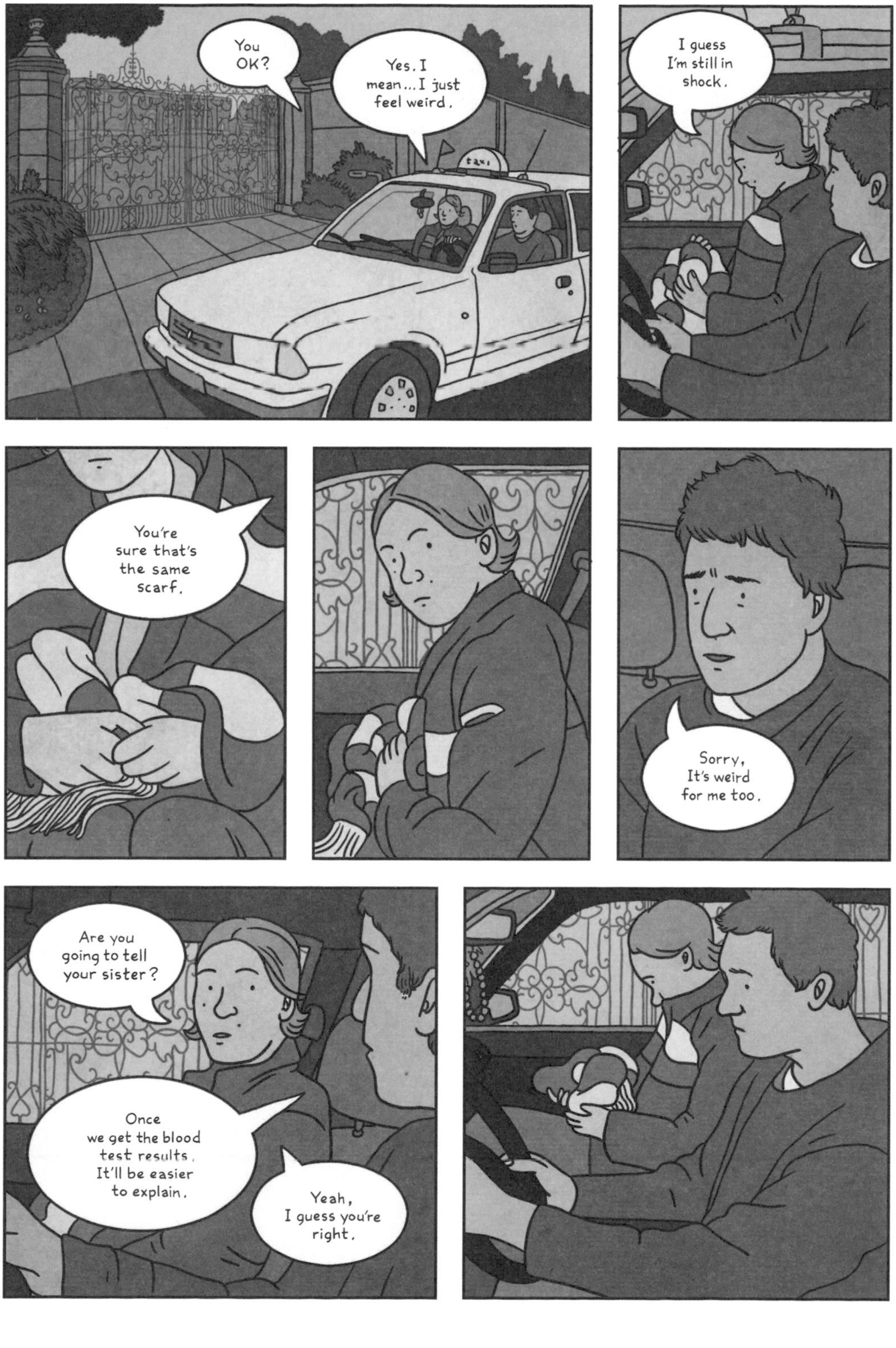
You OK?
Yes. I mean... I just feel weird.
I guess I'm still in shock.
You're sure that's the same scarf.
Sorry, It's weird for me too.
Are you going to tell your sister?
Once we get the blood test results. It'll be easier to explain.
Yeah, I guess you're right.

96

chapter three
riding the waves

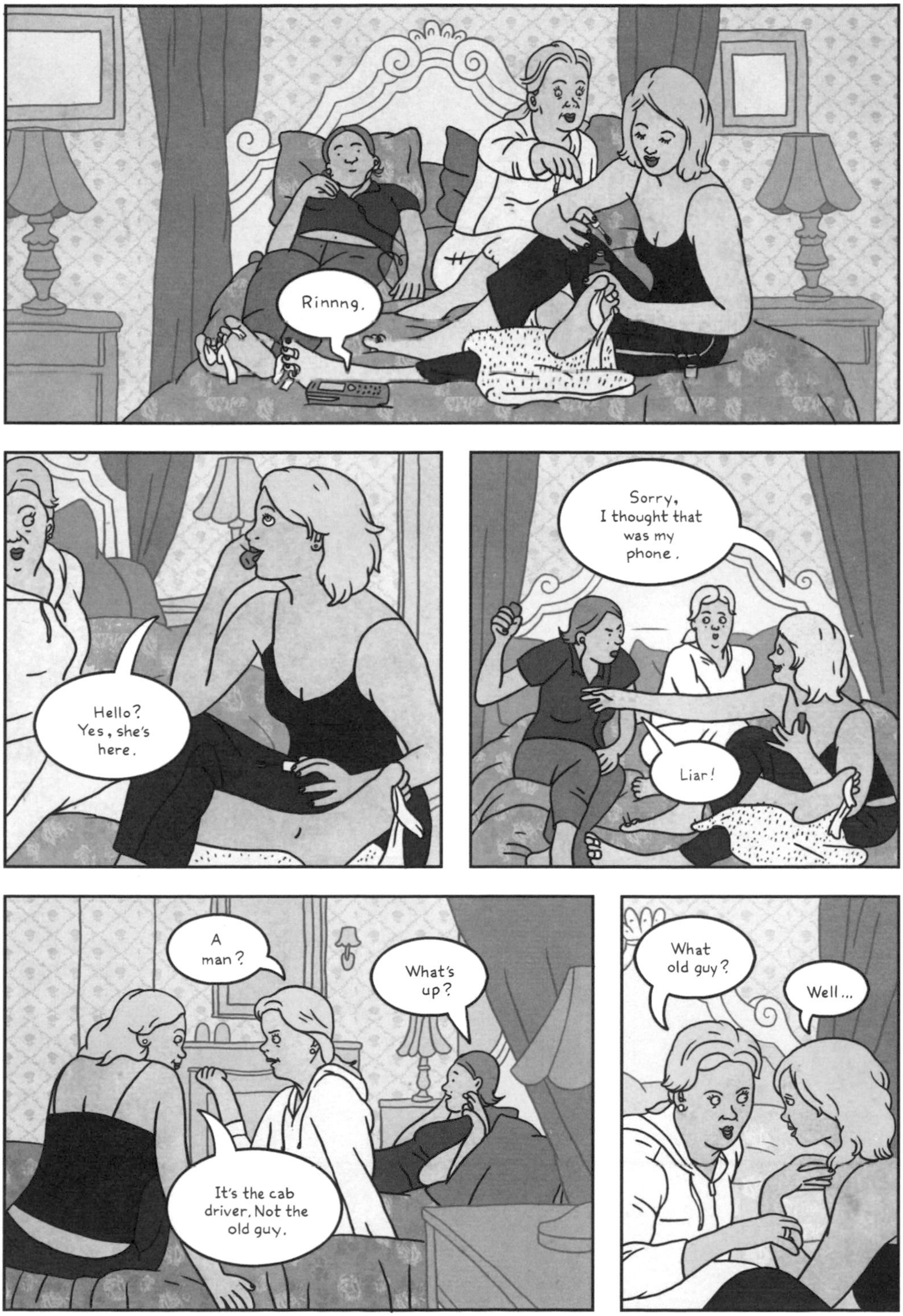
Rinnng.
Hello? Yes, she's here.
Sorry, I thought that was my phone.
Liar!
A man?
What's up?
It's the cab driver. Not the old guy.
What old guy?
Well...

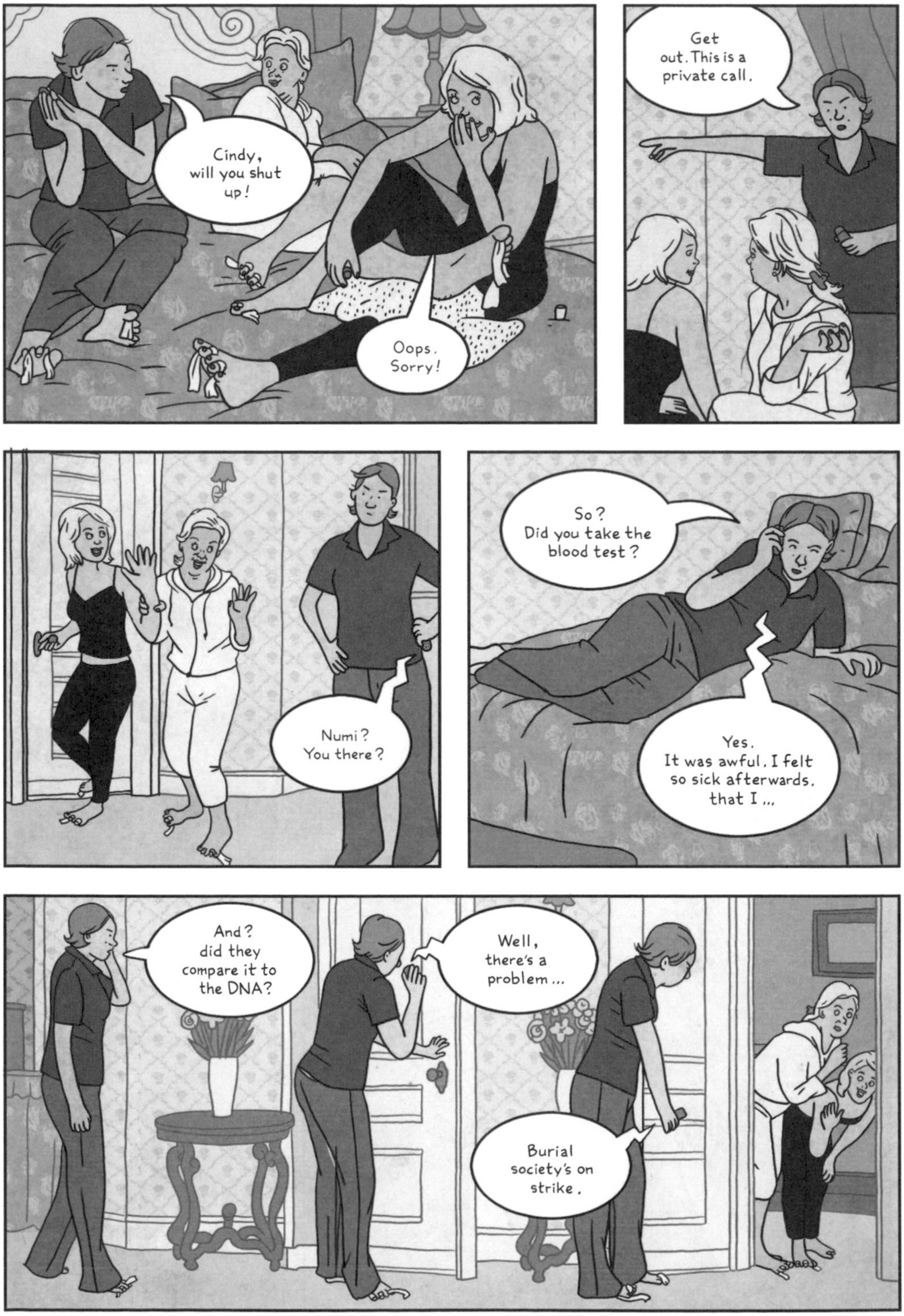

Cindy, will you shut up!
Oops. Sorry!
Get out. This is a private call.
Numi? You there?
So? Did you take the blood test?
Yes. It was awful. I felt so sick afterwards, that I ...
And? did they compare it to the DNA?
Well, there's a problem ...
Burial society's on strike.

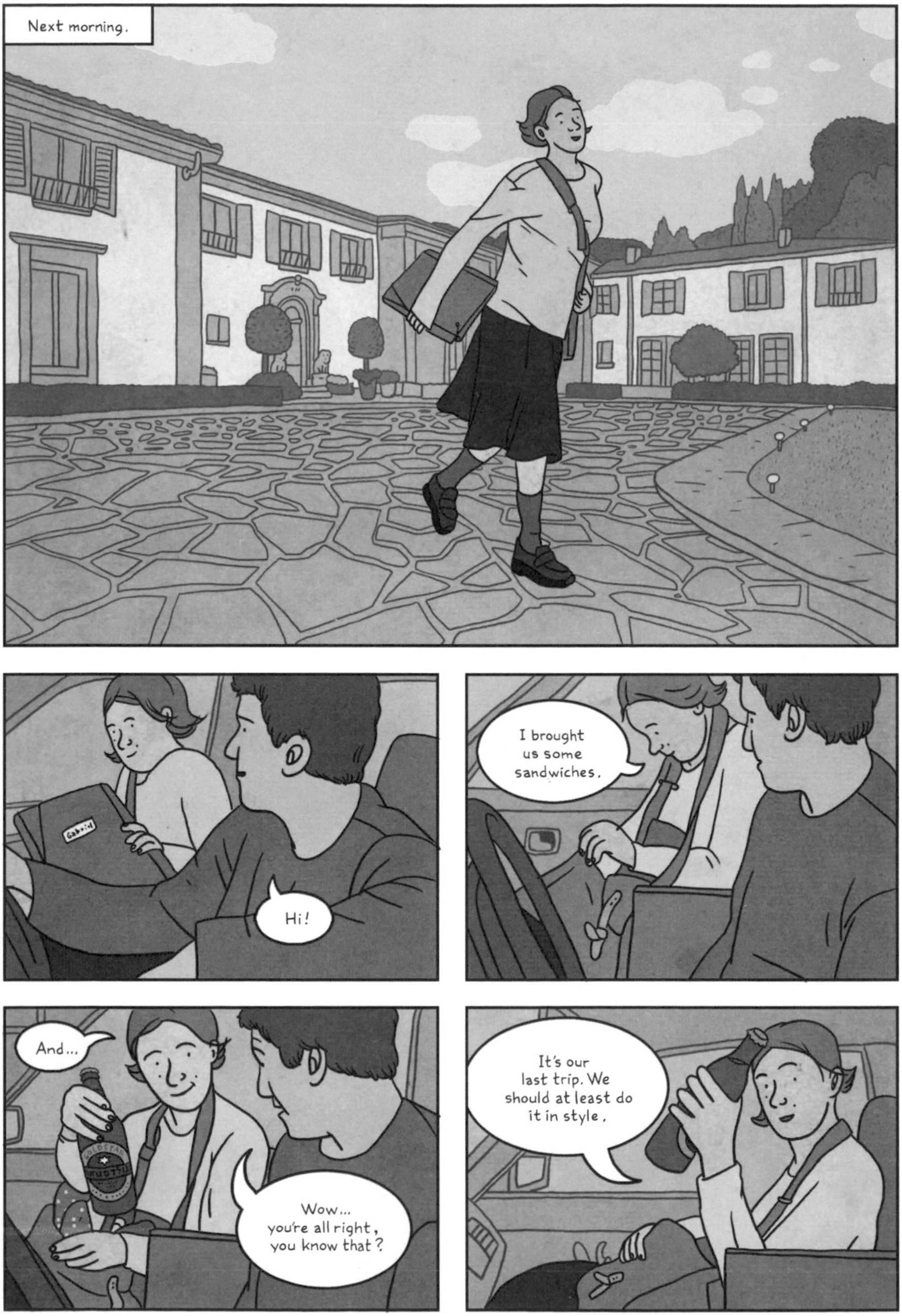
Next morning.
Hi!
I brought us some sandwiches.
And...
Wow... you're all right, you know that?
It's our last trip. We should at least do it in style.

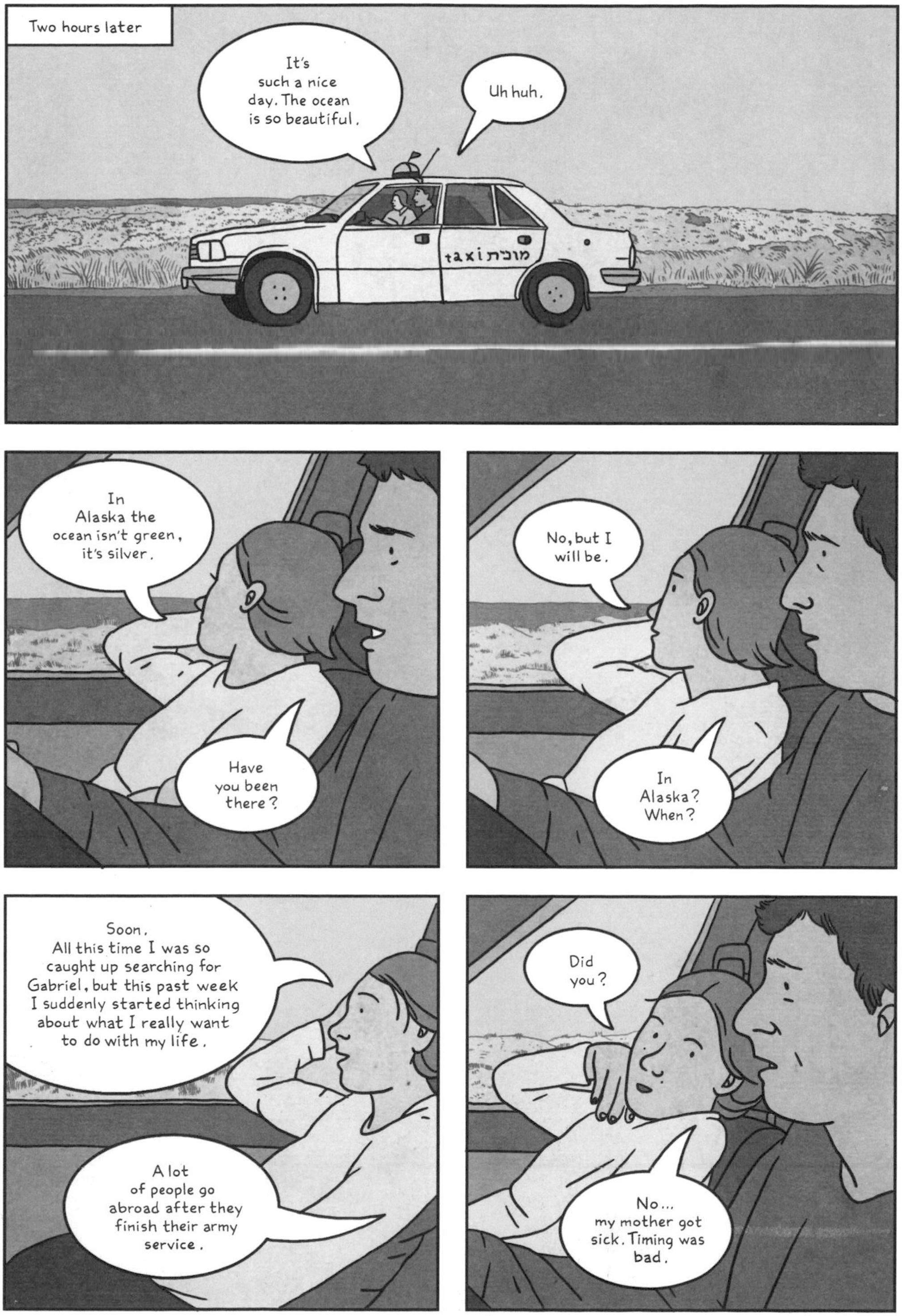
Two hours later
It's such a nice day. The ocean is so beautiful.
Uh huh.
taxi מונית
In Alaska the ocean isn't green, it's silver.
Have you been there?
No, but I will be.
In Alaska? When?
Soon. All this time I was so caught up searching for Gabriel, but this past week I suddenly started thinking about what I really want to do with my life.
A lot of people go abroad after they finish their army service.
Did you?
No... my mother got sick. Timing was bad.

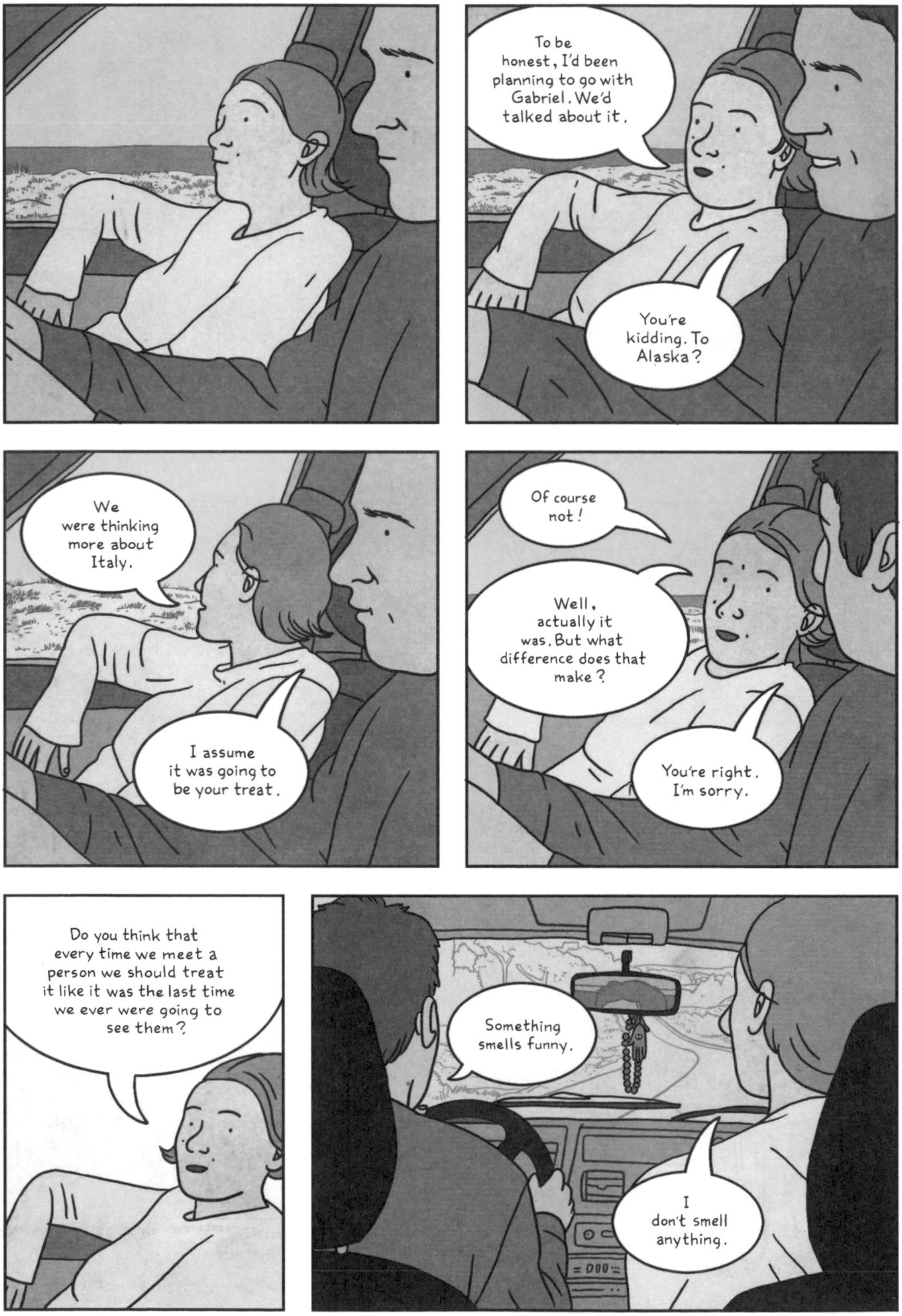
To be honest, I'd been planning to go with Gabriel. We'd talked about it.
You're kidding. To Alaska?
We were thinking more about Italy.
I assume it was going to be your treat.
Of course not!
Well, actually it was. But what difference does that make?
You're right. I'm sorry.
Do you think that every time we meet a person we should treat it like it was the last time we ever were going to see them?
Something smells funny.
I don't smell anything.

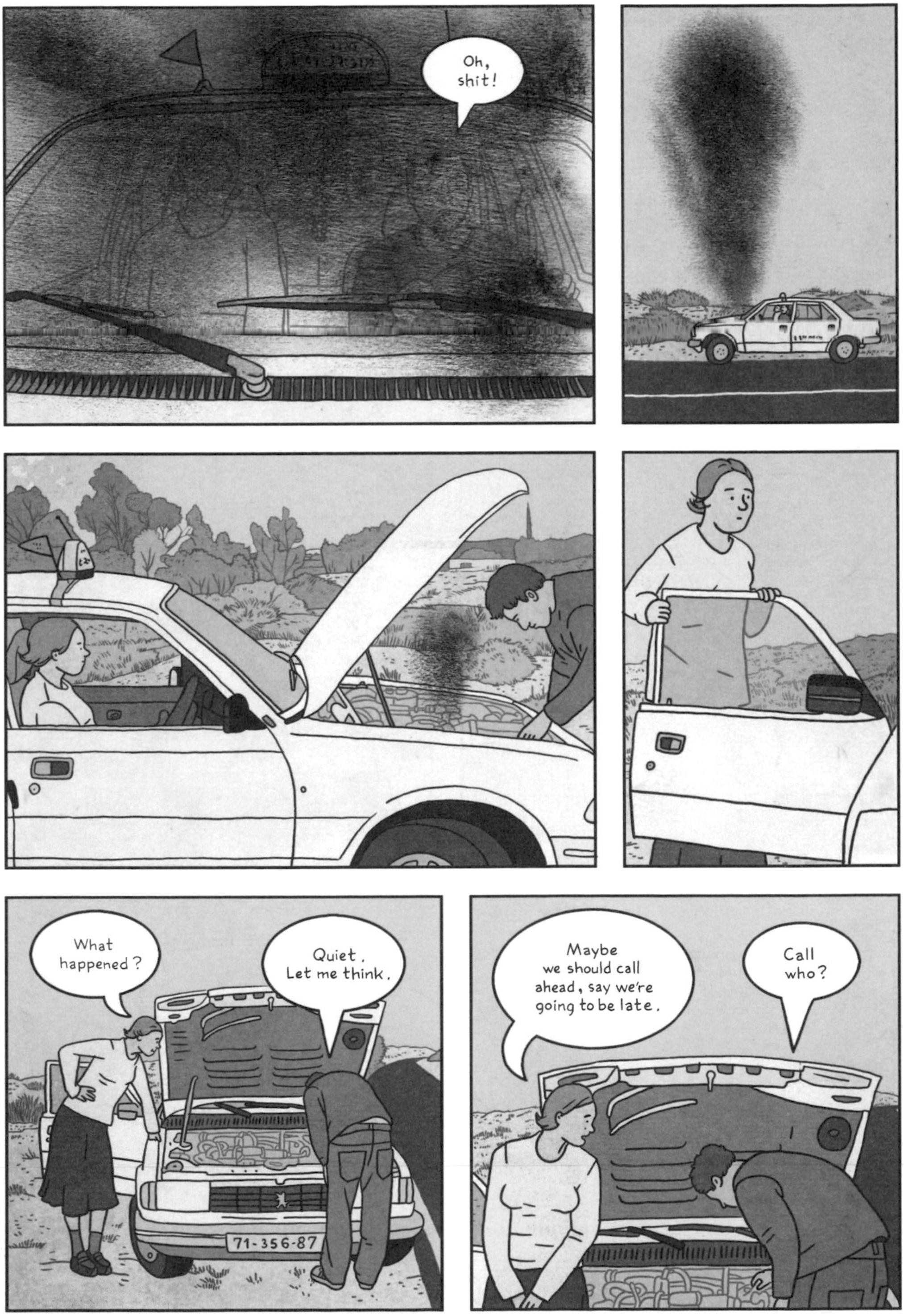
Oh, shit!
What happened?
Quiet. Let me think.
71-356-87
Maybe we should call ahead, say we're going to be late.
Call who?

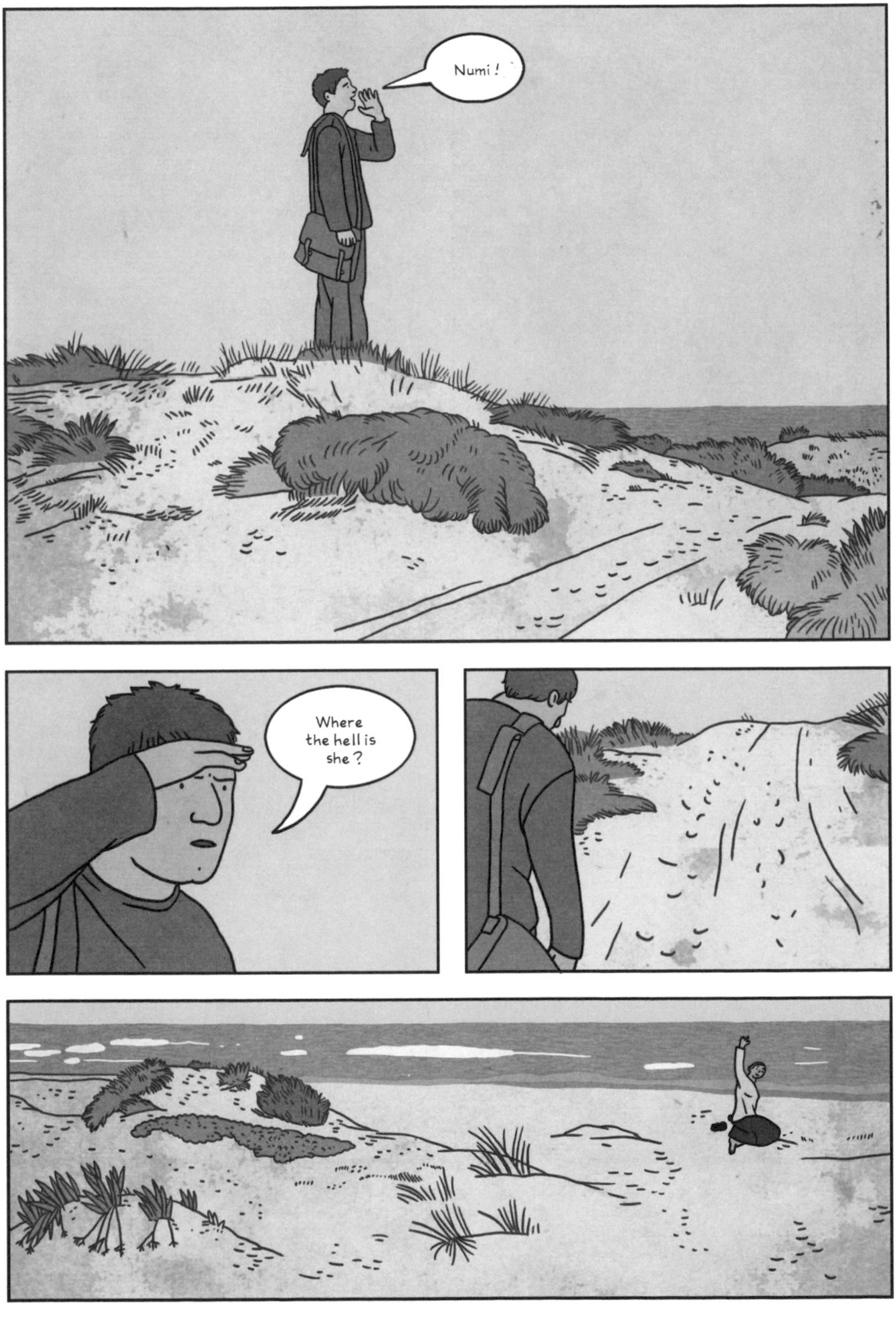
Numi!
Where the hell is she?

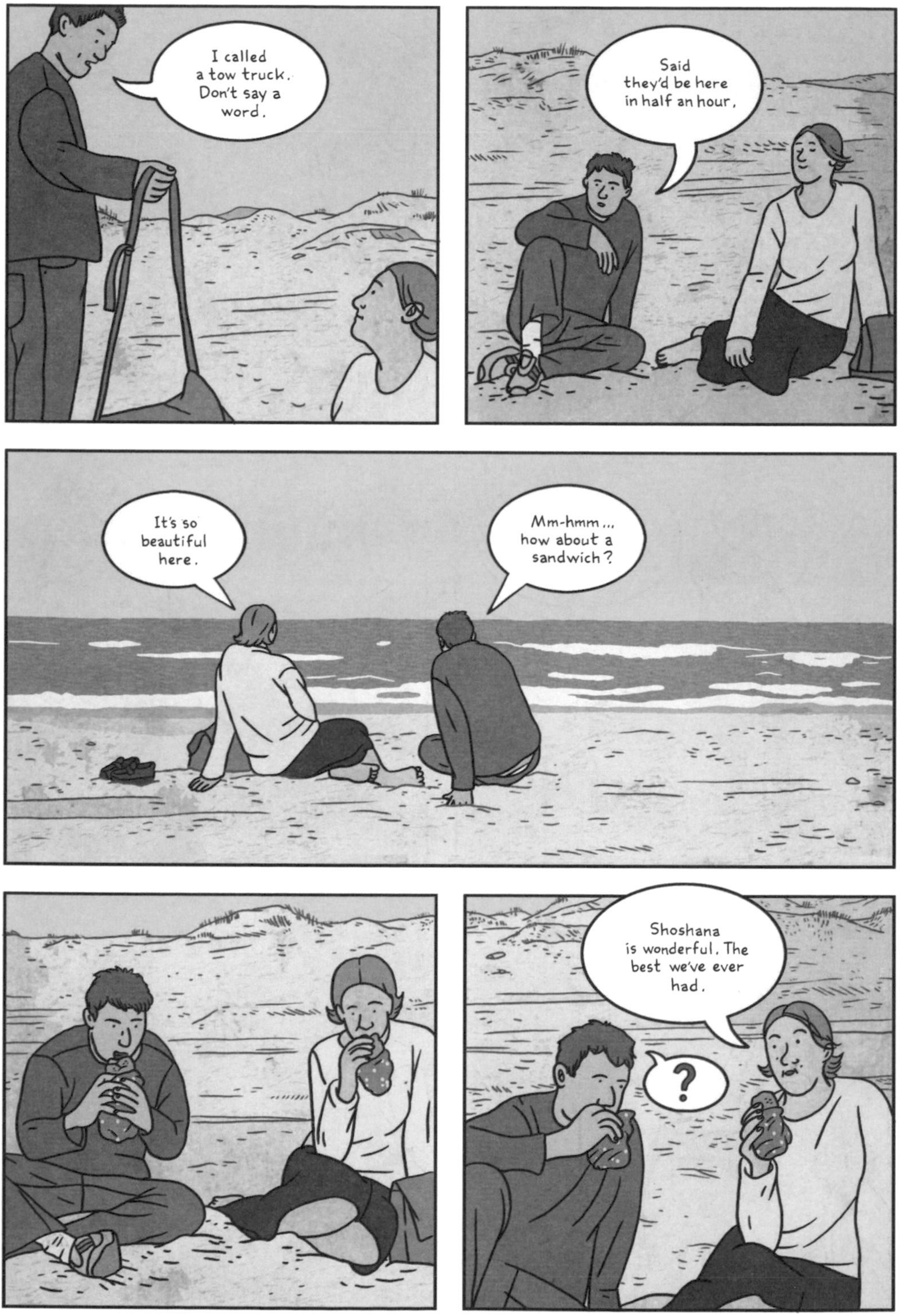
I called a tow truck. Don't say a word.
Said they'd be here in half an hour.
It's so beautiful here.
Mm-hmm... how about a sandwich?
Shoshana is wonderful. The best we've ever had.
?

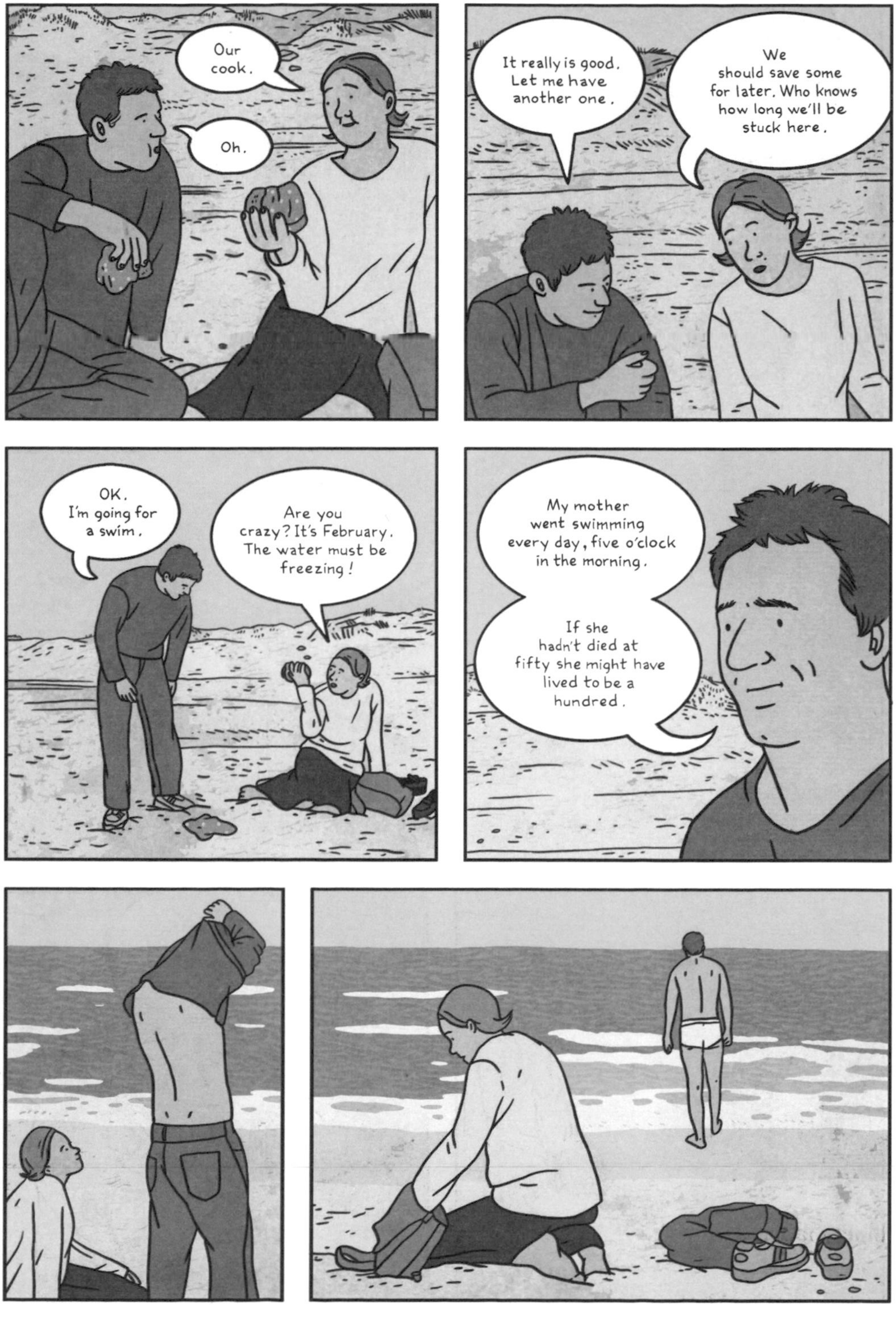
Our cook.
Oh.
It really is good. Let me have another one.
We should save some for later. Who knows how long we'll be stuck here.
OK. I'm going for a swim.
Are you crazy? It's February. The water must be freezing!
My mother went swimming every day, five o'clock in the morning.
If she hadn't died at fifty she might have lived to be a hundred.

Brrr...
How is it?
It's great! Come on in!
Don't look!
Liar! It's freezing!
Start swimming, you'll warm up.
Yeah, right.

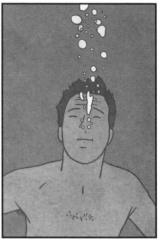

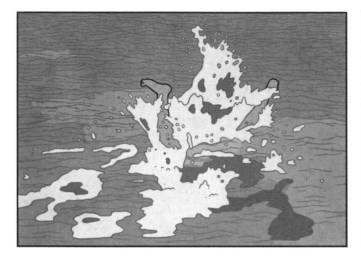

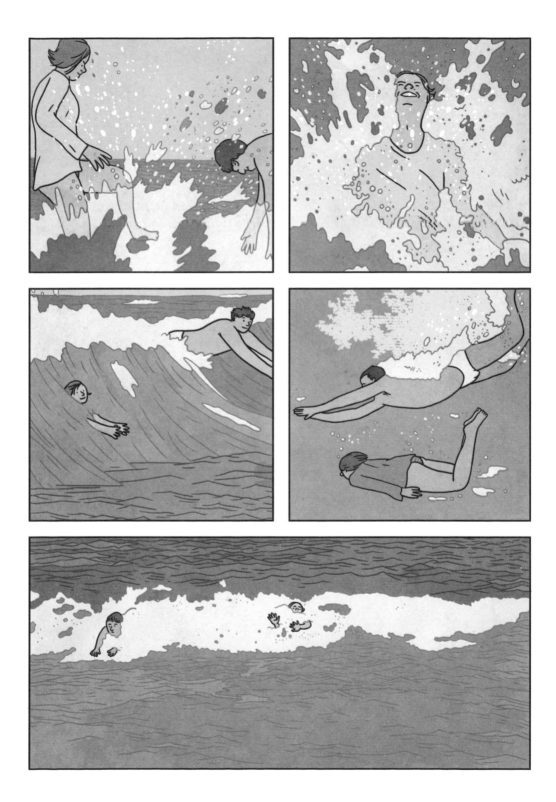

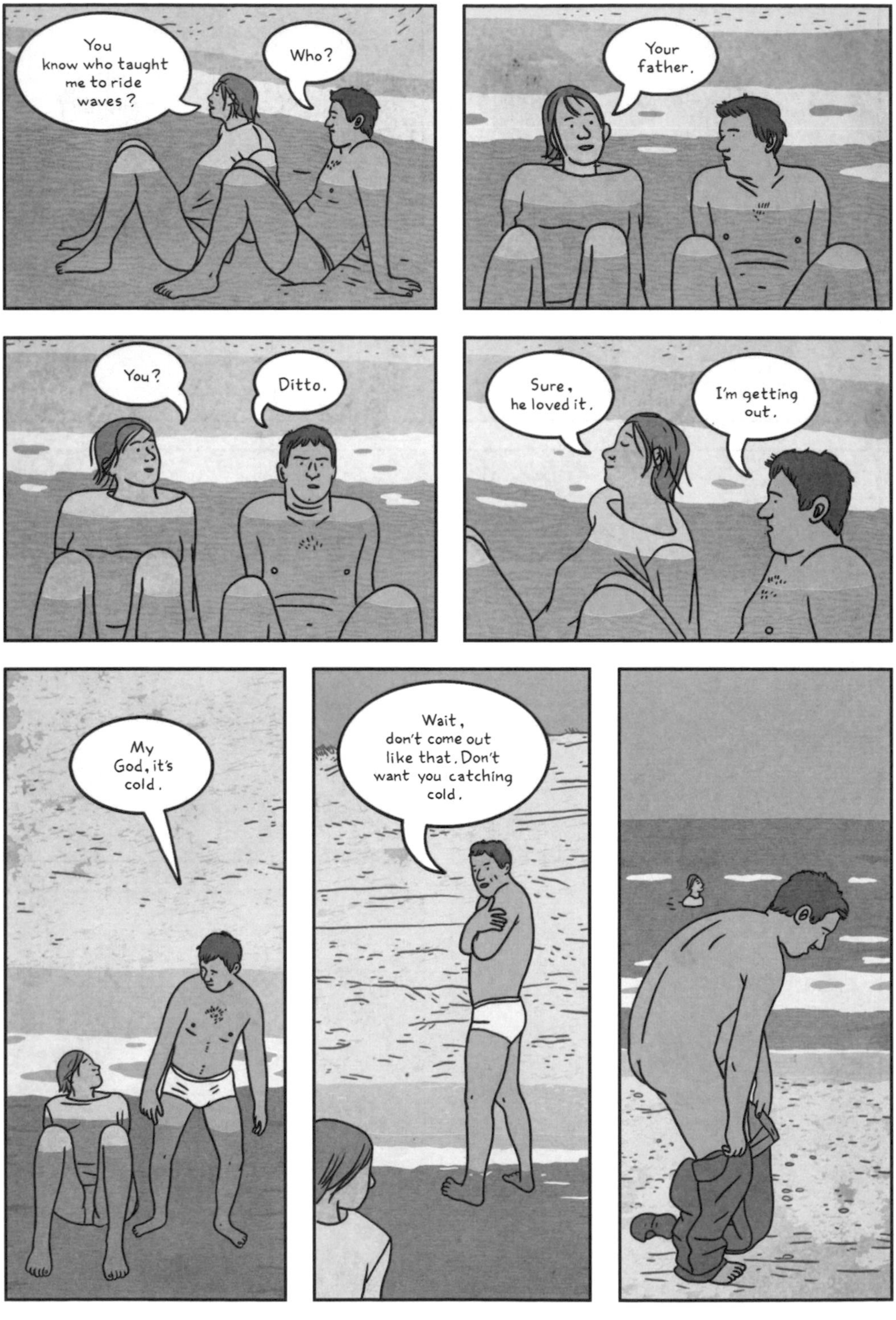
You know who taught me to ride waves?
Who?
Your father.
You?
Ditto.
Sure, he loved it.
I'm getting out.
My God, it's cold.
Wait, don't come out like that. Don't want you catching cold.

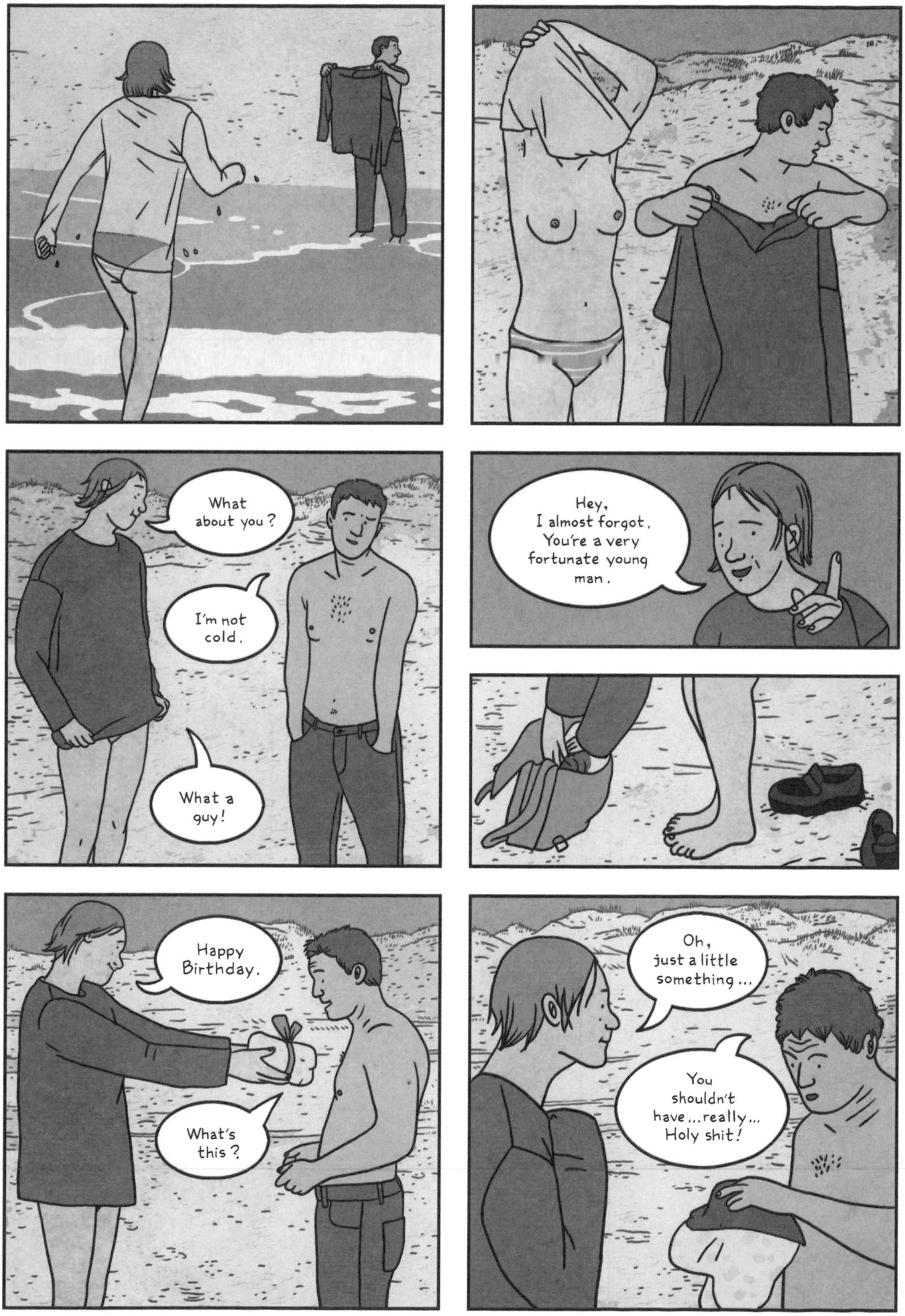
What about you?
I'm not cold.
What a guy!
Hey, I almost forgot. You're a very fortunate young man.
Happy Birthday.
What's this?
Oh, just a little something...
You shouldn't have...really... Holy shit!

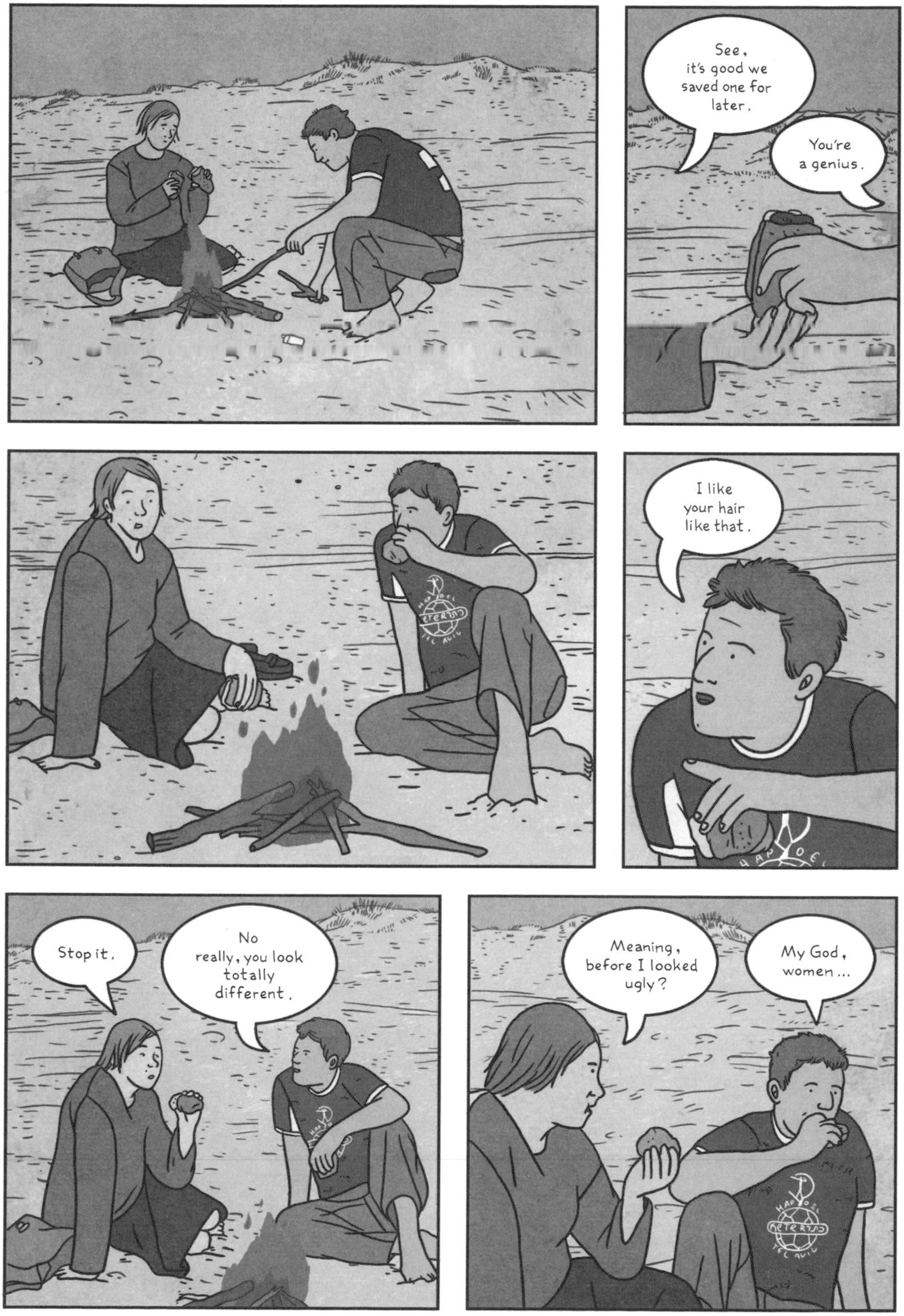

See, it's good we saved one for later.
You're a genius.
I like your hair like that.
Stop it.
No really, you look totally different.
Meaning, before I looked ugly?
My God, women...

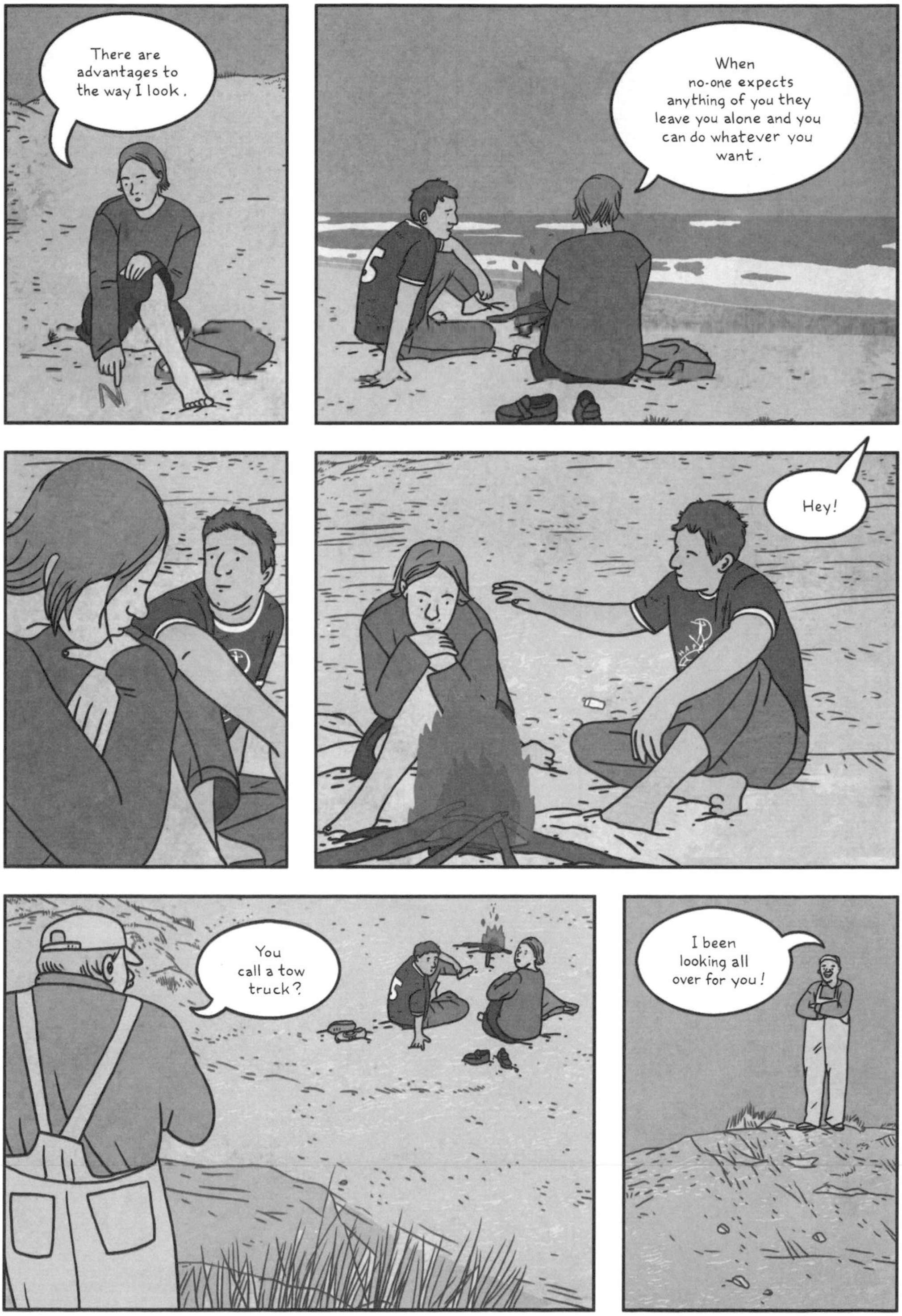
There are advantages to the way I look.
When no-one expects anything of you they leave you alone and you can do whatever you want.
Hey!
You call a tow truck?
I been looking all over for you!

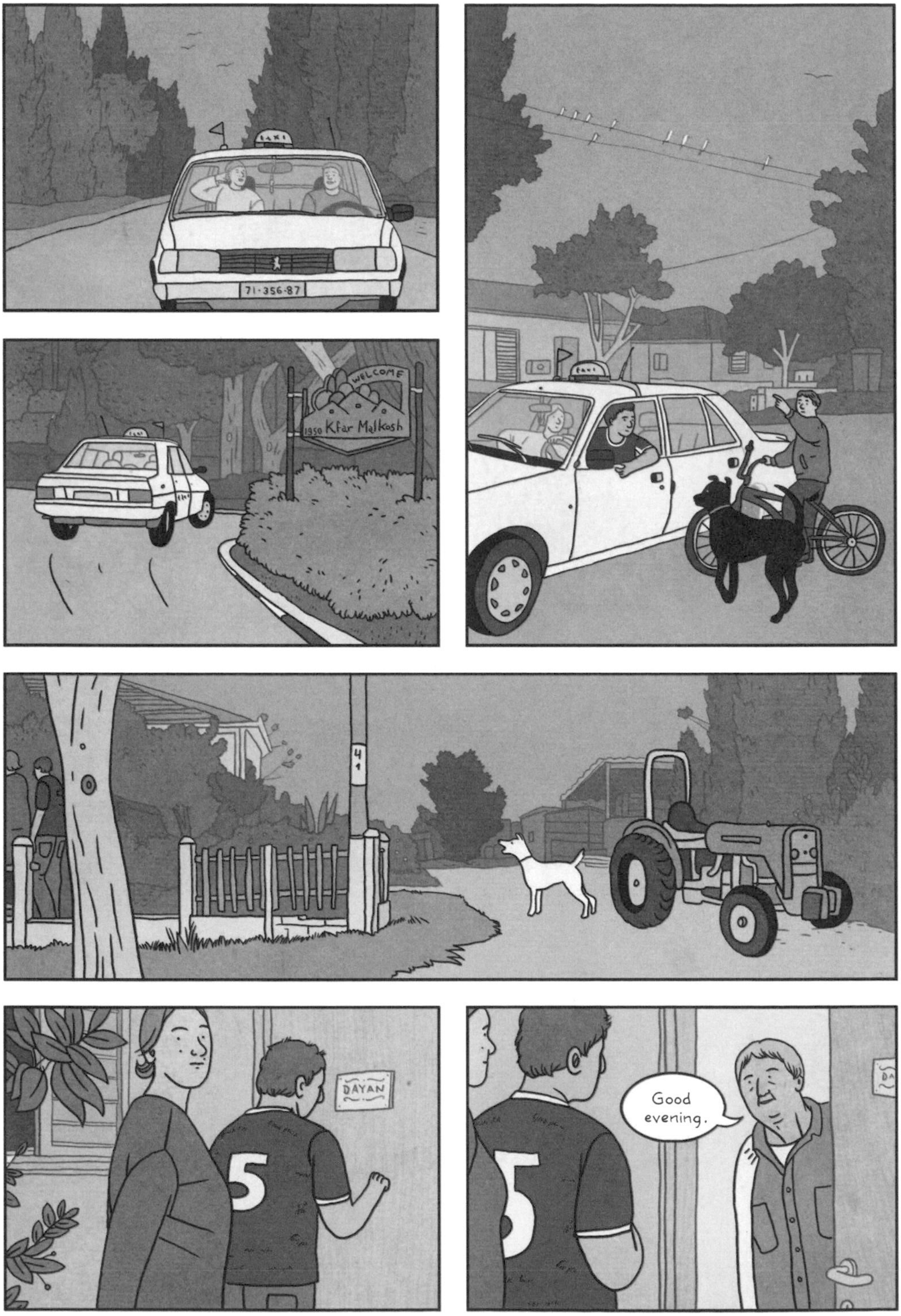
71-356-87
WELCOME
1950 Kfar Malkosh
DAYAN
Good evening.

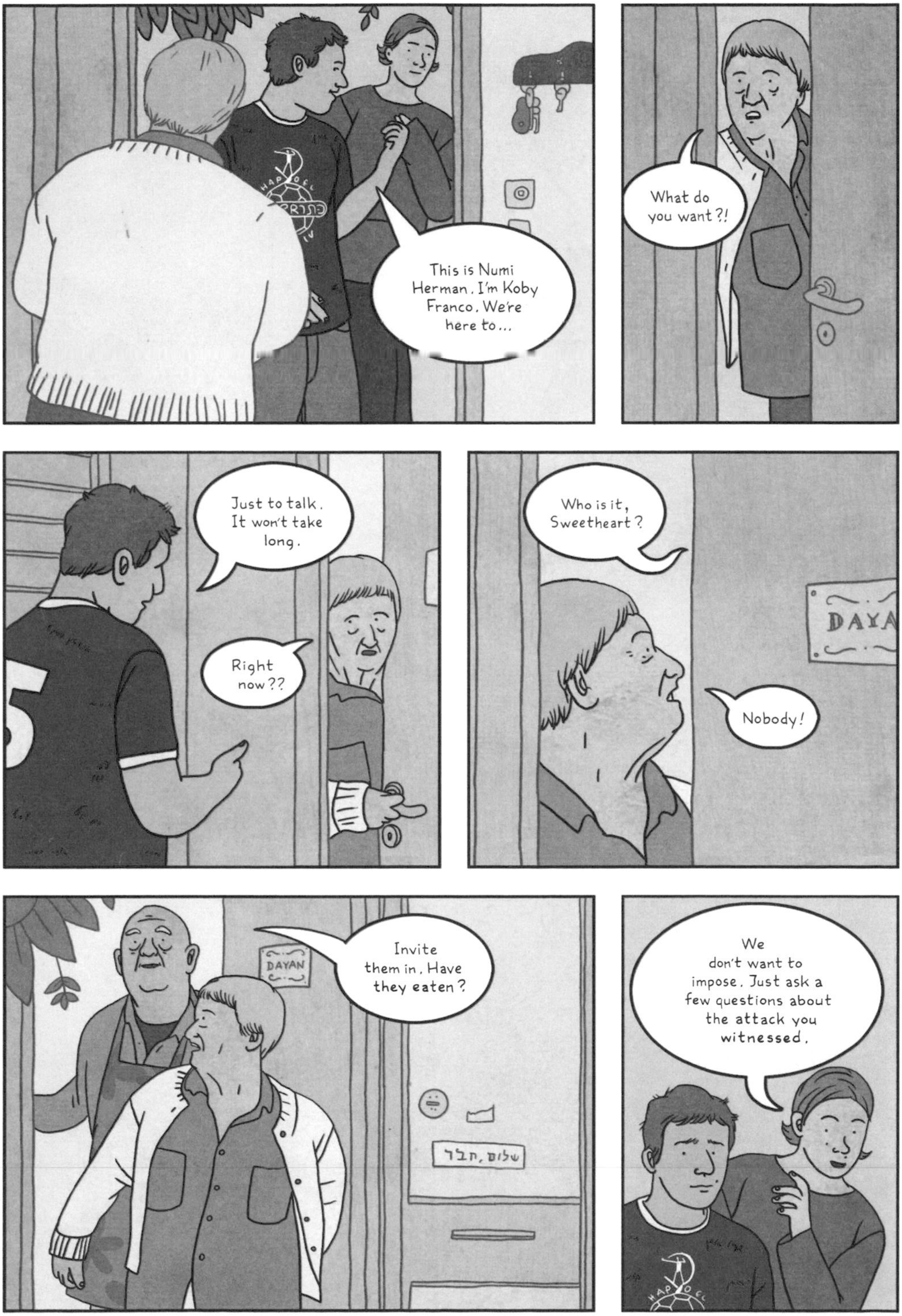
This is Numi Herman. I'm Koby Franco. We're here to...
What do you want?!
Just to talk. It won't take long.
Right now??
Who is it, Sweetheart?
DAYA
Nobody!
DAYAN
Invite them in. Have they eaten?
שלום, חבר
We don't want to impose. Just ask a few questions about the attack you witnessed.

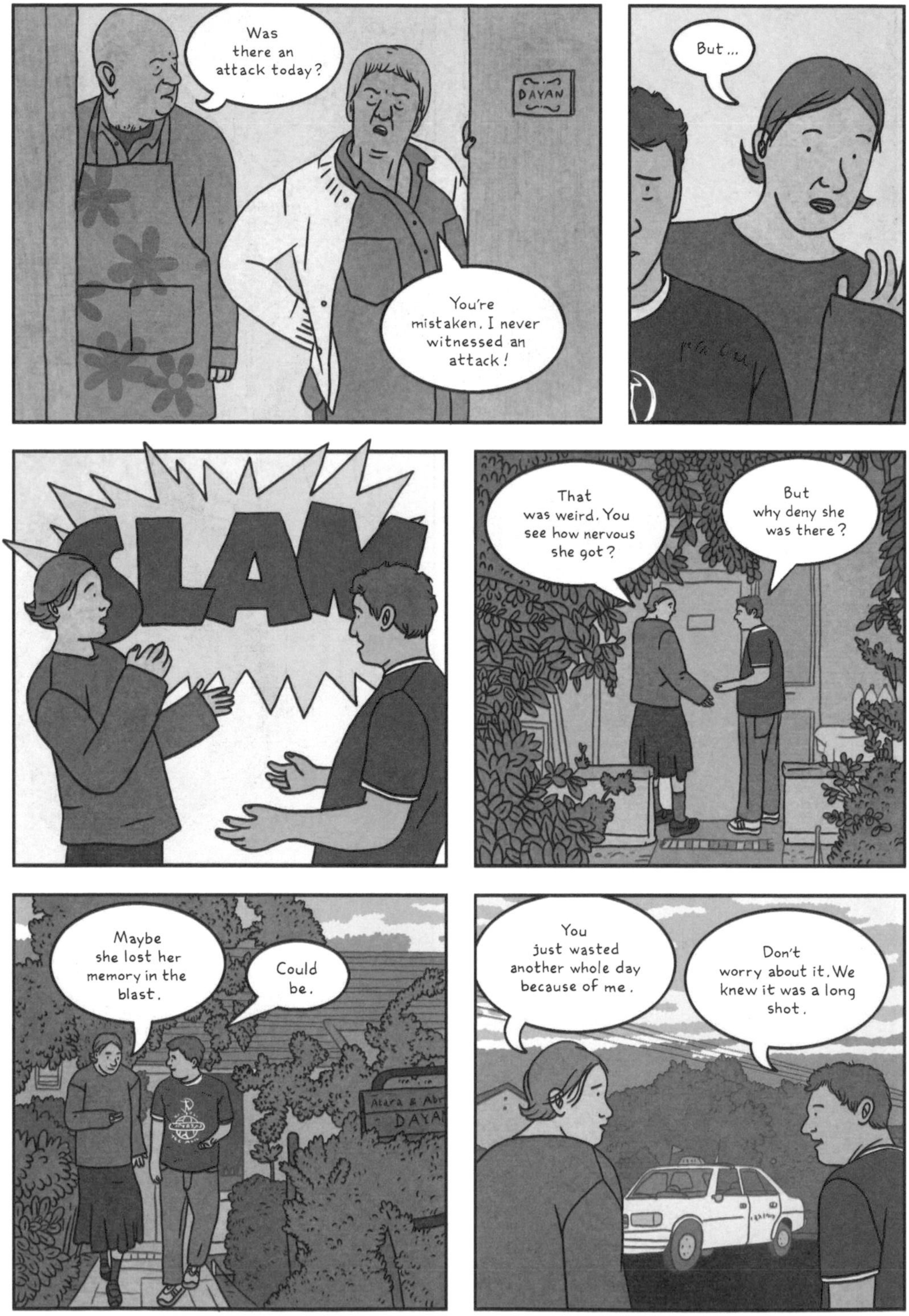
Was there an attack today?
DAYAN
You're mistaken. I never witnessed an attack!
But...
SLAM
That was weird. You see how nervous she got?
But why deny she was there?
Maybe she lost her memory in the blast.
Could be.
You just wasted another whole day because of me.
Don't worry about it. We knew it was a long shot.

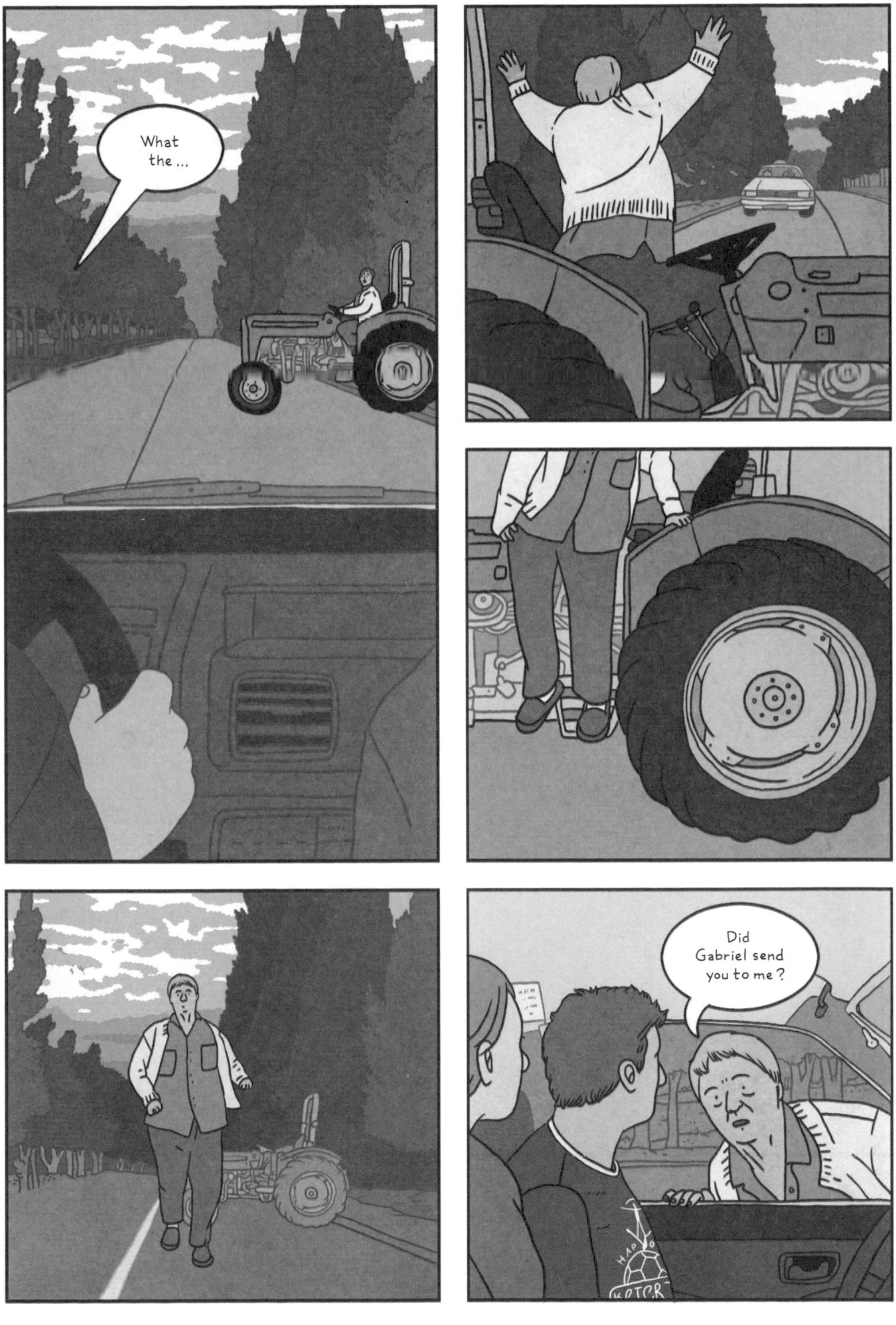
What the ...
Did Gabriel send you to me?

He said he'd come just to see me. We didn't even stay for the band. We went for a walk in the Carmel Mountains.

Forty five years, and it was like no time had passed at all.

I almost missed the bus back home.

I started traveling to Tel-Aviv every week. My husband was so impressed by my devotion to our grandchildren. It's good he didn't hear our daughter, Tami complaining, "You don't give a damn about the kids anymore."

The fact is, the kids were my alibi. I'd peek in on them, then hurry off to meet Gabriel. If Avraham asked, Tami would say I'd been there. But he never did.

In December Avraham went on a genealogy tour of Poland. That was my chance. I booked a room in a hotel in Tiberias. We planned to go away for the weekend.

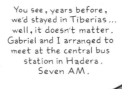

You see, years before, we'd stayed in Tiberias... well, it doesn't matter. Gabriel and I arranged to meet at the central bus station in Hadera. Seven AM.

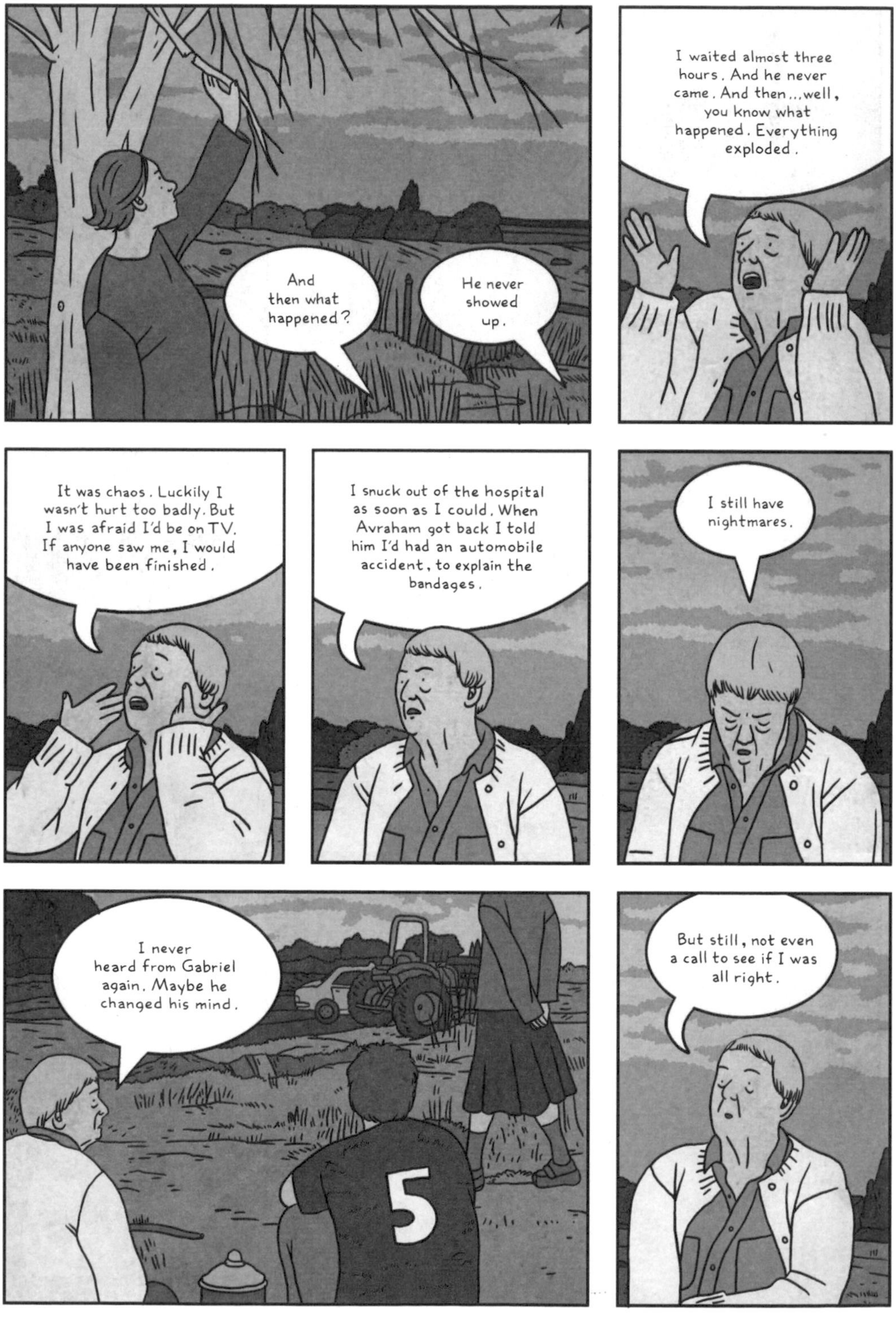
And then what happened?
He never showed up.
I waited almost three hours. And he never came. And then...well, you know what happened. Everything exploded.
It was chaos. Luckily I wasn't hurt too badly. But I was afraid I'd be on TV. If anyone saw me, I would have been finished.
I snuck out of the hospital as soon as I could. When Avraham got back I told him I'd had an automobile accident, to explain the bandages.
I still have nightmares.
I never heard from Gabriel again. Maybe he changed his mind.
5
But still, not even a call to see if I was all right.

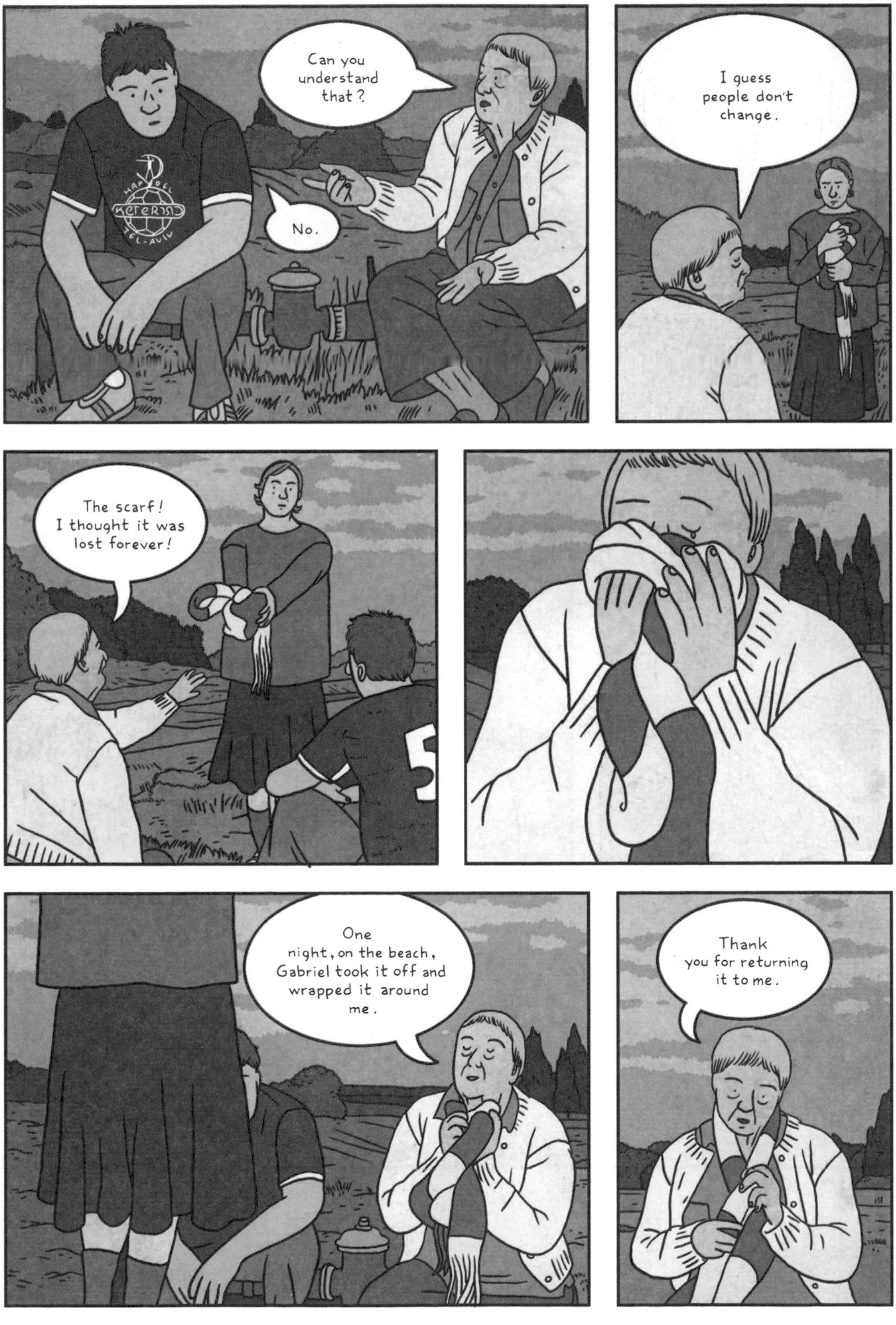
Can you understand that?
No.
I guess people don't change.
The scarf! I thought it was lost forever!
One night, on the beach, Gabriel took it off and wrapped it around me.
Thank you for returning it to me.

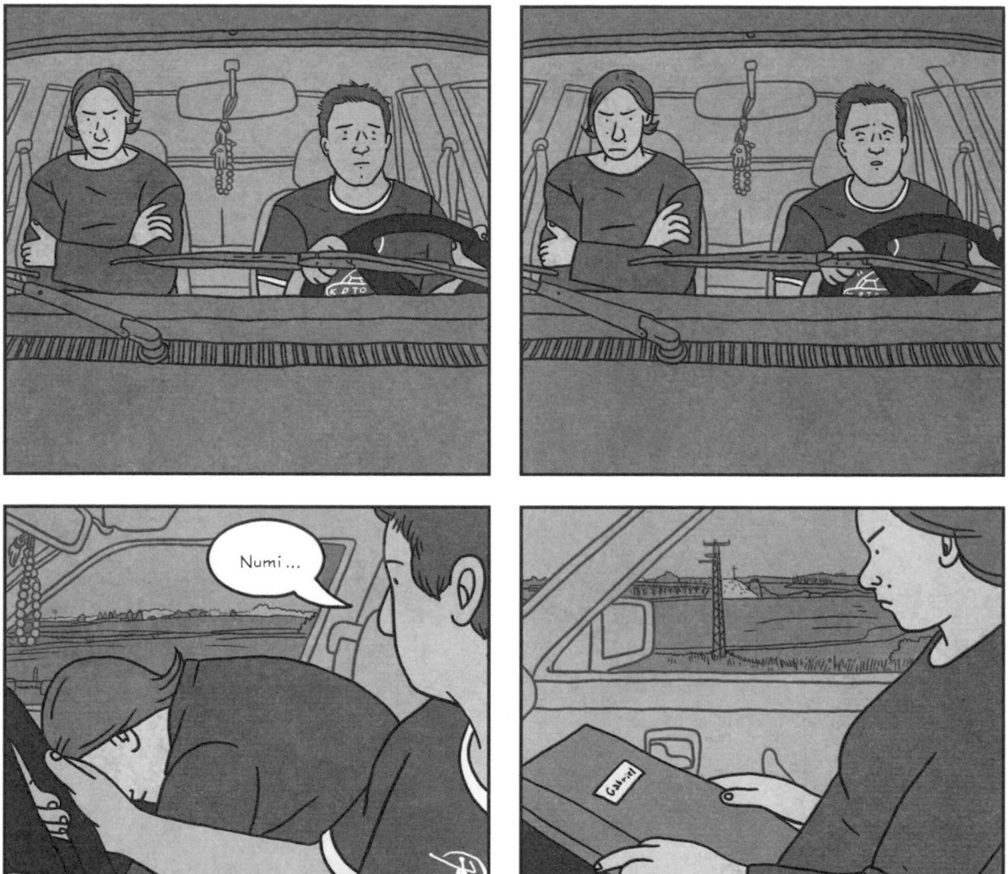
Numi ...
Gabriel

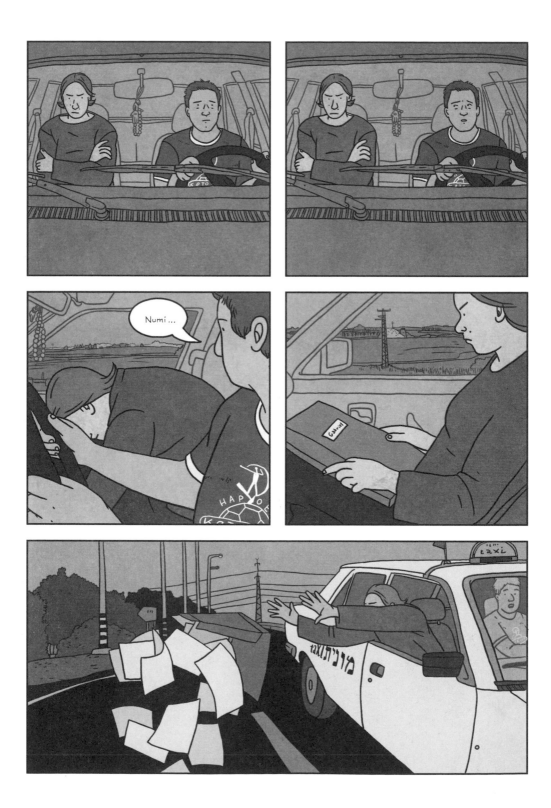

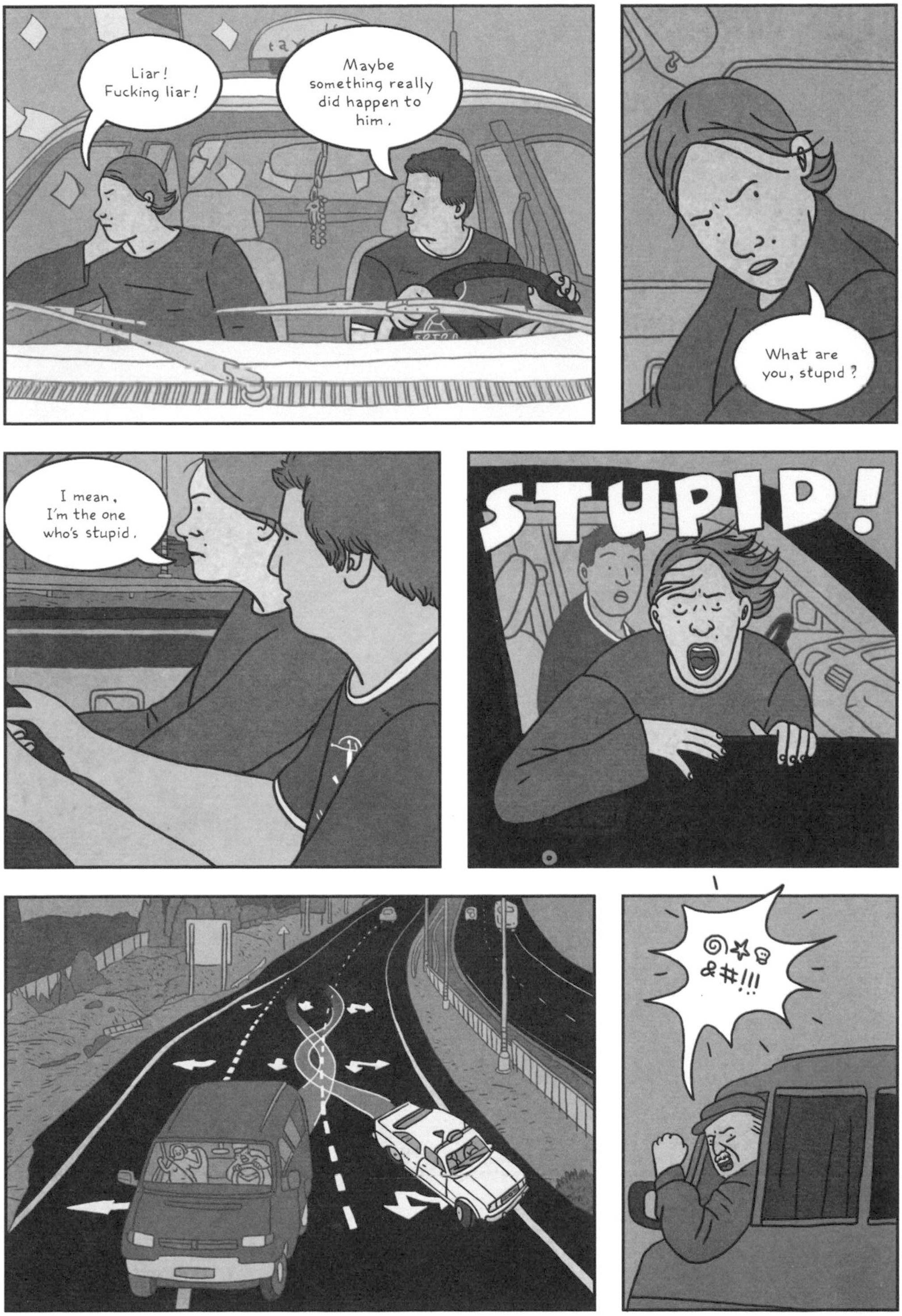
Liar! Fucking liar!
Maybe something really did happen to him.
What are you, stupid?
I mean, I'm the one who's stupid.
STUPID!
&#!!!

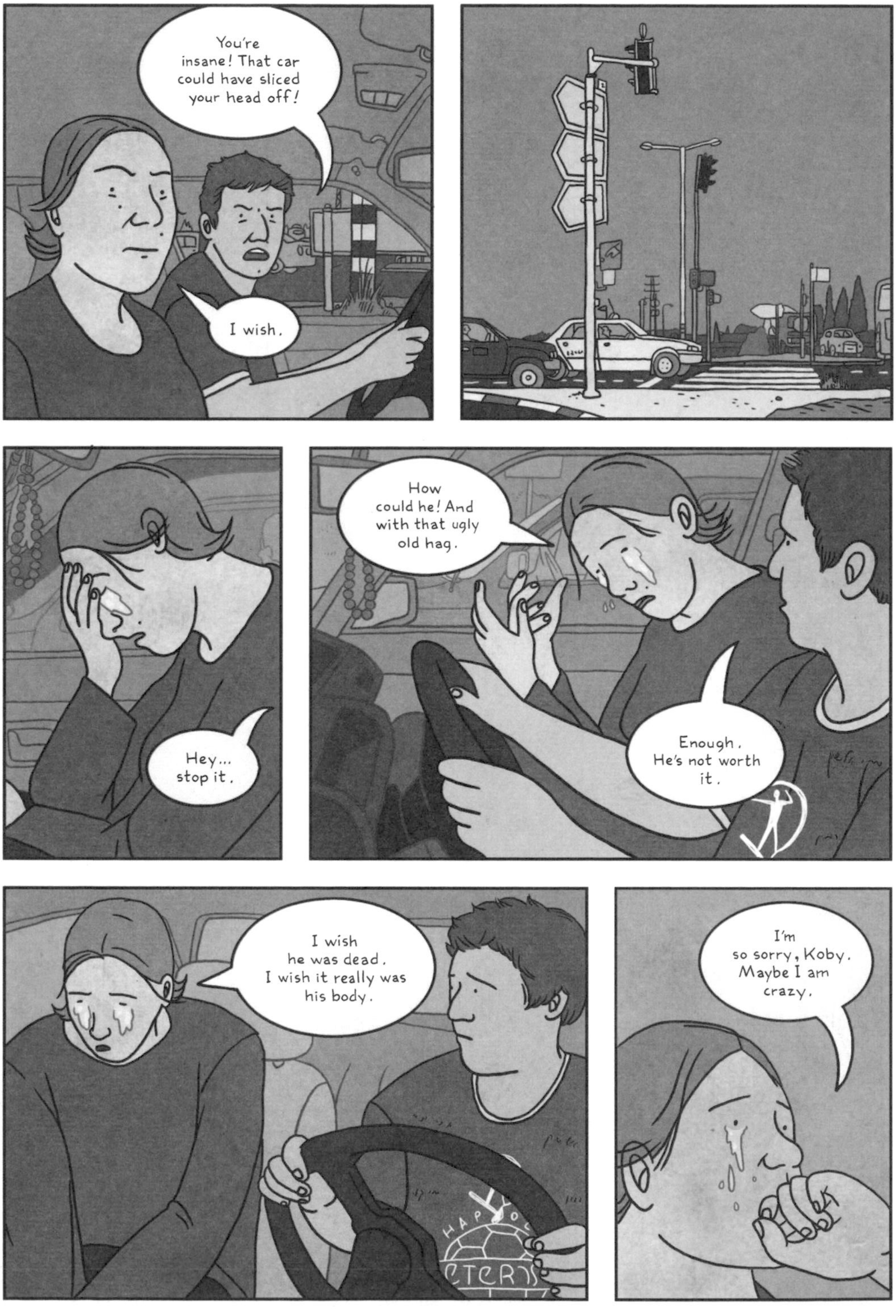
You're insane! That car could have sliced your head off!
I wish.
Hey... stop it.
How could he! And with that ugly old hag.
Enough. He's not worth it.
I wish he was dead. I wish it really was his body.
I'm so sorry, Koby. Maybe I am crazy.

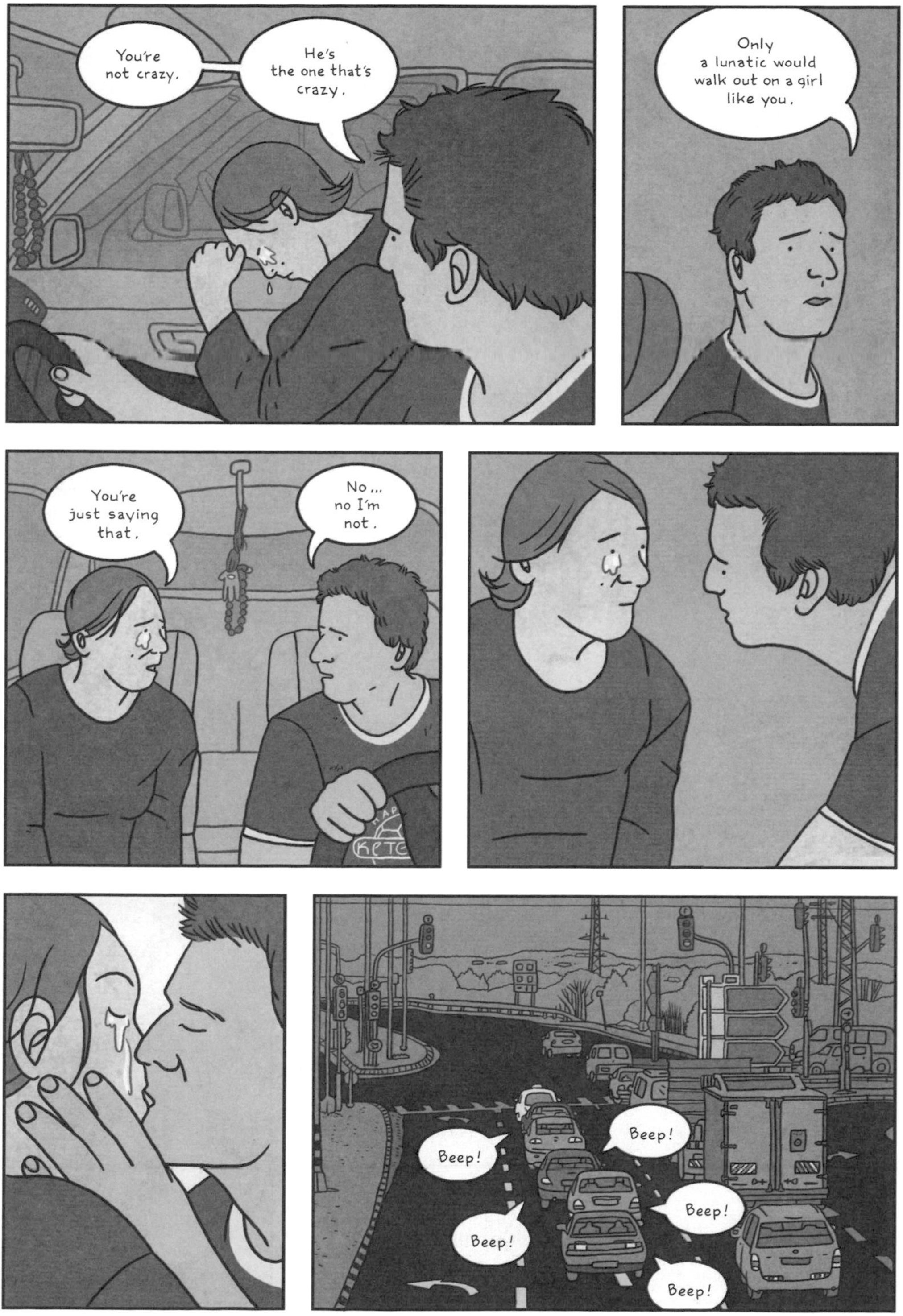
You're not crazy.
He's the one that's crazy.
Only a lunatic would walk out on a girl like you.
You're just saying that.
No... no I'm not.
Beep!
Beep!
Beep!
Beep!
Beep!

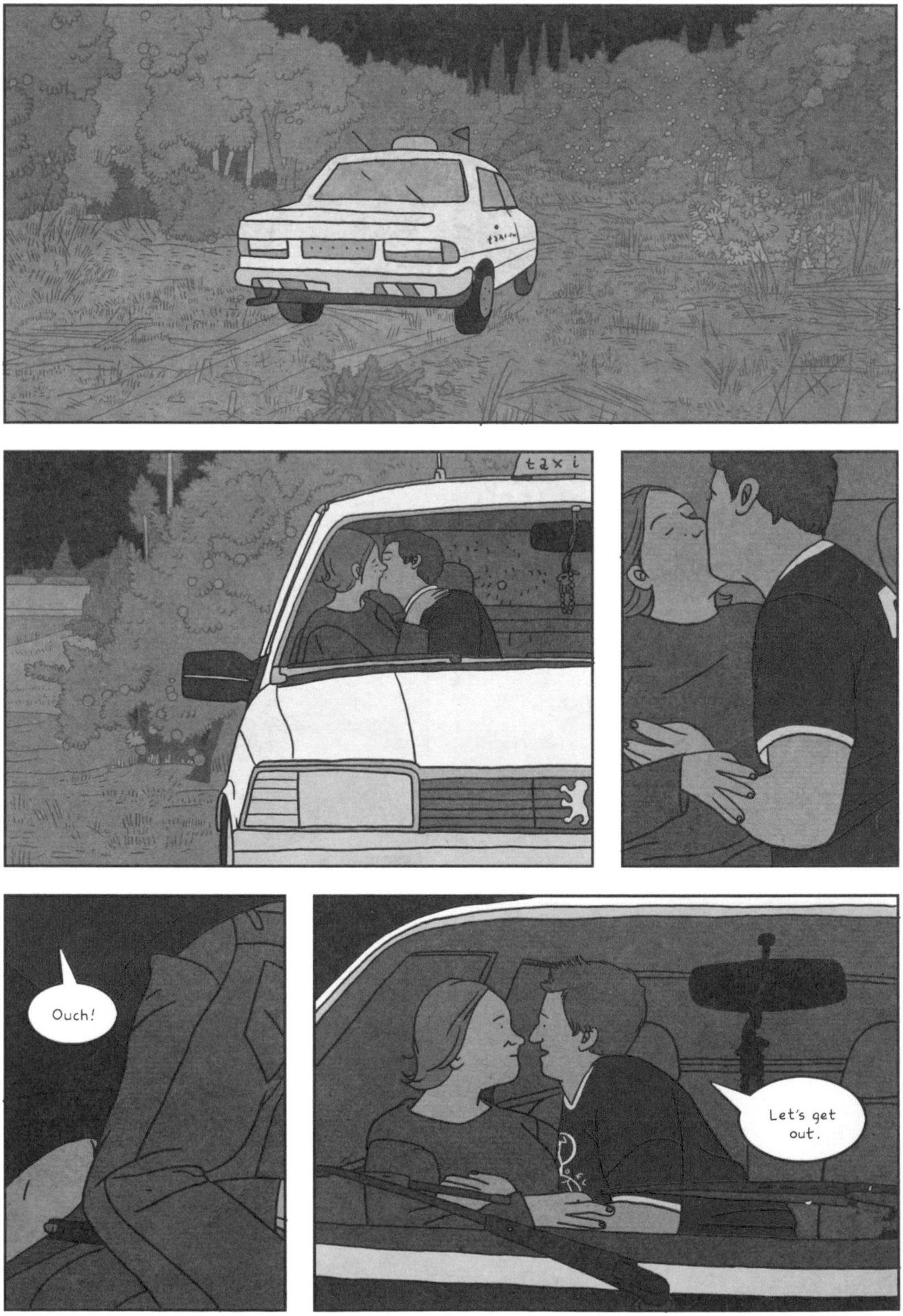
taxi
Ouch!
Let's get out.

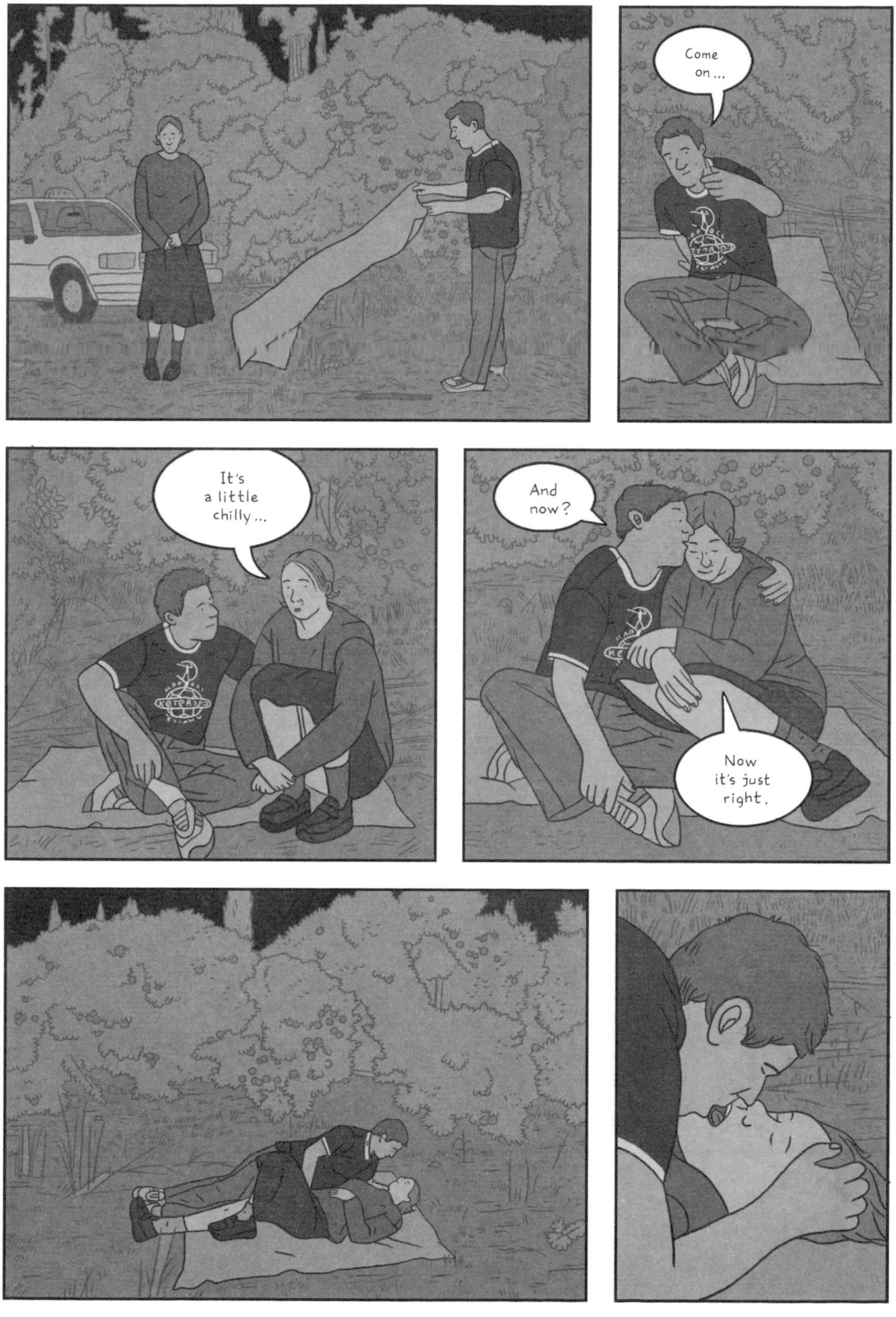
Come on...
It's a little chilly...
And now?
Now it's just right.

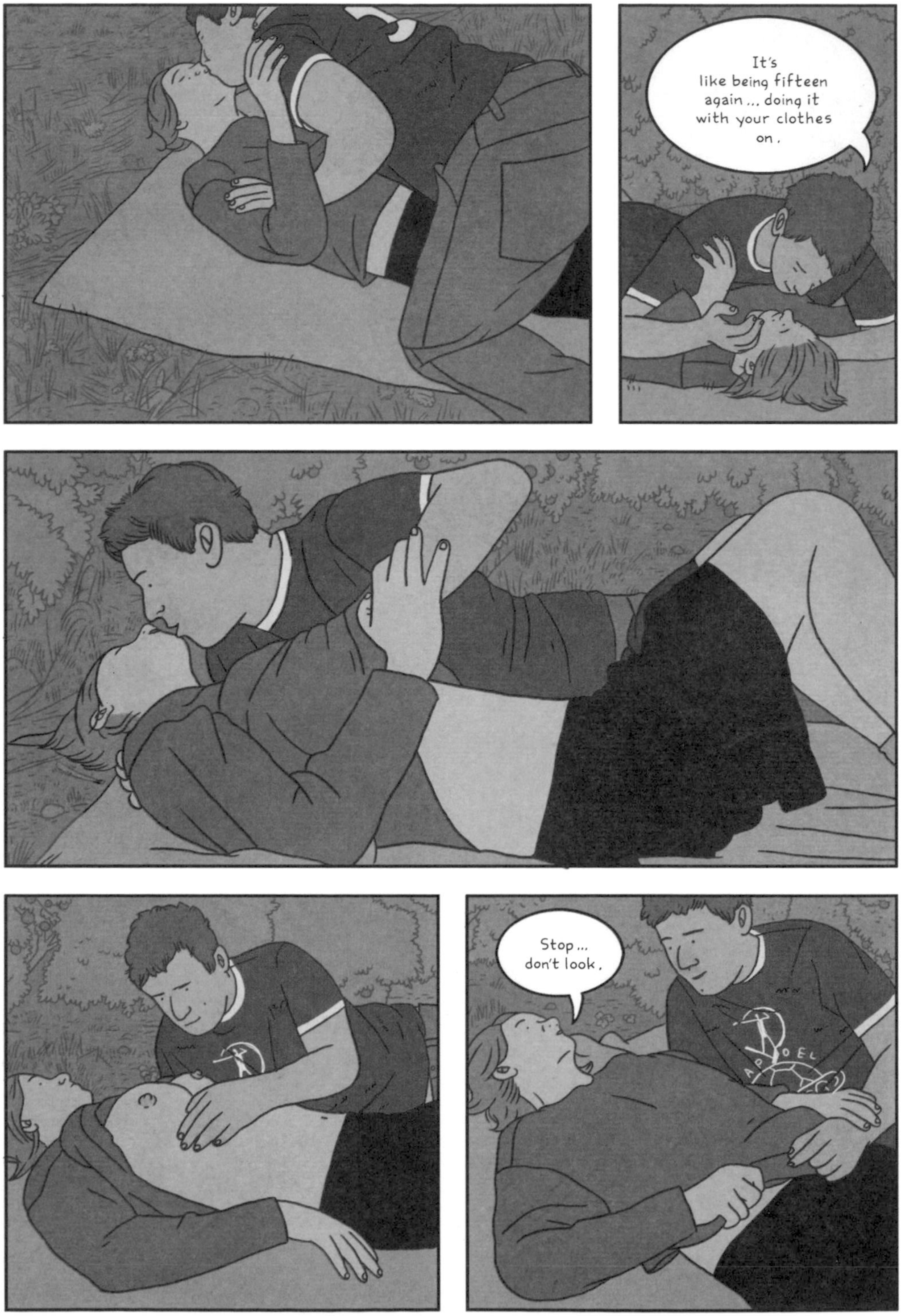
It's like being fifteen again ... doing it with your clothes on.
Stop ... don't look.

You're salty.

Does it bother you?

No, actually it's nice.

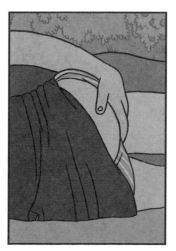

Let me... I'll do it.

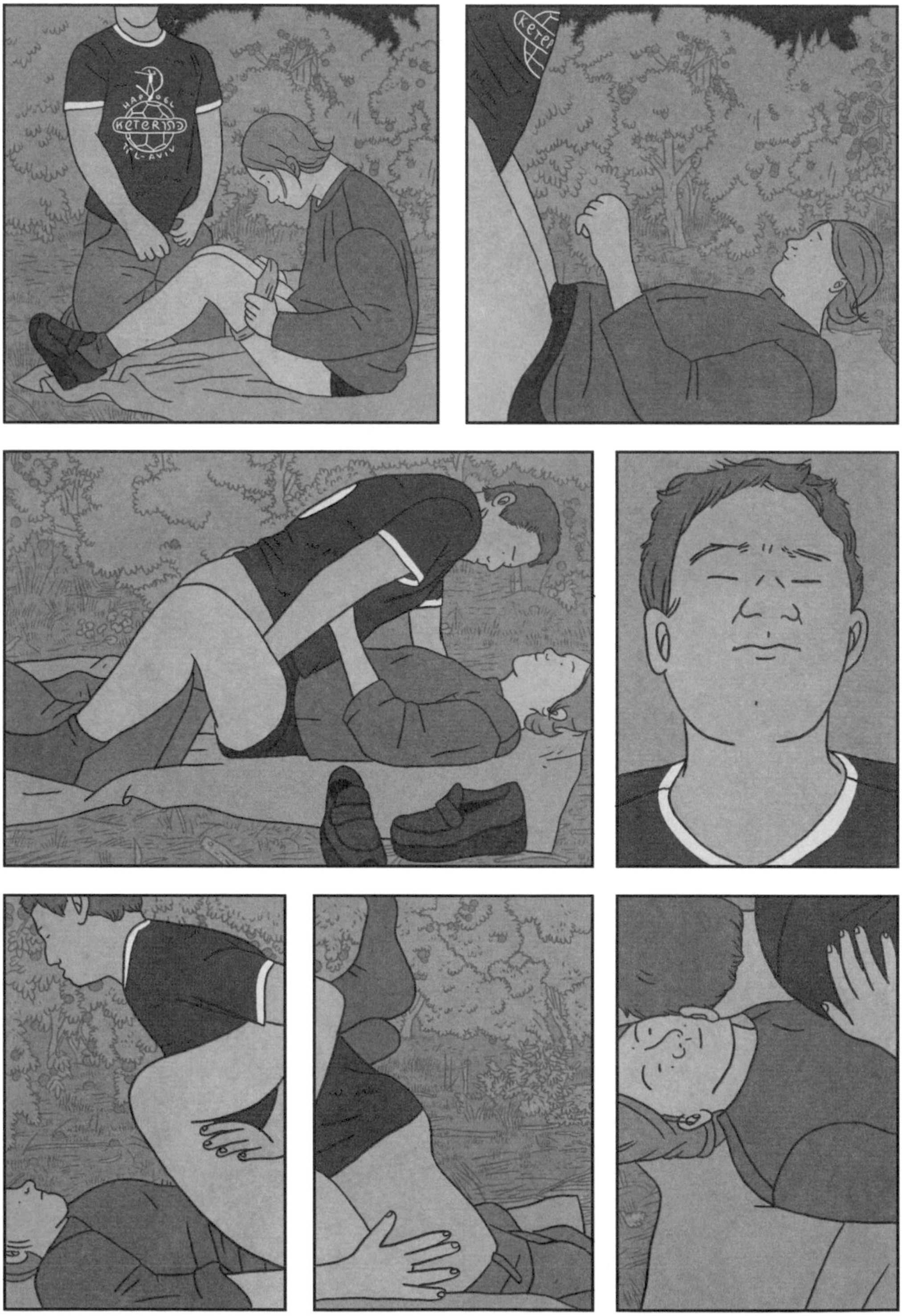
KETERING

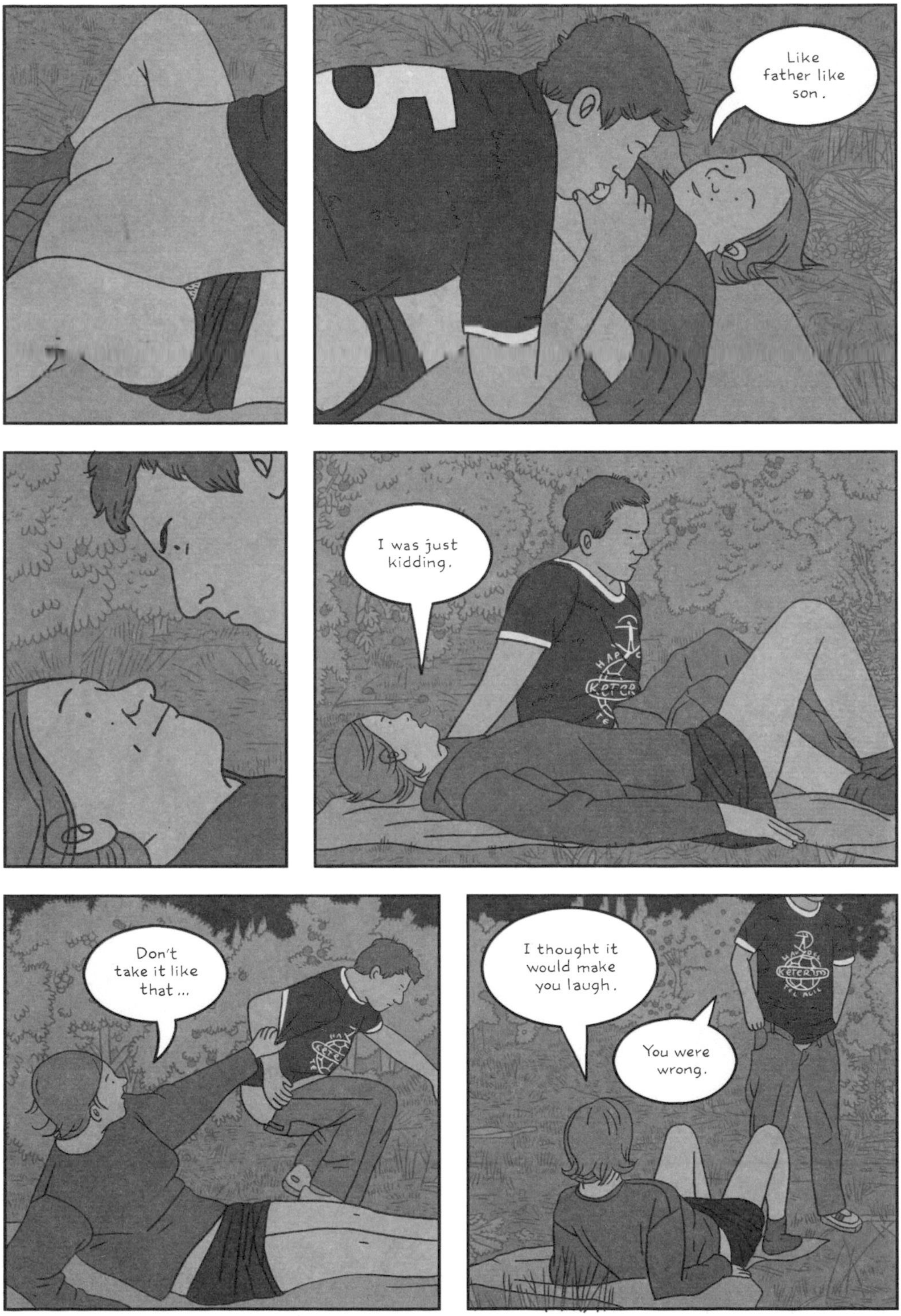
Like father like son.
I was just kidding.
Don't take it like that...
I thought it would make you laugh.
You were wrong.

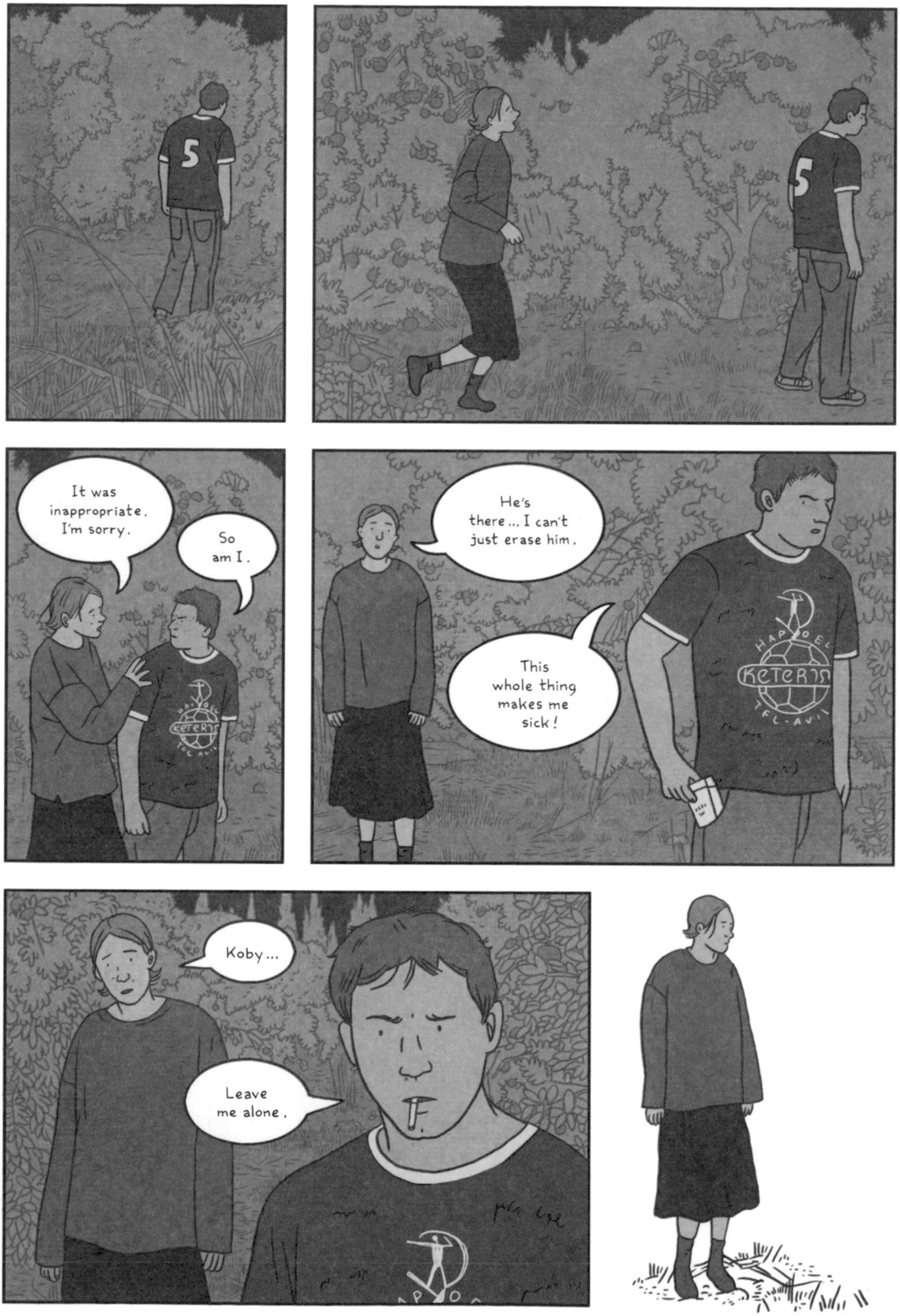
It was inappropriate. I'm sorry.
So am I.
He's there... I can't just erase him.
This whole thing makes me sick!
Koby...
Leave me alone.

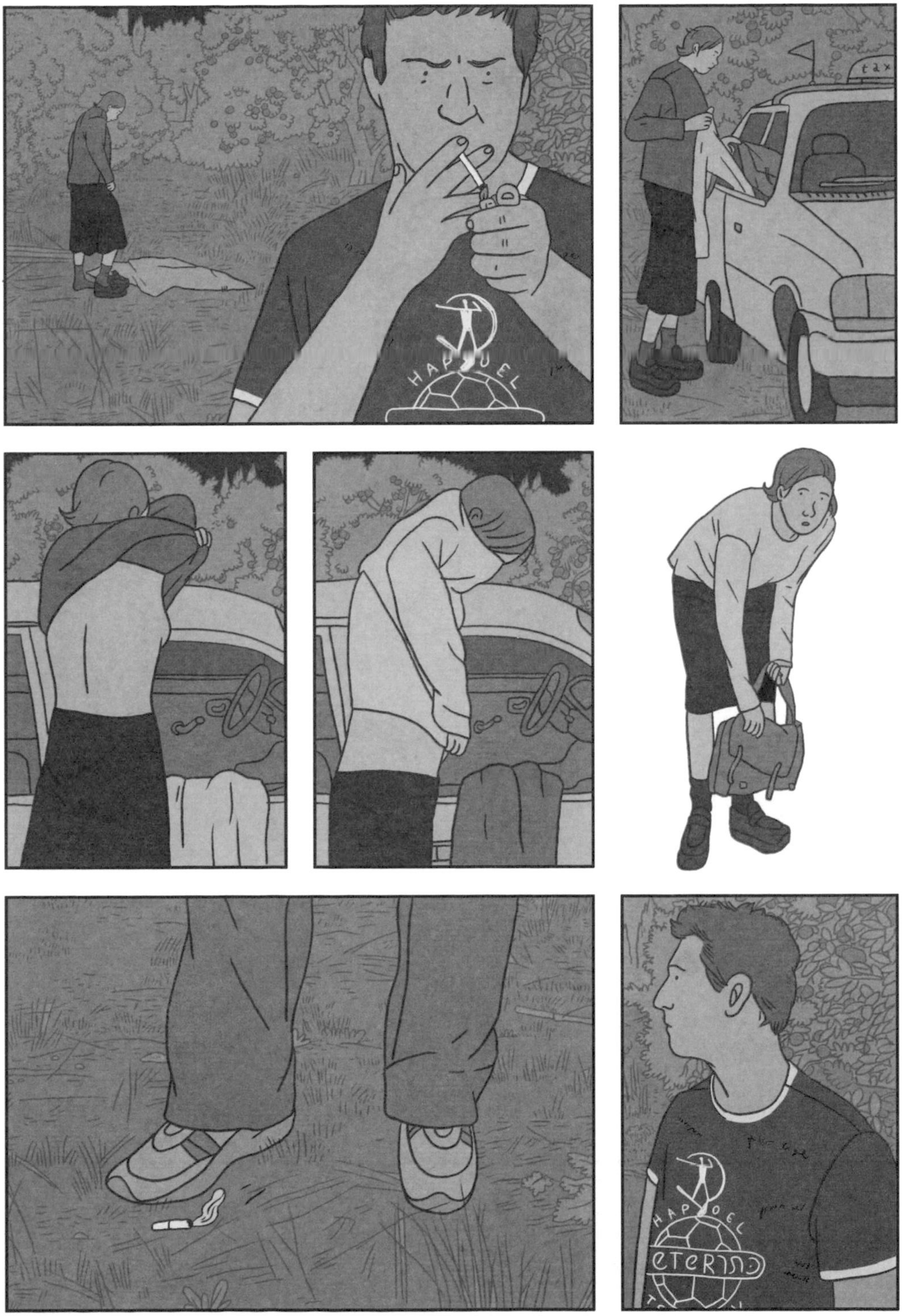

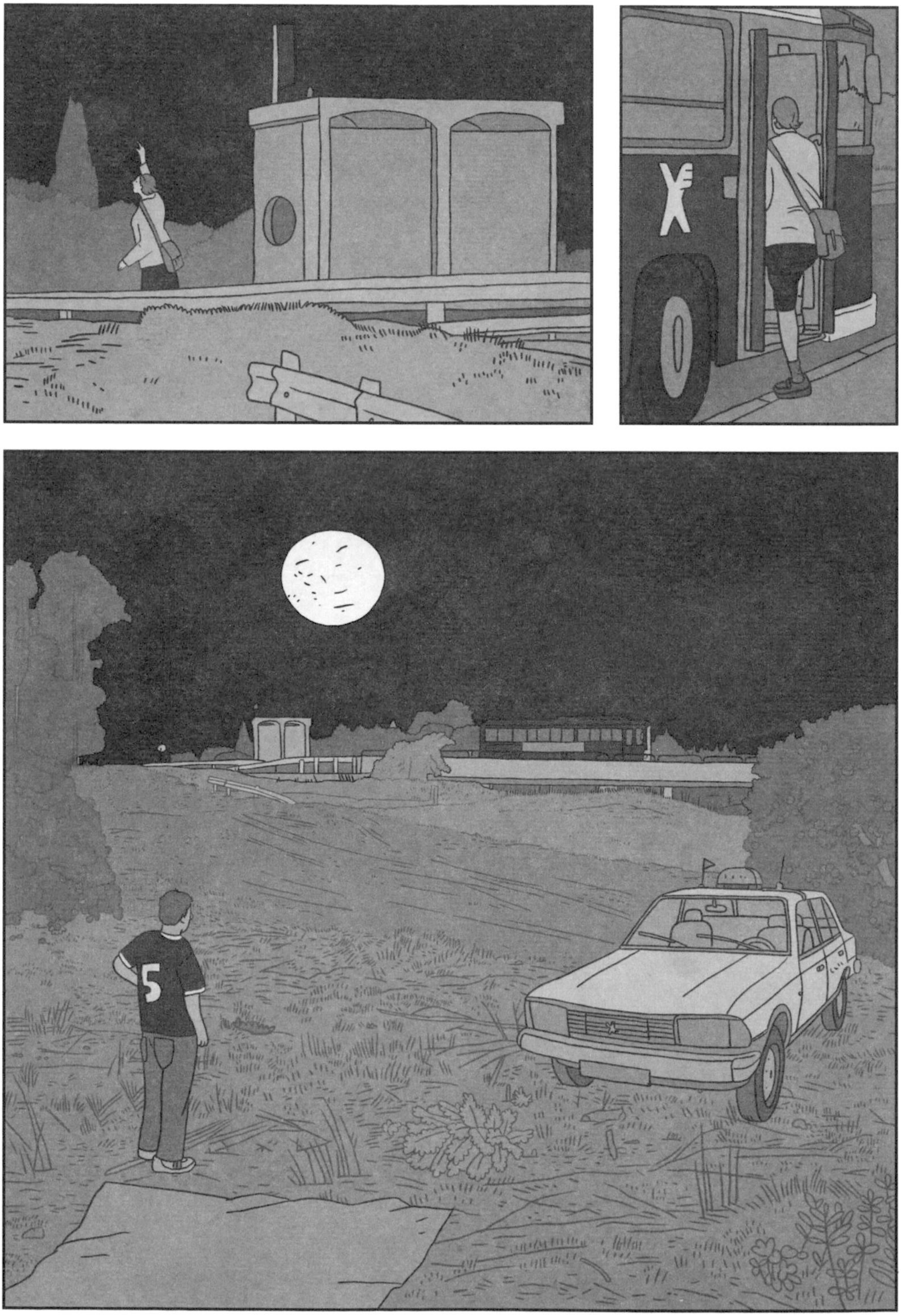

chapter four
resurrection

I worked like crazy for three months.

It had been raining non-stop almost till the end of April, and besides, people were afraid to ride the buses because of the bombings.

11.30 shekels please.

On top of that Aunt Ruthie had to have surgery. Nothing serious, but I started doing her shifts too.

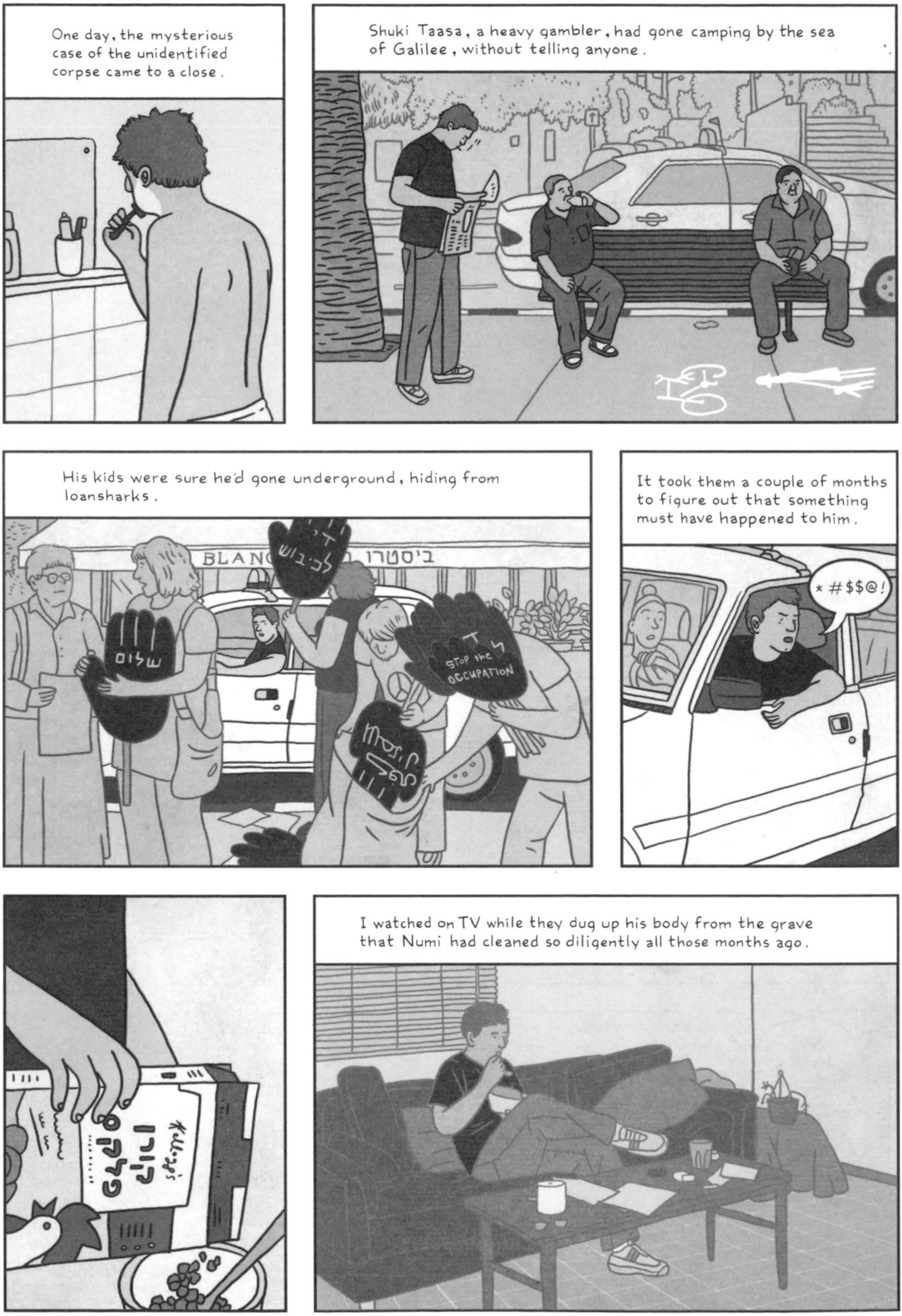
One day, the mysterious case of the unidentified corpse came to a close.
Shuki Taasa, a heavy gambler, had gone camping by the sea of Galilee, without telling anyone.
His kids were sure he'd gone underground, hiding from loanshark.
BLANC
ביסטרו
לכיבוש
שלום
STOP the OCCUPATION
It took them a couple of months to figure out that something must have happened to him.
*#$$@!
I watched on TV while they dug up his body from the grave that Numi had cleaned so diligently all those months ago.

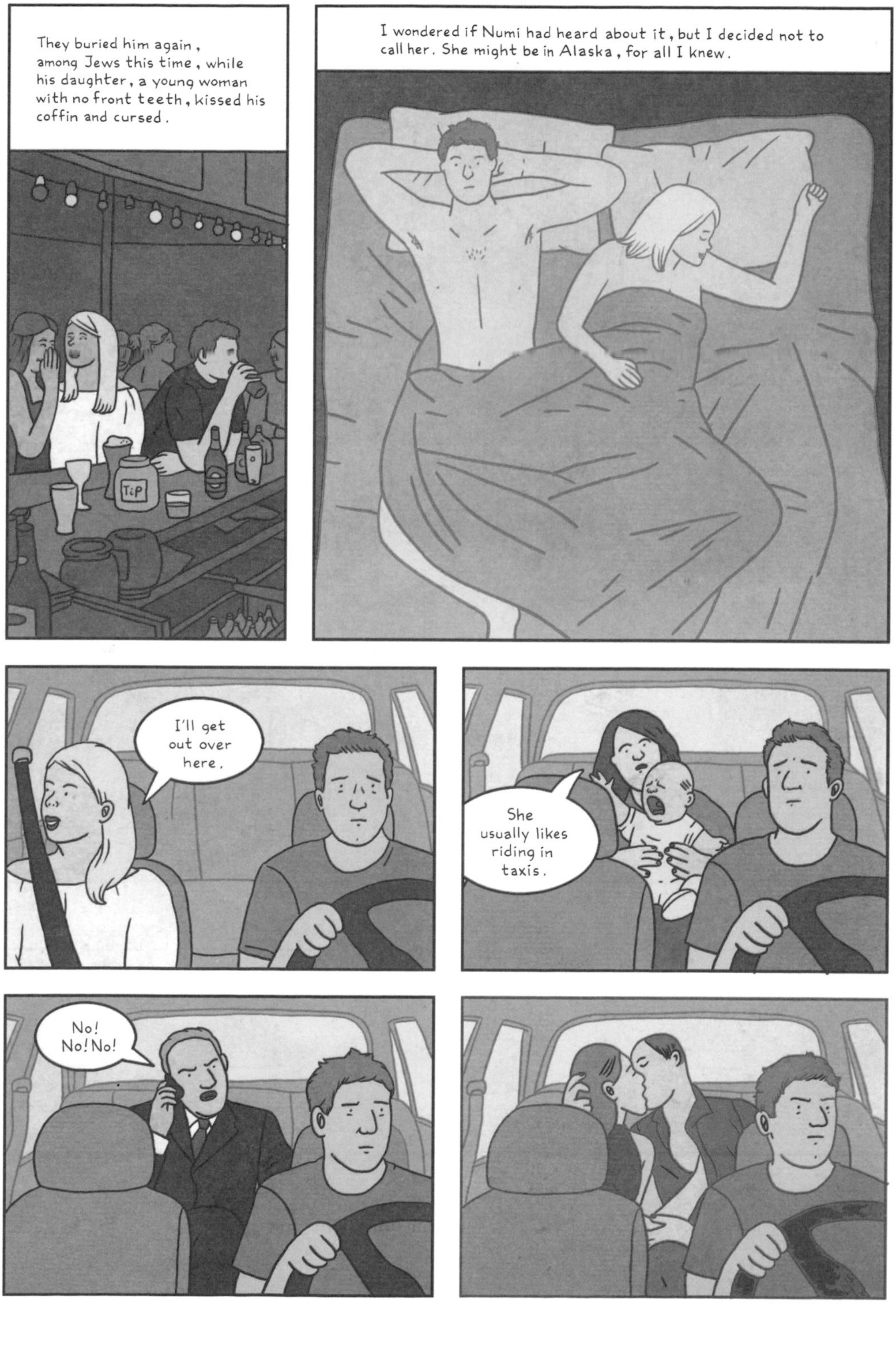
They buried him again, among Jews this time, while his daughter, a young woman with no front teeth, kissed his coffin and cursed.
TIP
I wondered if Numi had heard about it, but I decided not to call her. She might be in Alaska, for all I knew.
I'll get out over here.
She usually likes riding in taxis.
No! No! No!

I developed a theory, as yet unfounded, that my father had been having an affair with Aunt Ruthie.

Despite her eternal animosity towards him - or maybe because of it ... it explains too many things.

I don't have any proof, but that time, long ago, when he kicked me out of his house, he had been so uptight. And Aunt Ruthie had been there, after all.

The way I see it now, if i'd shown up just fifteen minutes earlier I might have caught them in the act.

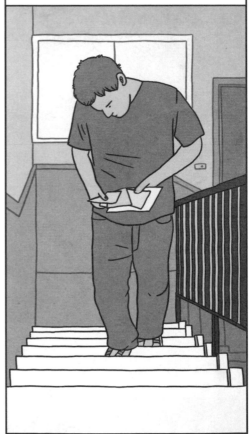

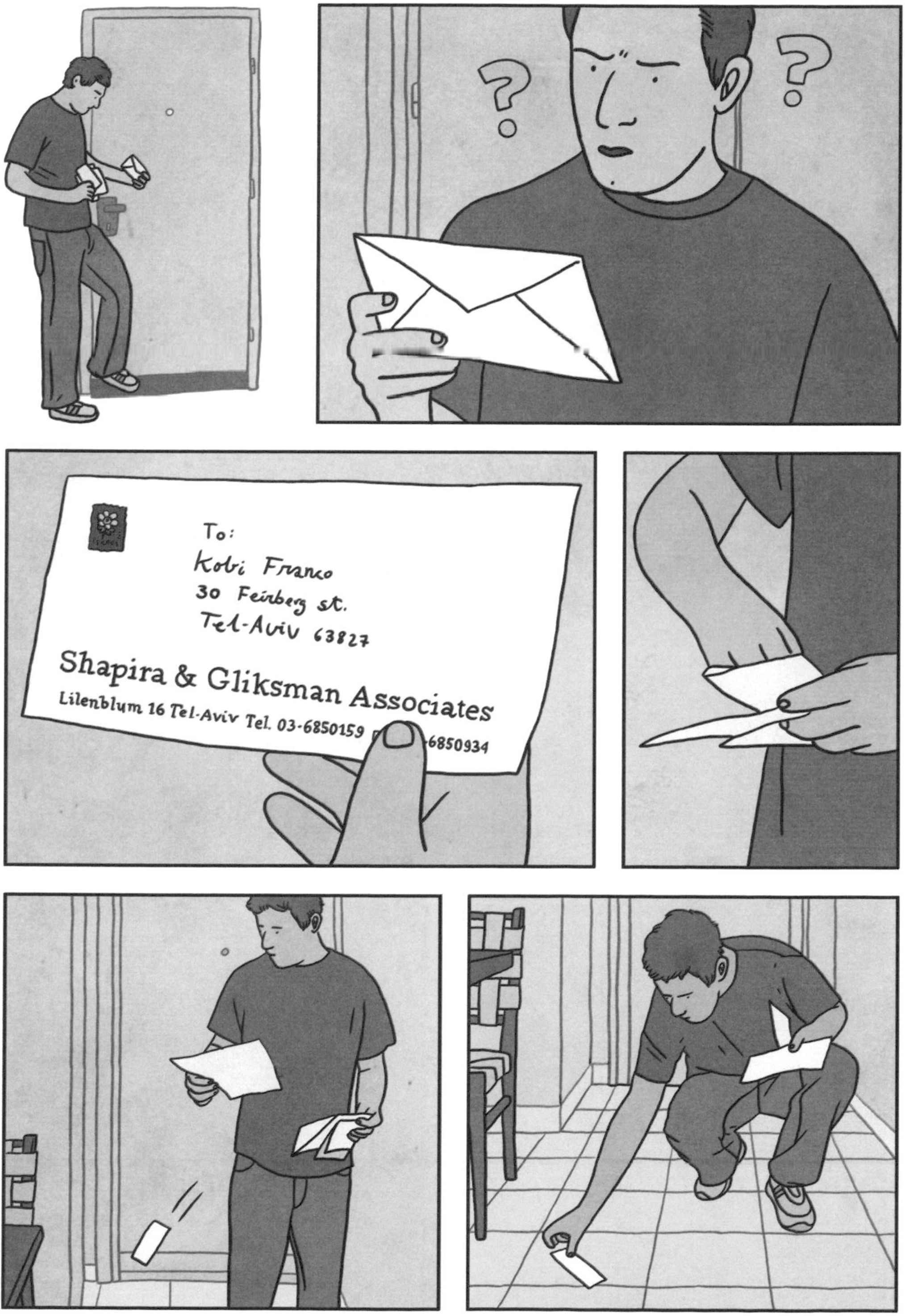
?
?
To:
Kobi Franco
30 Feirberg st.
Tel-Aviv 63827
Shapira & Gliksman Associates
Lilenblum 16 Tel-Aviv Tel. 03-6850159
6850934

בנק לאומי
bank leumi
FRANCO GABRIEL
ID 059372
ACCOUNT No 506138/79
BRANCH 811
PAY Kobi Franco
176,000xx
One hundred Seventy six thousand Shekels
N.I.S
5/6/2002
DATE
G. Franco
SIGNATURE
"1150618879 ≈10-21131= 454
What the fuck!

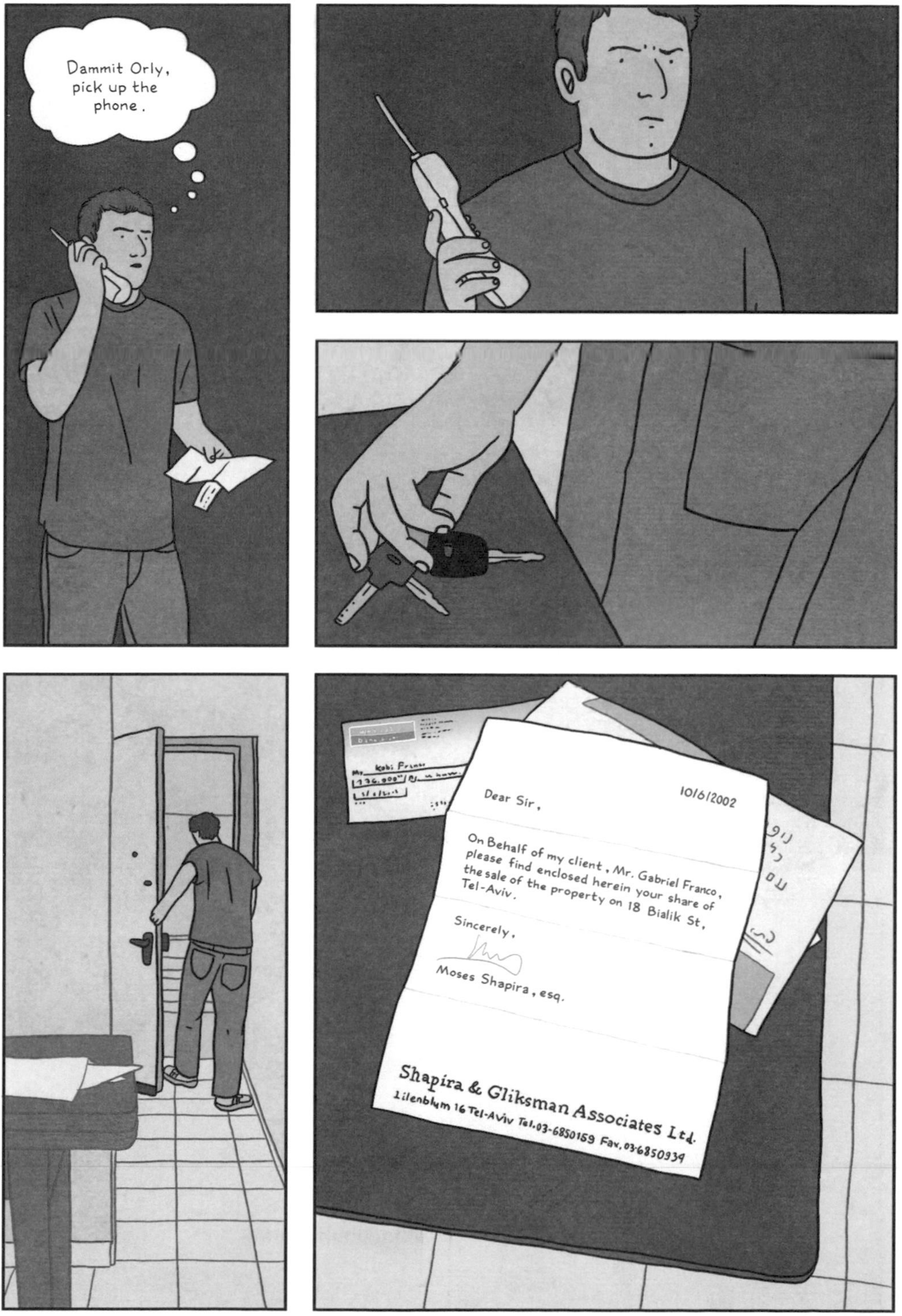
Dammit Orly, pick up the phone.
Dear Sir,
10/6/2002
On Behalf of my client, Mr. Gabriel Franco, please find enclosed herein your share of the sale of the property on 18 Bialik St, Tel-Aviv.
Sincerely,
Moses Shapira, esq.
Shapira & Gliksman Associates Ltd.
Lilenblum 16 Tel-Aviv Tel.03-6850159 Fax.03-6850934

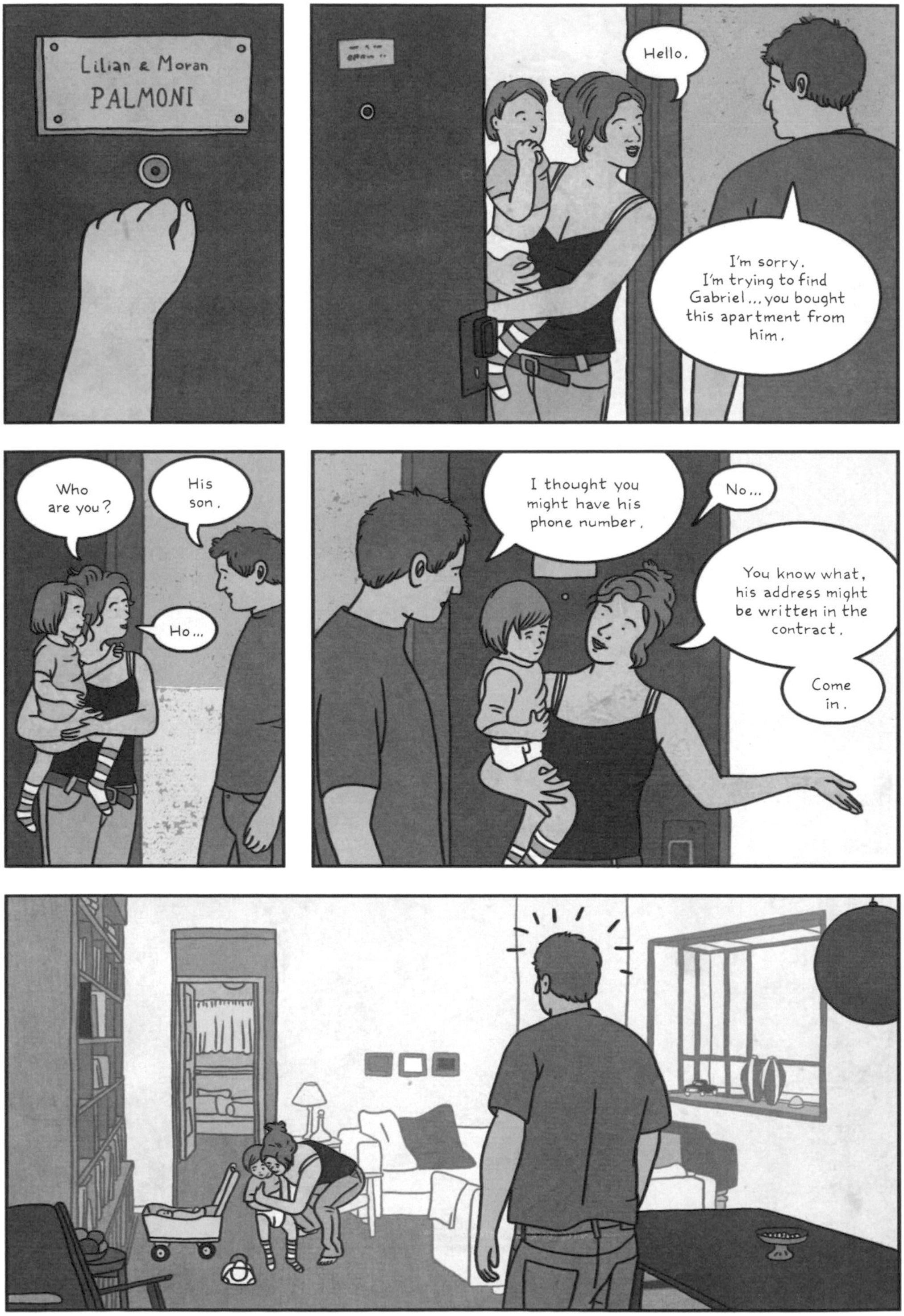
Lilian & Moran
PALMONI
Hello.
I'm sorry. I'm trying to find Gabriel... you bought this apartment from him.
Who are you?
His son.
Ho...
I thought you might have his phone number.
No...
You know what, his address might be written in the contract.
Come in.

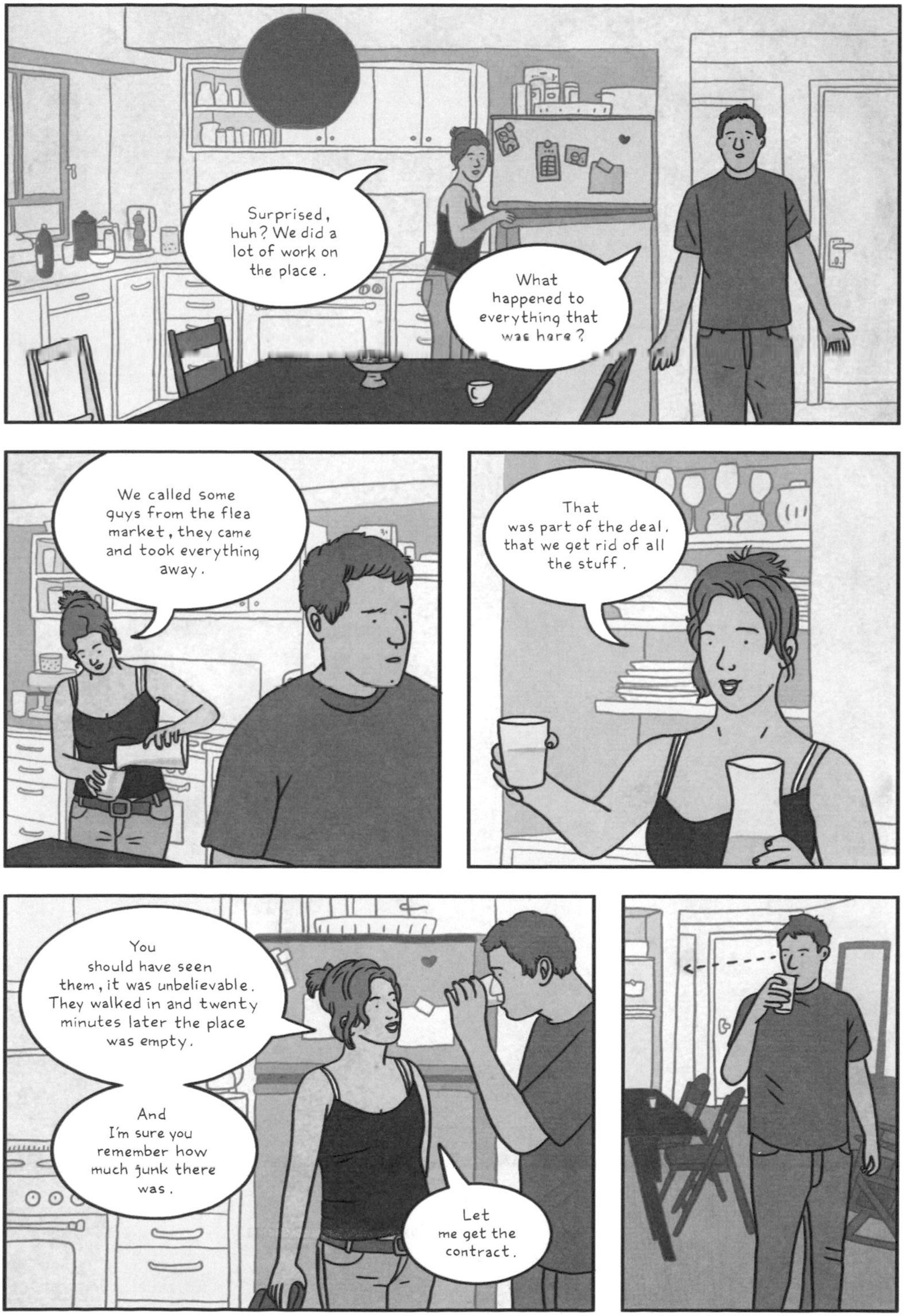
Surprised, huh? We did a lot of work on the place.
What happened to everything that was here?
We called some guys from the flea market, they came and took everything away.
That was part of the deal, that we get rid of all the stuff.
You should have seen them, it was unbelievable. They walked in and twenty minutes later the place was empty.
And I'm sure you remember how much junk there was.
Let me get the contract.

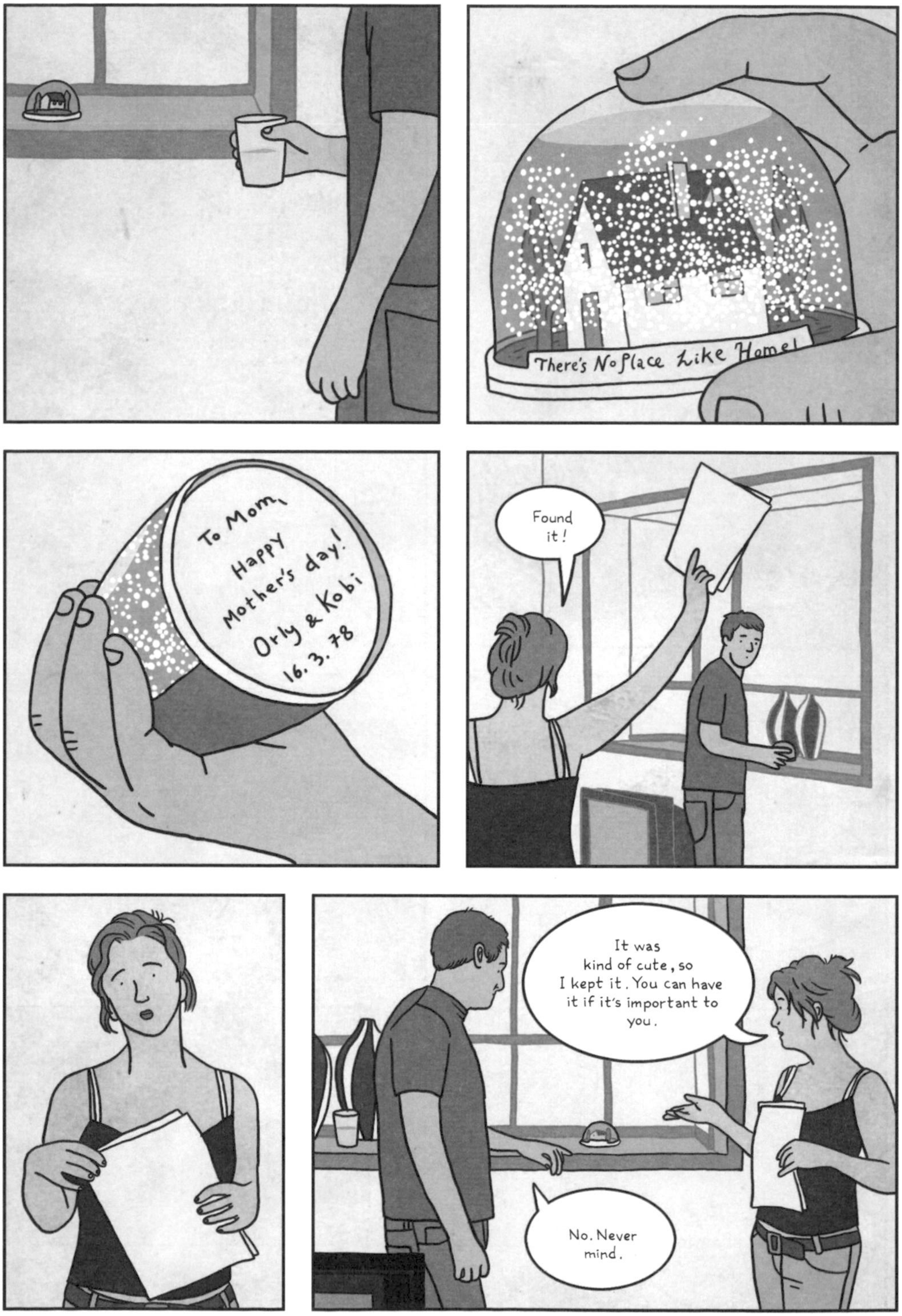
There's No Place Like Home!
To Mom,
Happy Mother's day!
Orly & Kobi
16.3.78
Found it!
It was kind of cute, so I kept it. You can have it if it's important to you.
No. Never mind.

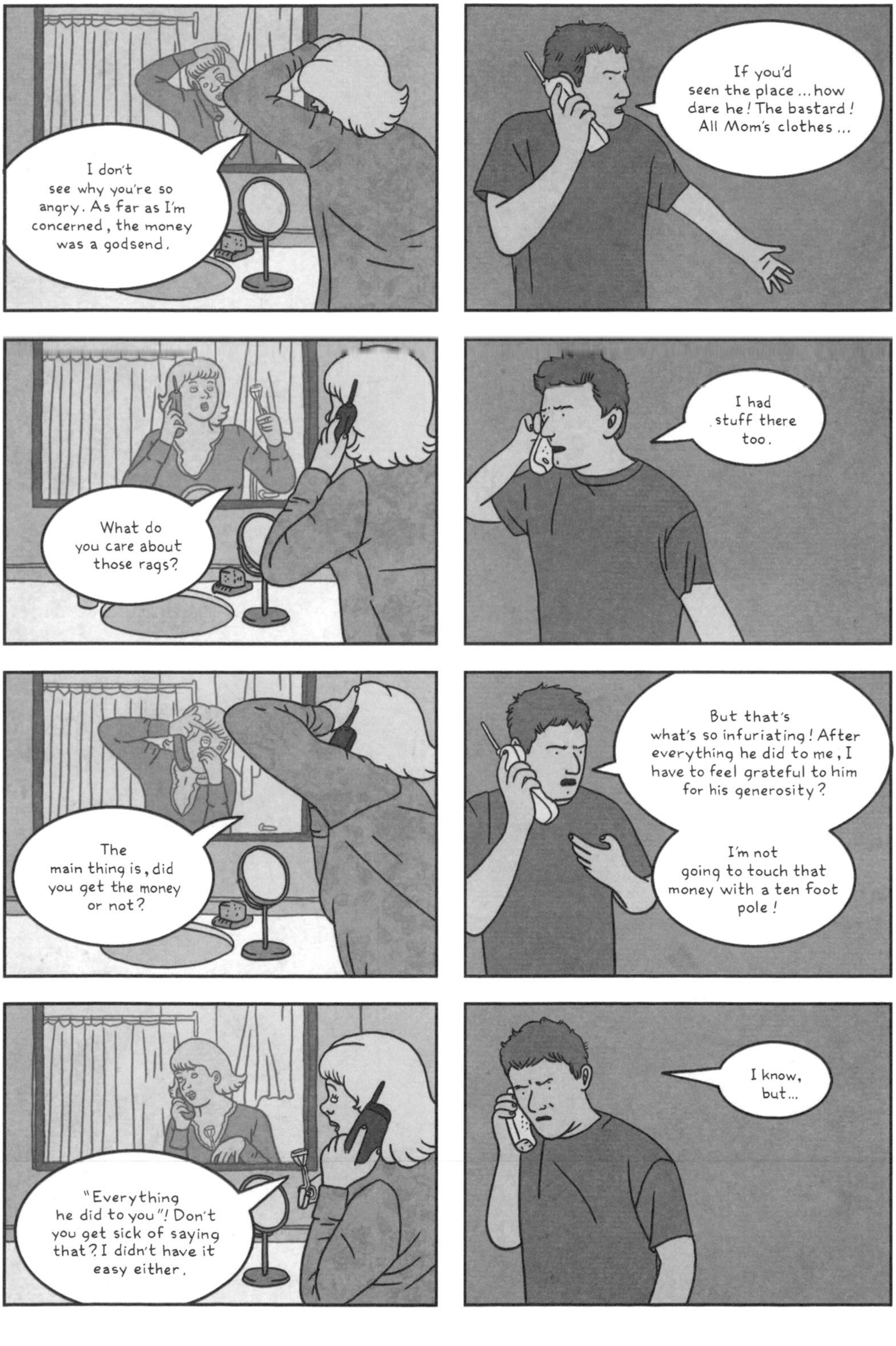
I don't see why you're so angry. As far as I'm concerned, the money was a godsend.
If you'd seen the place ... how dare he! The bastard! All Mom's clothes ...
What do you care about those rags?
I had stuff there too.
The main thing is, did you get the money or not?
But that's what's so infuriating! After everything he did to me, I have to feel grateful to him for his generosity?
I'm not going to touch that money with a ten foot pole!
"Everything he did to you"! Don't you get sick of saying that? I didn't have it easy either.
I know, but...

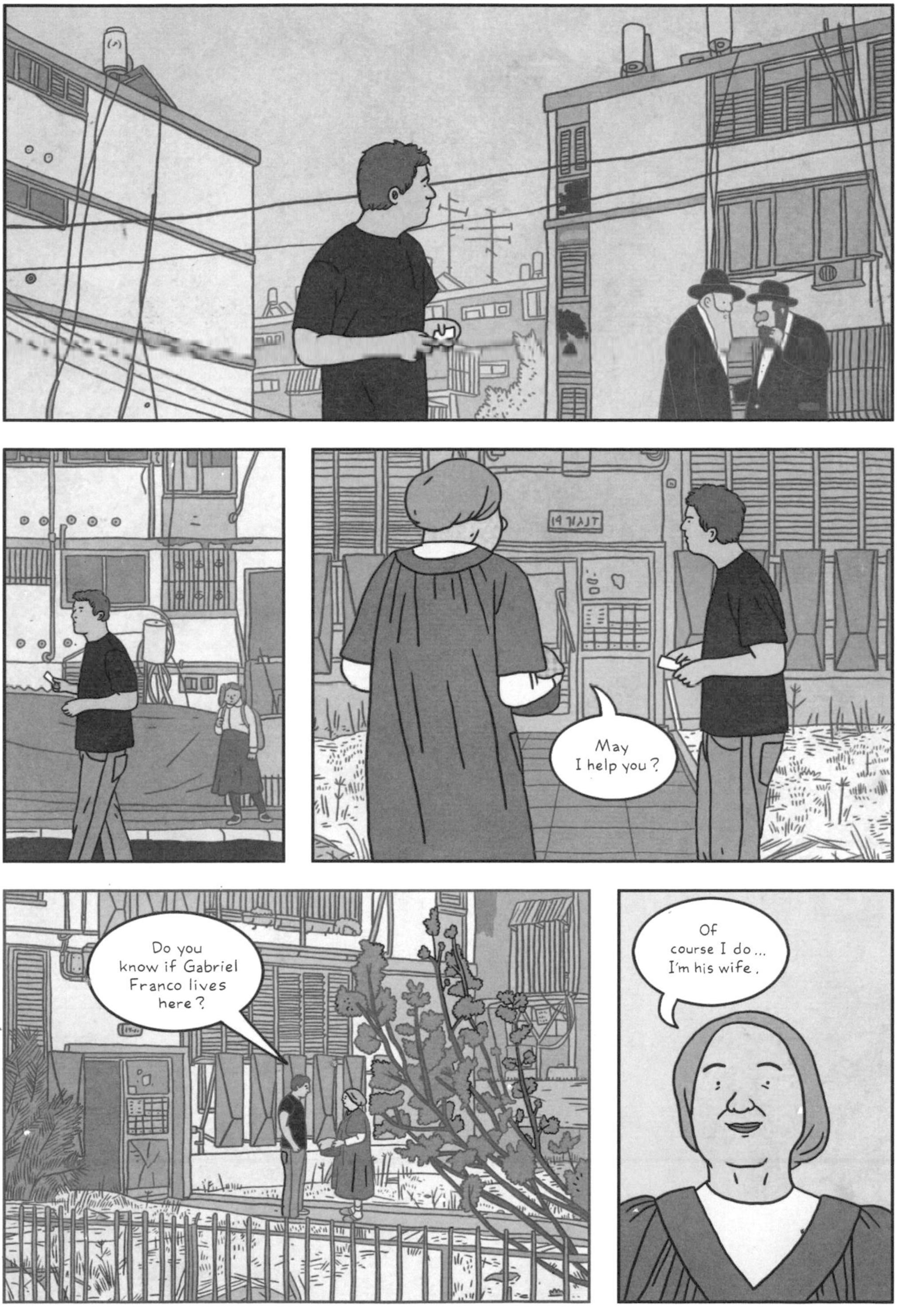
May I help you?
Do you know if Gabriel Franco lives here?
Of course I do... I'm his wife.

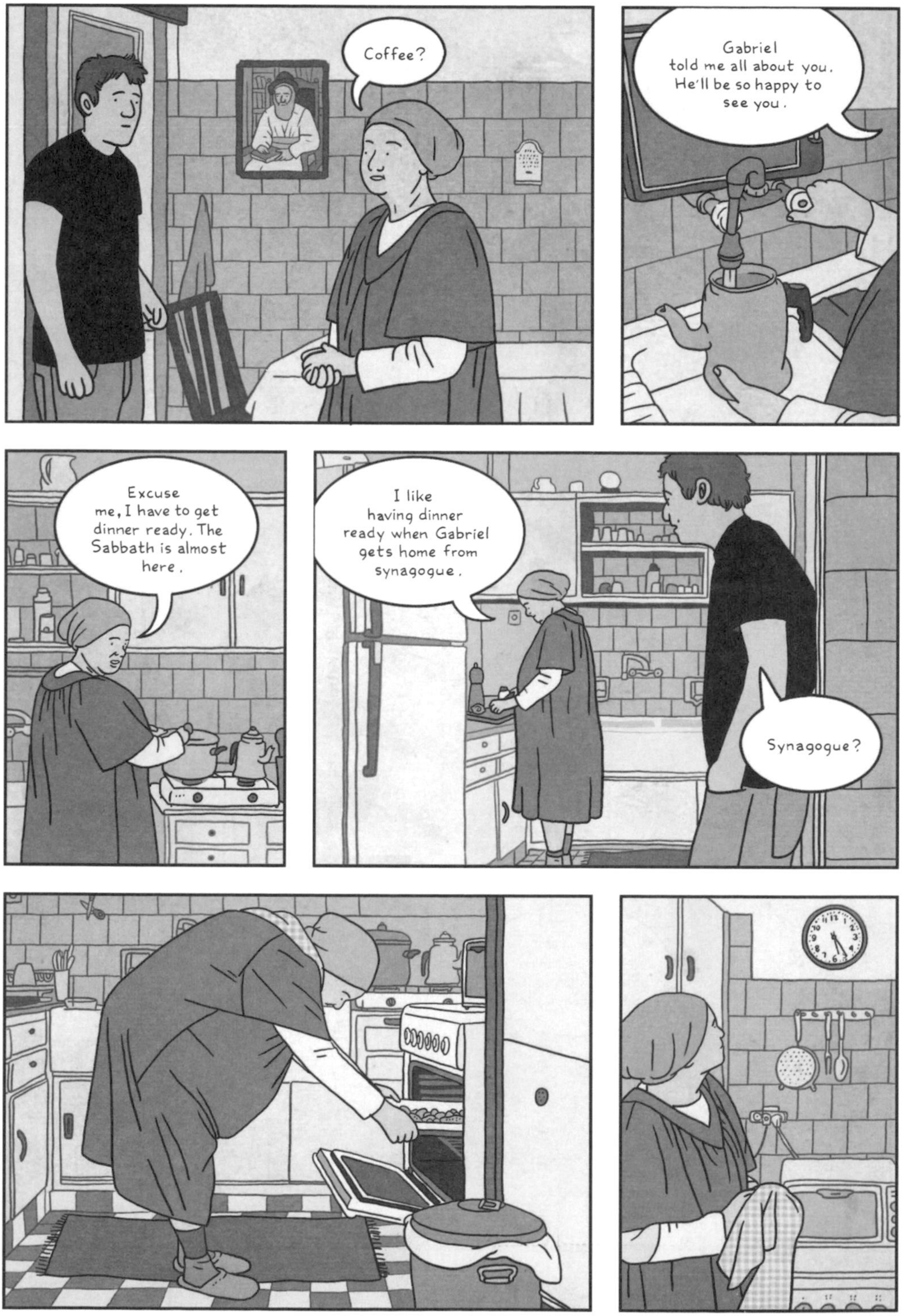
Coffee?
Gabriel told me all about you. He'll be so happy to see you.
Excuse me, I have to get dinner ready. The Sabbath is almost here.
I like having dinner ready when Gabriel gets home from synagogue.
Synagogue?

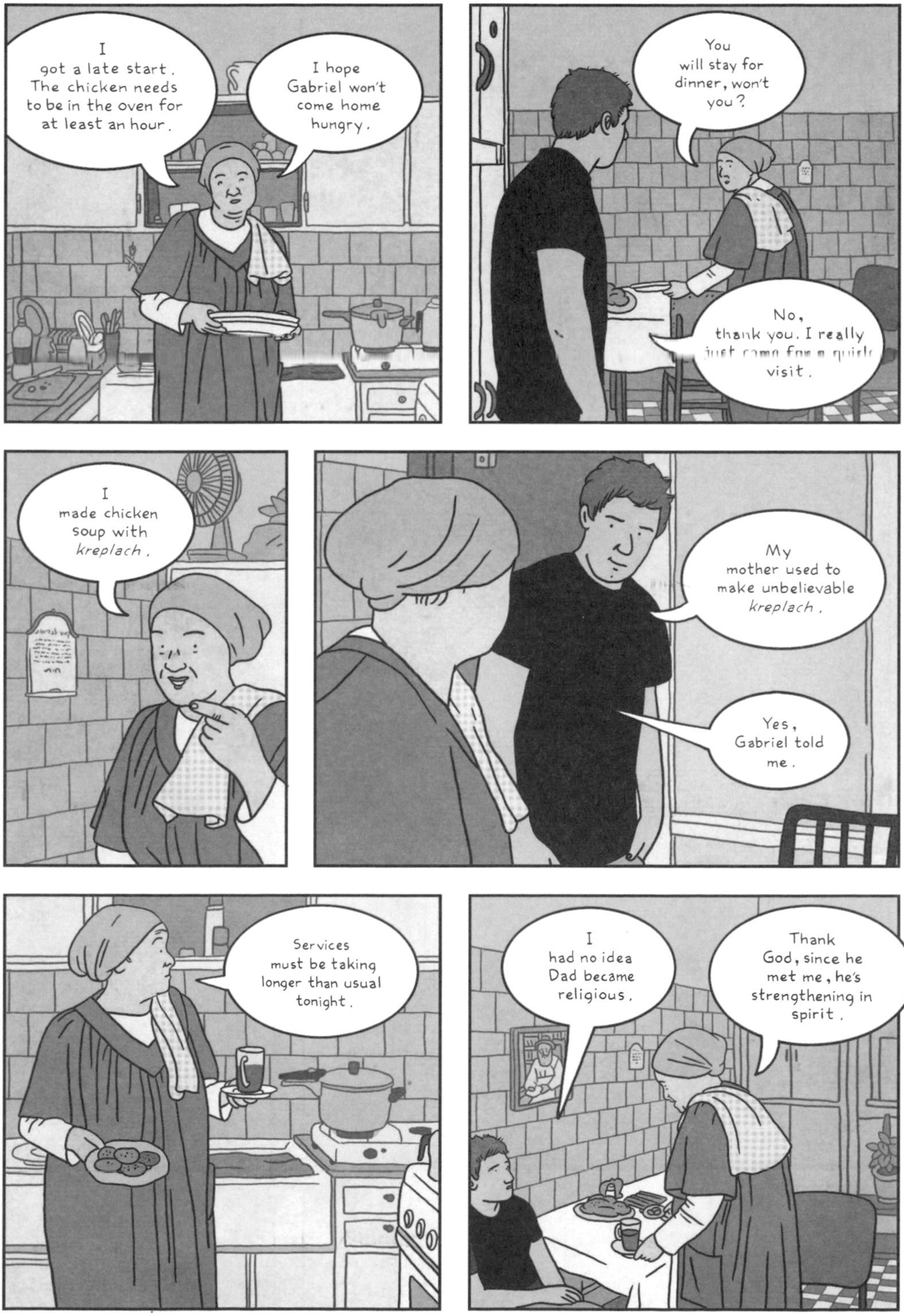
I got a late start. The chicken needs to be in the oven for at least an hour.
I hope Gabriel won't come home hungry.
You will stay for dinner, won't you?
No, thank you. I really just came for a quick visit.
I made chicken soup with *kreplach*.
My mother used to make unbelievable *kreplach*.
Yes, Gabriel told me.
Services must be taking longer than usual tonight.
I had no idea Dad became religious.
Thank God, since he met me, he's strengthening in spirit.

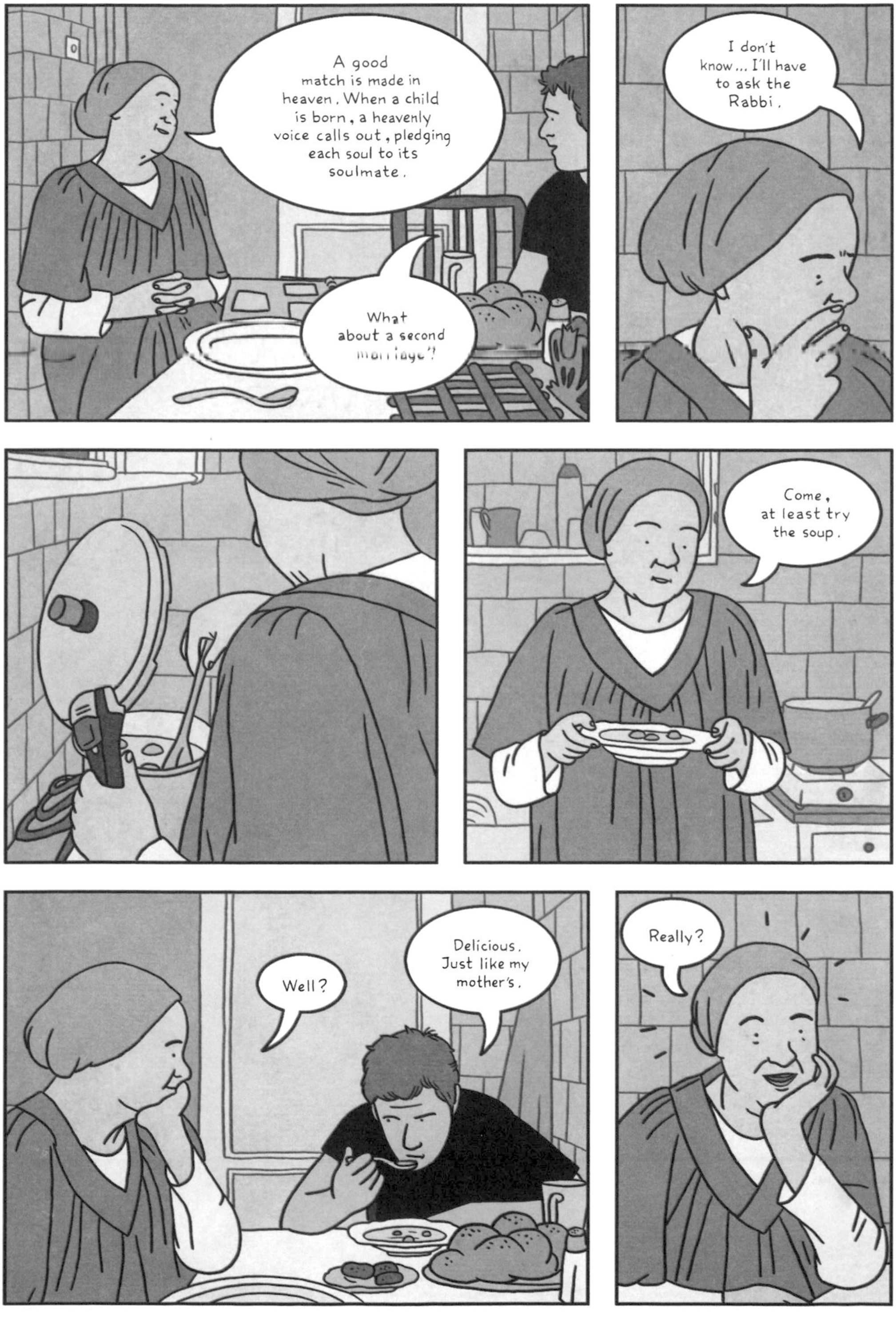
A good match is made in heaven. When a child is born, a heavenly voice calls out, pledging each soul to its soulmate.
What about a second marriage?
I don't know... I'll have to ask the Rabbi.
Come, at least try the soup.
Well?
Delicious. Just like my mother's.
Really?

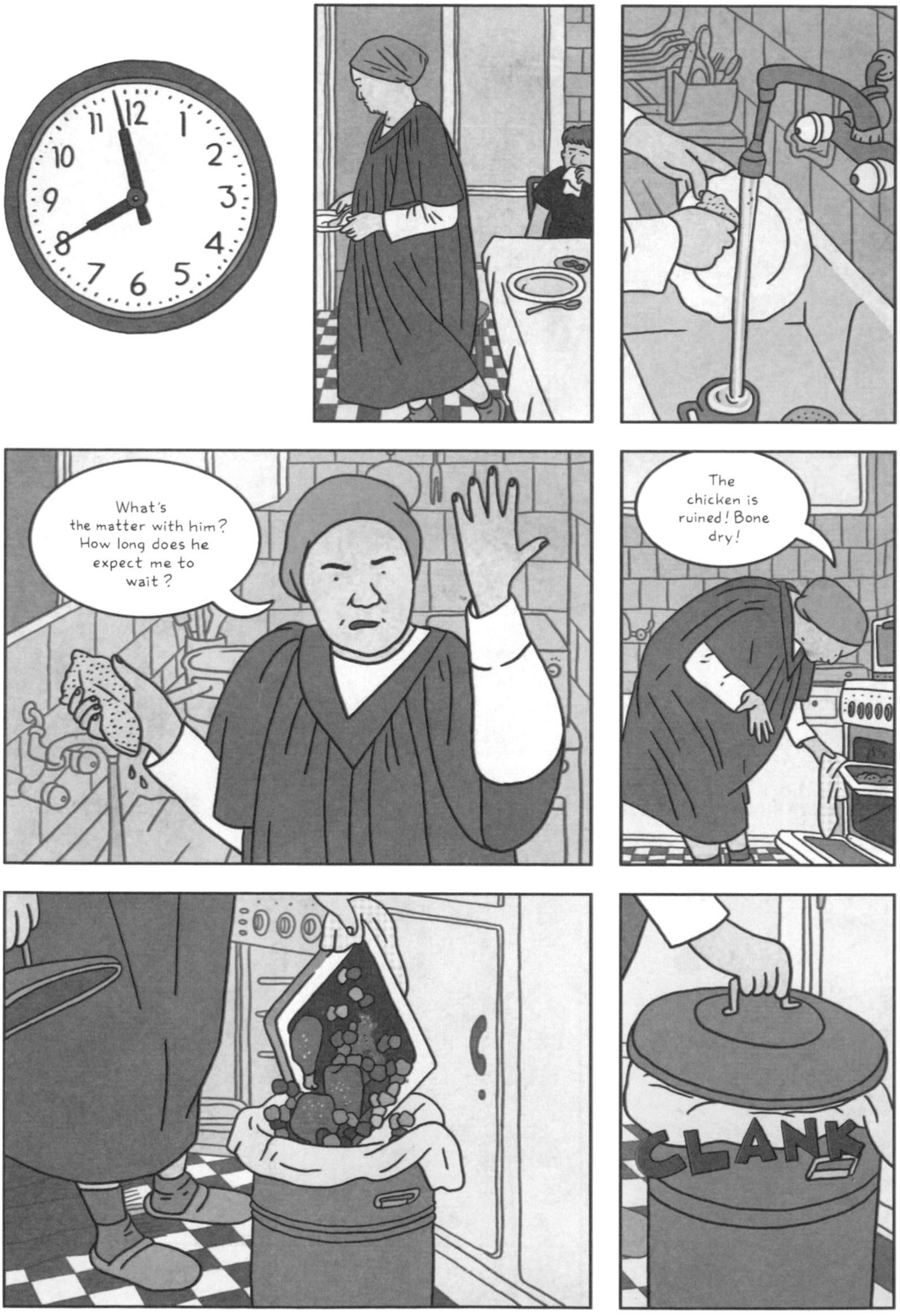
What's the matter with him? How long does he expect me to wait?
The chicken is ruined! Bone dry!
CLANK

One hour later.

I shouldn't have thrown it away. I could have made chicken salad.

I really should go.

Why? Gabriel will be here any minute.

I've waited enough.

It's a shame you missed each other. Do you want to leave him a message?

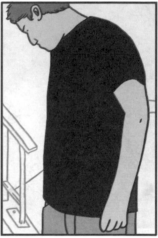

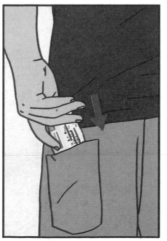

No. Just tell him I was here.

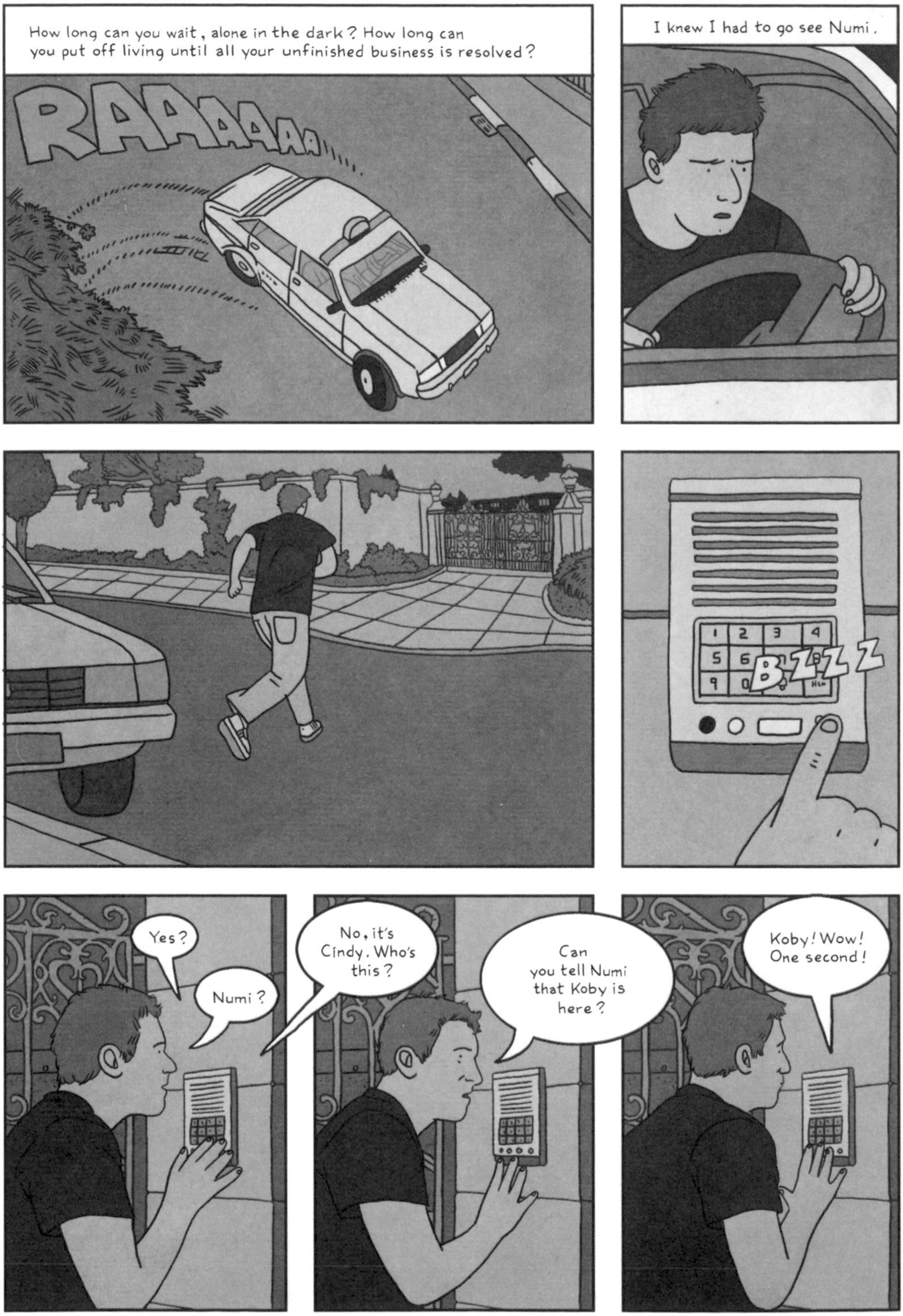
How long can you wait, alone in the dark? How long can you put off living until all your unfinished business is resolved?
RAAAAAA
I knew I had to go see Numi.
BZZZZ
Yes?
Numi?
No, it's Cindy. Who's this?
Can you tell Numi that Koby is here?
Koby! Wow! One second!

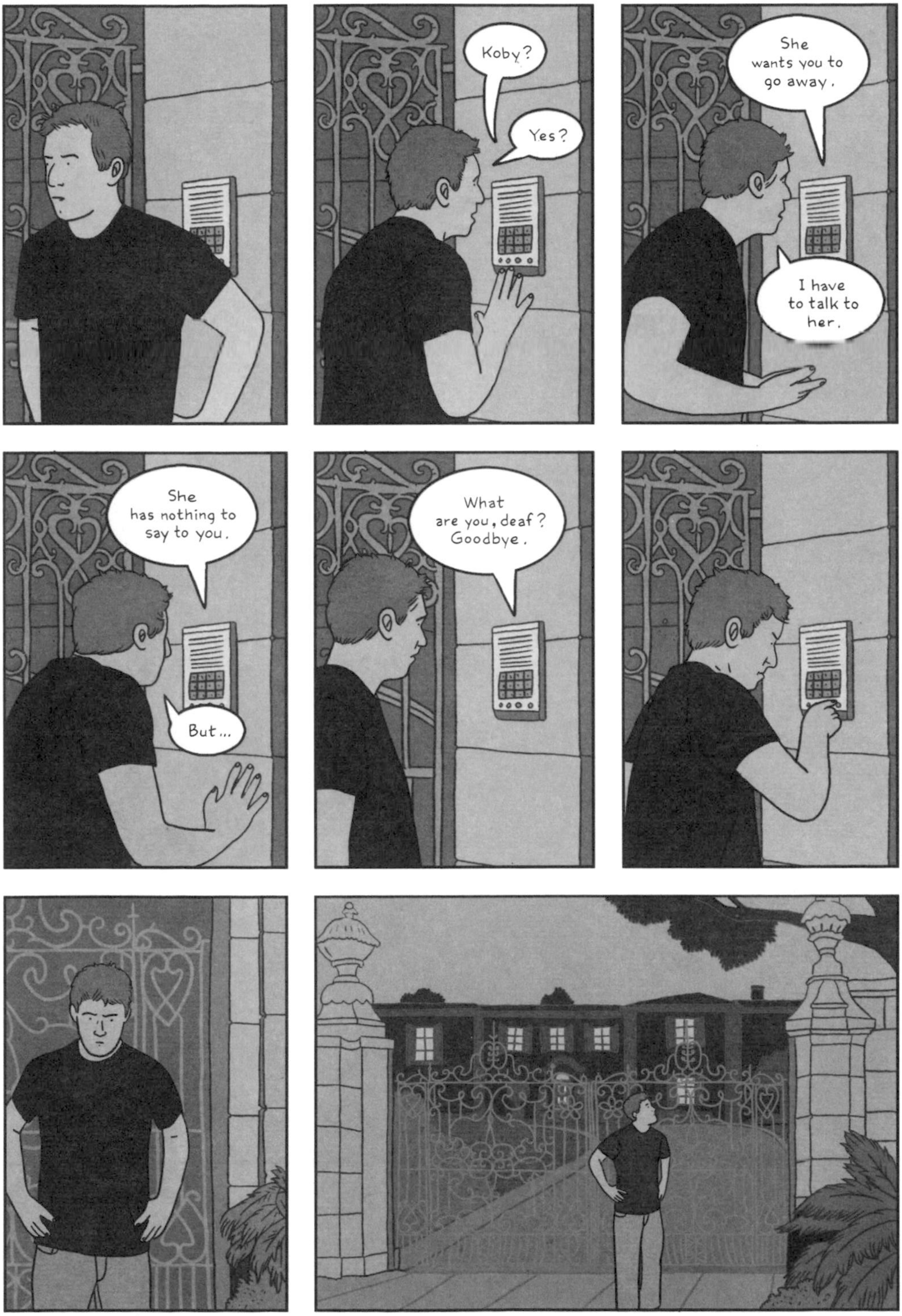
Koby?
Yes?
She wants you to go away.
I have to talk to her.
She has nothing to say to you.
But...
What are you, deaf? Goodbye.

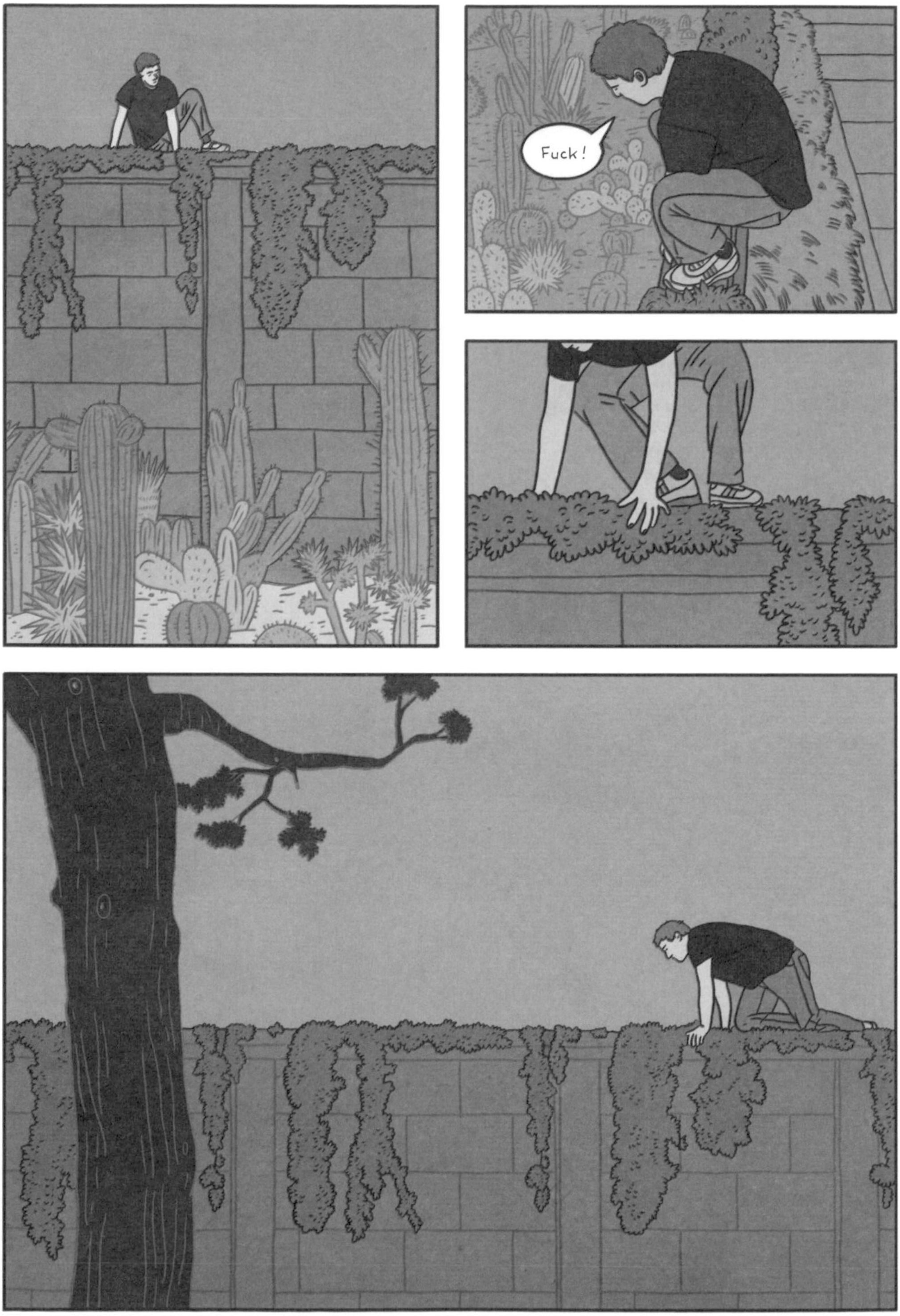
Fuck!

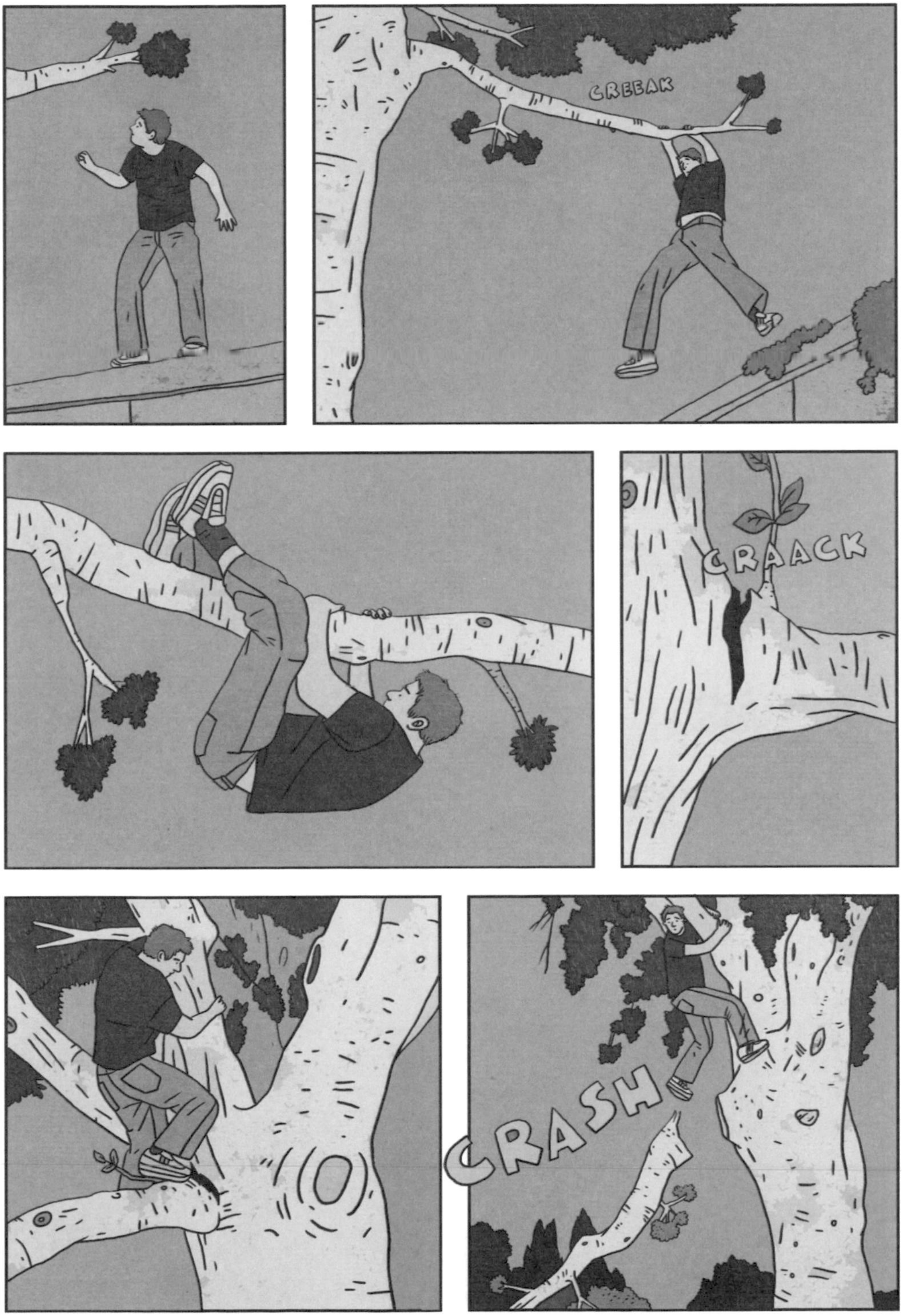
CREEAK
CRAACK
CRASH

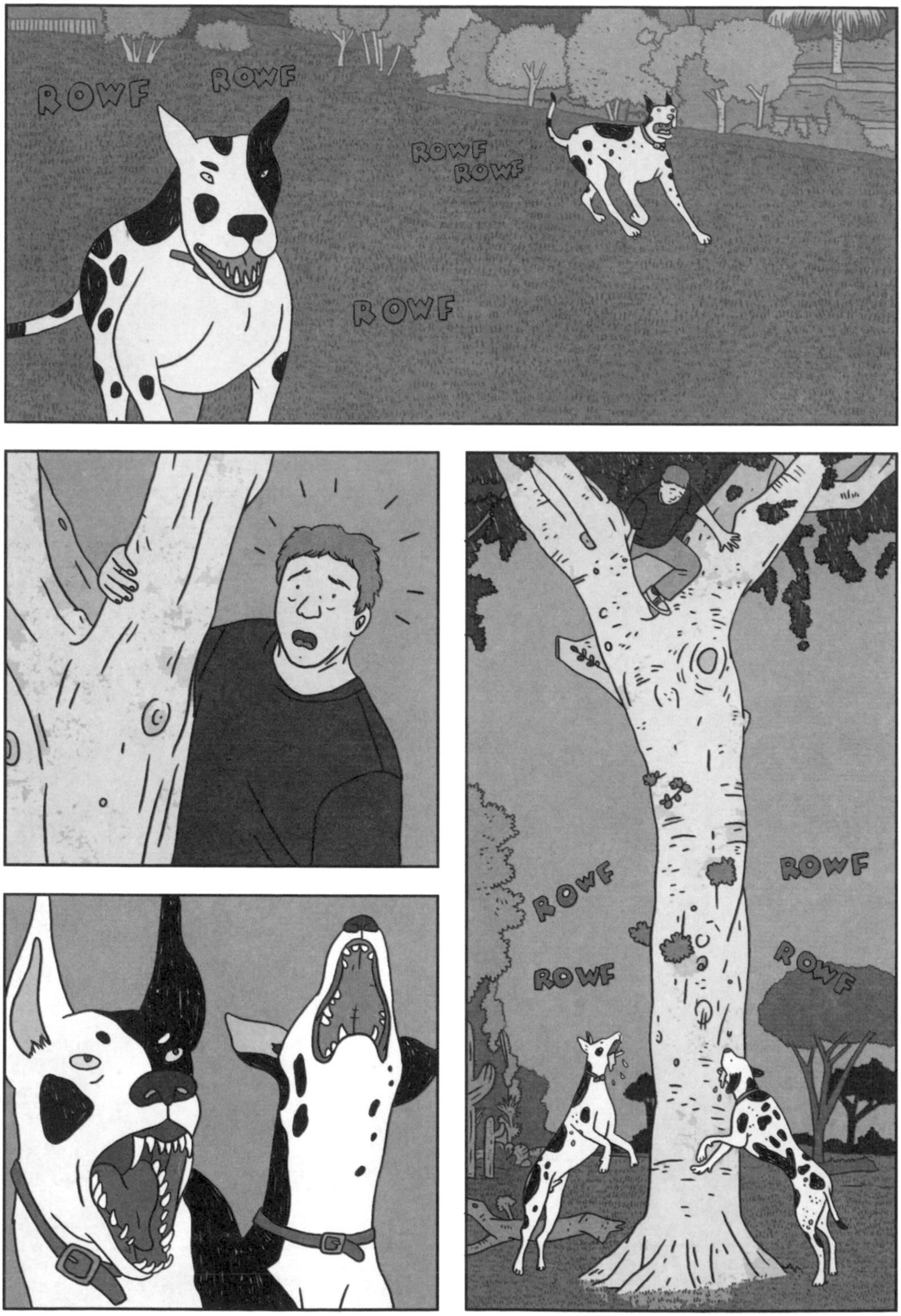
ROWF
ROWF
ROWF
ROWF
ROWF
ROWF
ROWF
ROWF
ROWF

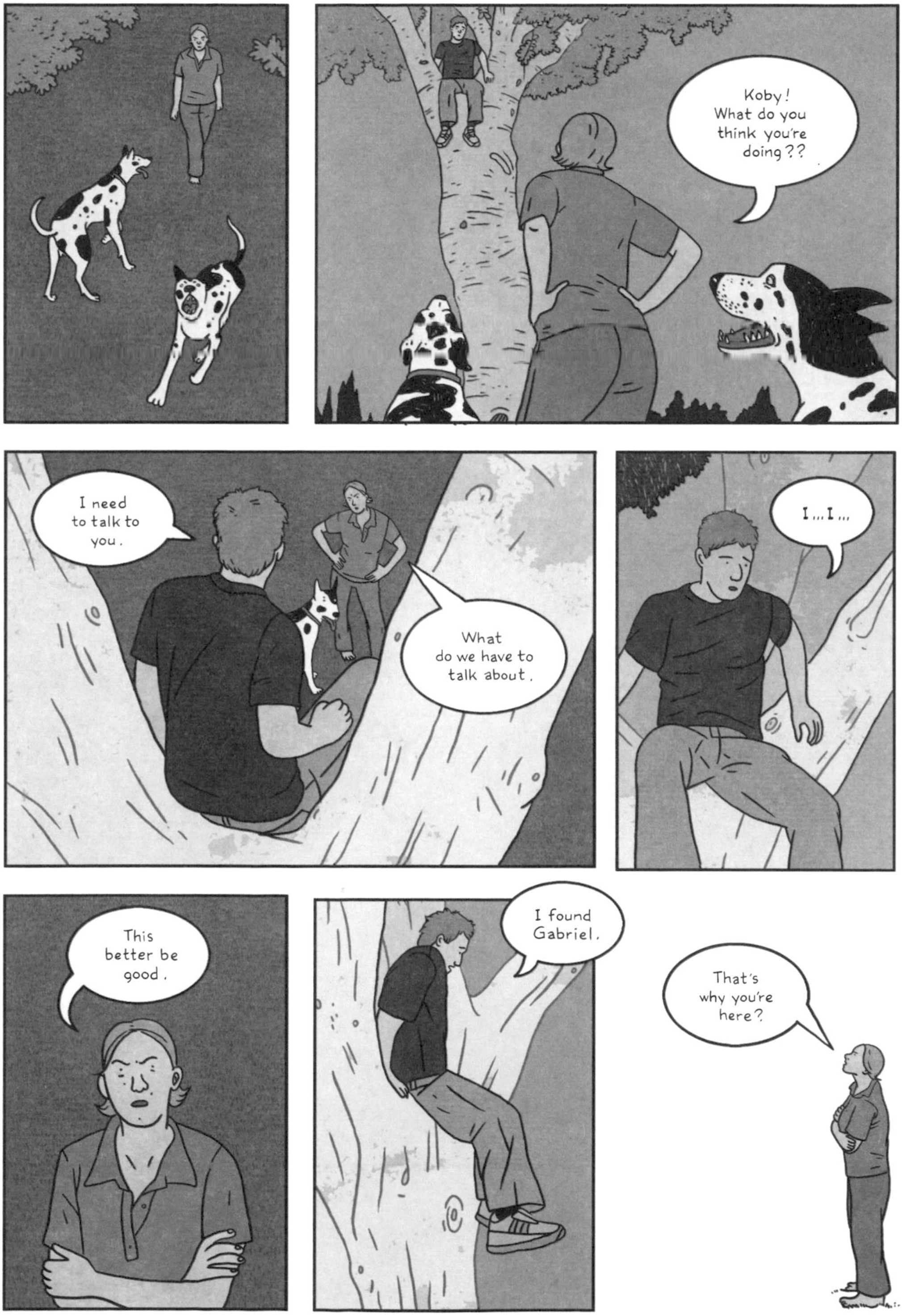
Koby! What do you think you're doing??
I need to talk to you.
What do we have to talk about.
I...I...
This better be good.
I found Gabriel.
That's why you're here?

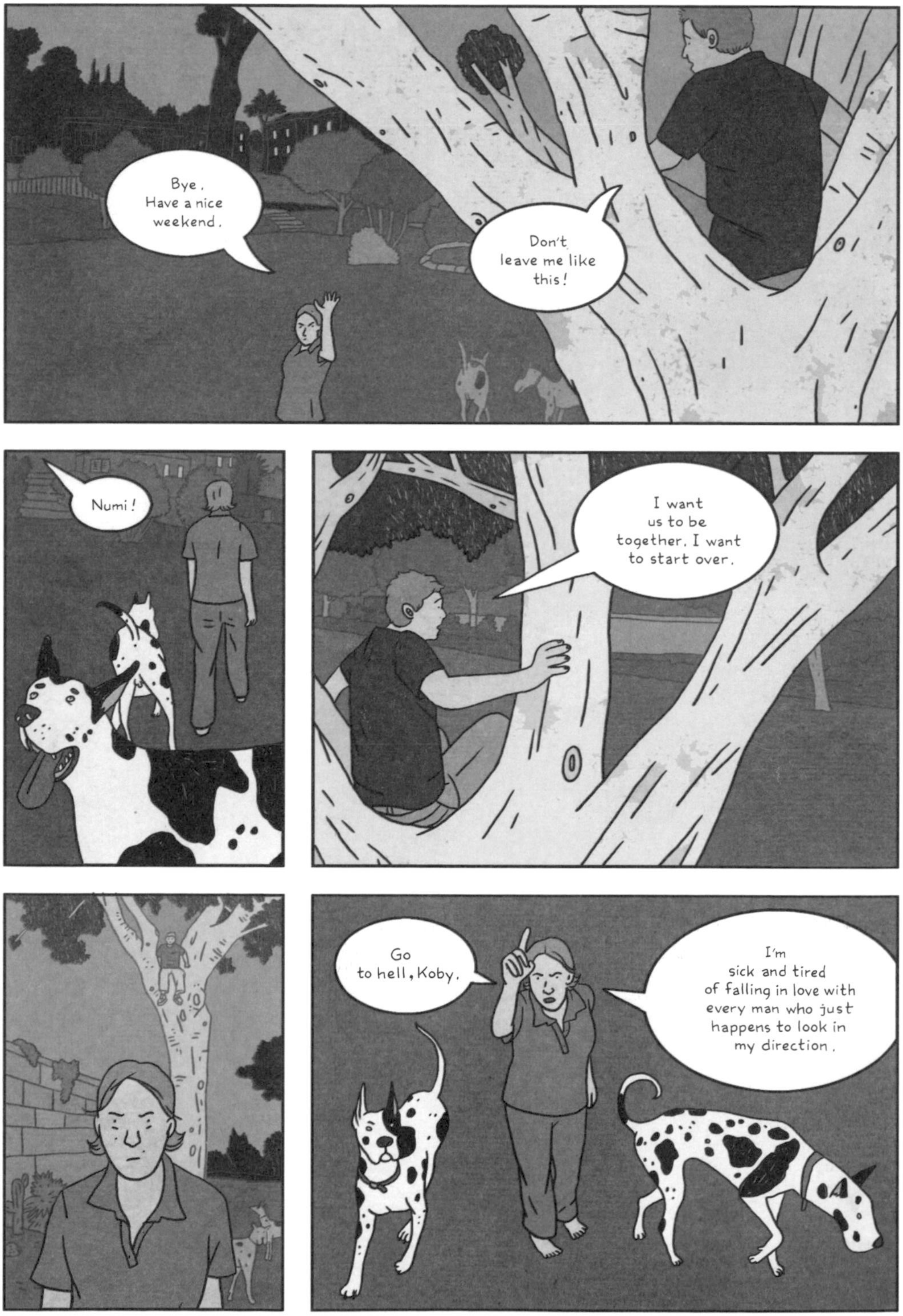
Bye. Have a nice weekend.
Don't leave me like this!
Numi!
I want us to be together. I want to start over.
Go to hell, Koby.
I'm sick and tired of falling in love with every man who just happens to look in my direction.

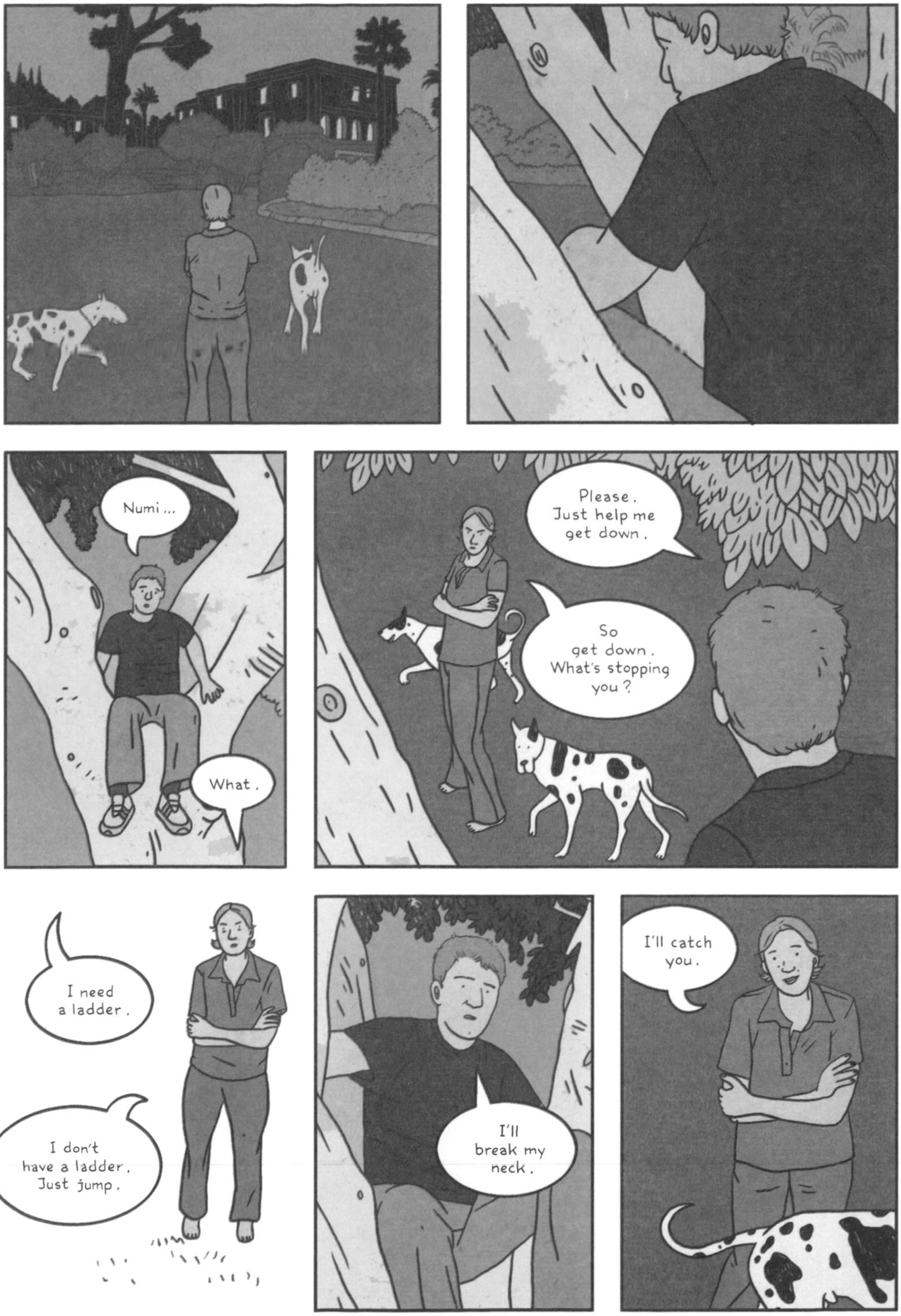

Numi ...
What.
Please. Just help me get down.
So get down. What's stopping you?
I need a ladder.
I don't have a ladder. Just jump.
I'll break my neck.
I'll catch you.

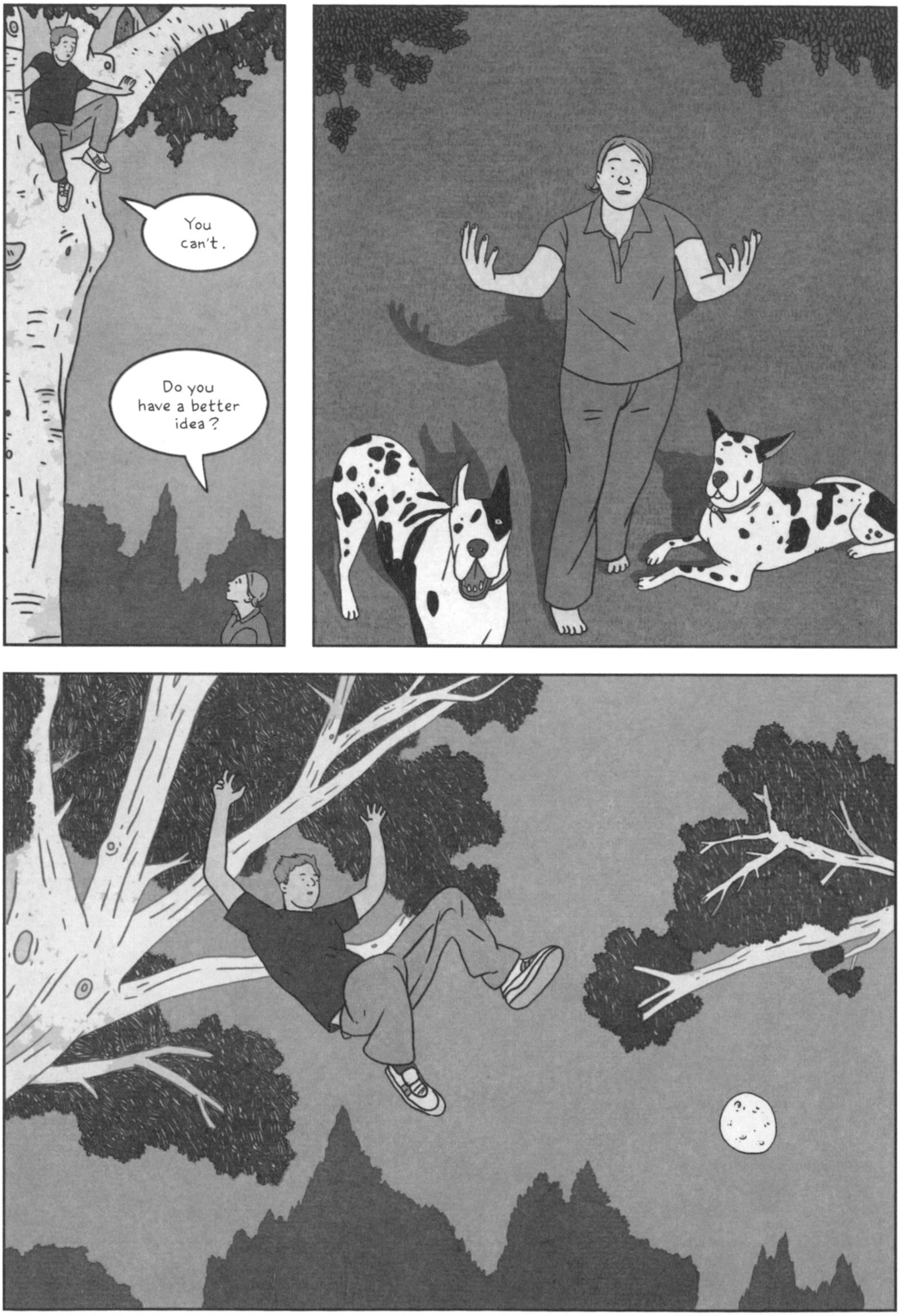
You can't.
Do you have a better idea?

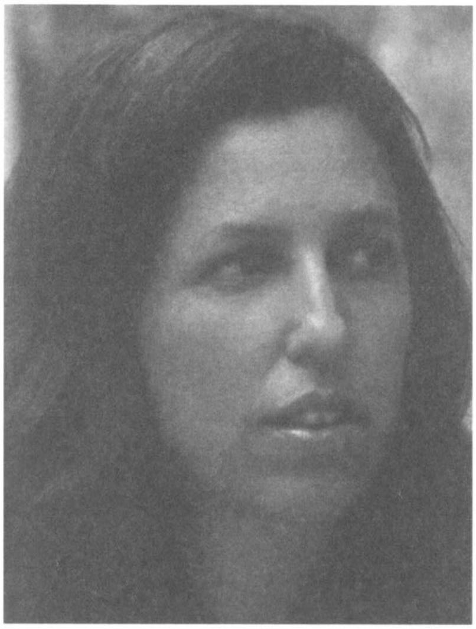

Photo by Ephrat Beloosesky

Rutu Modan was born in Tel-Aviv in 1966. She graduated *cum laude* from the Bezalel Academy of Art and Design in Jerusalem. After graduating, she began regularly writing and illustrating comic strips and stories for Israel's leading daily newspapers, as well as co-editing the Israeli edition of *MAD* magazine. She is a co-founder of Actus Tragicus, an alternative comic artists collective and independent publishing house. She collaborated with Israeli author Etgar Keret on her first graphic novel, *Nobody Said it Was Going to Be Fun*, an Israeli bestseller. Modan has worked as an illustrator for magazines and books in Israel and abroad, including *The New York Times*, *New Yorker* and *Le Monde*, and others. She is the recipient of four Best Illustrated Children's Book Awards from the Israel Museum in Jerusalem, the Young Artist of the Year by the Israel Ministry of Culture, the International Board on Books for Young People Honor List for Children's Book Illustration and is a chosen artist of the Israel Cultural Excellence Foundation since 2005. She has been nominated for the Angoulême Festival's Goccini Award, Eisner, and Ignatz Awards.

Modan currently teaches comics and illustration at the Bezalel Academy of Art and Design and lives in Tel-Aviv with her family.